D1478846

BYZANTIUM AND BULGARIA

A comparative study across the early medieval frontier

Byzantium and Bulgaria

A comparative study
across the early medieval frontier

ROBERT BROWNING

UNIVERSITY OF CALIFORNIA PRESS
Berkeley and Los Angeles, California

University of California Press
Berkeley and Los Angeles, California
ISBN 0-520-02670-5
LC 73-91665
© 1975 Robert Browning
First published in Great Britain 1975
by Maurice Temple Smith Ltd
37 Great Russell Street, London WC1
Printed in Great Britain

Contents

For Ruth

THE BYZANTINE EMPIRE c.1025

━━━ Extent c.1025

┅┅ Acquisitions after 1025 (with dates)

| 0 | 100 | 300 miles |
| 0 | 100 | 400 kilometres |

R. Drava

R. Sava

Sirmium

Morava

Singidunum

Vidin   Nicopolis

River Danube   Silistria

Zara

Nish

Balkan Mts

Trnovo   Pliska

Varna

Mesembria

Spalato

Ragusa

Serdica   *R. Maritsa*

Sozopolis

Pristina

Philippopolis   Adrianople

Prilep

Melnik   *1*

2

3 *4*

Ohrid   Strumitsa

Dyrrhachium

Prespa

Thessalonika

Nic

Bari

Avlona

Lemnos

Pergamum

Larissa

Lesbos

Smyrna

Nicopolis

Chios   *R. Meand*

CATEPANATE OF ITALY

Thebes

Ephesus

Athens

Miletus

Corinth

Taormina

1038-1043

Syracuse

Crete

Cherson

Caucasus Mts

Ani **1045**

Kars   Dvin

Sinope

R Araxes

Trebizond

Manzikert

Sangarius
Ancyra

R. Halys

Amida

Mosul

Amorium

Germanicea

Edessa   **1052**

Adana

Tarsus

R. Tigris

Attalia

Seleucia

Aleppo

Antioch

R Euphrates

Cyprus

Beirut

Damascus

Caesarea

Jerusalem

Index to towns
1 Didymotichus
2 Bulgarophygon
3 Constantinople
4 Chrysopolis
5 Nicomedia

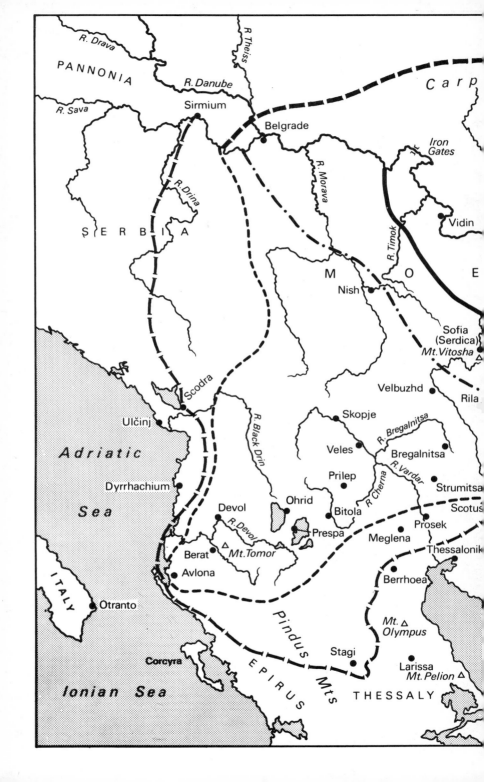

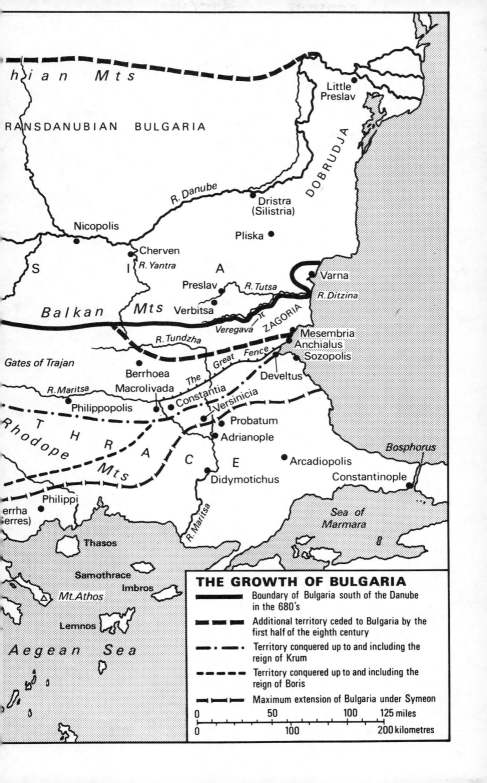

h i a n M t s

RANSDANUBIAN BULGARIA

Little
Preslav

R. Danube

DOBRUDJA

Dristra
(Silistria)

Nicopolis

Pliska ●

Cherven
R. Yantra

A

S   I

Preslav
Verbitsa

R. Tutsa

Varna ●

R. Ditzina

Balkan   Mts

Veregava ZAGORIA

R. Tundzha

Mesembria

Gates of Trajan

Berrhoea

The   Great   Fence

Anchialus
Sozopolis

Macrolivada

Constantia

Develtus

R. Maritsa

Versinicia

Philippopolis

Probatum

Bosphorus

Adrianople

T

Rhodope

H   R

Arcadiopolis

Constantinople ●

A   C

E

Mts

Didymotichus

R. Maritsa

errha
Serres)

Philippi

Sea of
Marmara

B

Thasos

Samothrace

Imbros

△ Mt.Athos

Aegean   Sea

Lemnos

THE GROWTH OF BULGARIA

▬▬▬	Boundary of Bulgaria south of the Danube in the 680's
▬ ▬ ▬	Additional territory ceded to Bulgaria by the first half of the eighth century
▬·▬·▬	Territory conquered up to and including the reign of Krum
▬ ▬ ▬	Territory conquered up to and including the reign of Boris
▬╌▬╌▬	Maximum extension of Bulgaria under Symeon

0   50   100   125 miles

0   100   200 kilometres

Preface

I first set foot in Bulgaria in October 1944, as an officer on the staff of the Allied Control Commission. Since then I have made several visits, and learnt to know something of the country, its people, and their history. Gradually the conviction has grown upon me that the course of the relations between Bulgaria and the Byzantine empire in the ninth and tenth centuries is not merely an interesting example of the complexity of the process of acculturation; it established a pattern for Byzantine relations with the other peoples of Eastern Europe as one after another they embraced Christianity; it determined the main features of the culture and of the developing national identity of these peoples, among whom the Russians were the most numerous and powerful. In a sense, then, the events in this ill-defined no-man's-land of the northern Balkans a thousand years ago played a not insignificant part in shaping Europe as a historical entity. I was therefore very glad to be invited to contribute a volume on Bulgaria and Byzantium in the present series of comparative studies. If it has turned out longer and different in form from other books in the series, I can only plead that a straightforward synchronic comparative study would have been valueless, and probably impossible.

My warmest thanks are due in the first place to the many Bulgarian scholars who through their works and through personal contact have broadened and deepened my understanding of the early history of their country. In particular I should like to acknowledge my debt to Academician Veselin Beševliev and to Professors Dimitŭr Angelov and Ivan Dujčev. Byzantine historians are numerous, and I have learnt much from many among them. My debt in the present work to Professor George Ostrogorsky and Professor Paul Lemerle is evident. Maurice Temple Smith and August Frugé both gave encouragement and were uncommercial enough to undertake the publication of a book whose sales are bound to be limited. Finally, the book would never have been published were it not for Susan Archer, who typed the manuscript, much of it twice.

ROBERT BROWNING

1   Introduction

The Byzantine empire and Bulgaria in the ninth and tenth centuries did not resemble each other closely. If one undertakes a comparative study of them, it is not in order to distinguish the differences between two societies which appear to have advanced much the same distance along the same road, as one might compare say, Lübeck and Venice in the thirteenth century, Rome and Carthage in the third century B.C., or the Roman empire and Han China. The obvious counterpart to the middle Byzantine empire in such a comparison is the Abbasid Caliphate. An examination of their resemblances and their differences would be well worth undertaking. But it would be beyond the capacity of the present writer. And some of the essential preliminary researches are still unattempted.

The first reason for examining Bulgaria and Byzantium together is their geographical proximity. At the period in question they divided the Balkan peninsula between them and had a long common frontier. What difference did it make to an individual or a community to be on this or that side of the long frontier?

As we introduce further historical considerations, fresh points of contrast emerge. The Byzantine empire was the direct continuation of the Roman empire of classical times, with a political and administrative tradition running back uninterrupted for many centuries. The Bulgarian Kingdom was a relatively new arrival on the political map of medieval Europe. As a newcomer, it had open options, and could within certain limits choose the role it was to play. For the Byzantines there was little choice.

Another way of looking at the matter is suggested by the fact that the territory of the Bulgarian Kingdom had all—with the exception of the Transdanubian area, which was soon lost—formed a part of the Roman empire until the age of the successors of Justinian, and was reabsorbed into the Byzantine empire again at the beginning of the eleventh century. Did the few centuries of separation from the great Mediterranean world state lead to irreversible changes in the structure and functioning of society in these lost provinces? The question is an interesting one, and the answer may throw light on some aspects of the history of western Europe, where the separation was a permanent one.

If we look at the matter from the viewpoint of the economic historian, fresh questions pose themselves. In medieval terms the Byzantine empire—like the Muslim caliphate—was an economically advanced state, a super-power. Bulgaria belonged to the underdeveloped world. How did the difference in the level of their economic development affect their relations and the internal development of each of them? When we remember that during much of the period under study the frontier between Byzantium and Bulgaria ran within 200 kilometres of Constantinople, and within only 40 kilometres of Thessalonica, the second city of the empire, the steepness of the gradient of economic development becomes apparent. The rich and the poor of the medieval world faced one another across a very narrow gap, which the armies of either side could cross at will.

The sociologically-inclined historian will be struck by the rapid and decisive changes which took place in Bulgarian society in the period under examination. For him Byzantine-Bulgarian relations may be primarily the occasion for a study in acculturation, and in resistance to it. If Bulgaria formed part of what Professor Obolensky so aptly called 'the Byzantine Commonwealth,' it certainly did not become a mere carbon copy of Byzantium. There were striking differences. Some of the features of Bulgarian society recall the barbarian west rather than the Mediterranean lands of ancient culture. And even what is taken over directly from Byzantine models often shows a different profile in Bulgaria, though we may be hard put to it to define the difference.

It was the reflection of Byzantine civilisation in Bulgaria which served in its turn as model for Serbia and, more important, for Kievan and later Muscovite Russia. Thus the relations between Byzantium and Bulgaria in the ninth and tenth centuries were of far more than local and contemporary significance. It was through them that certain lasting features of the Orthodox Slavonic world were formed, features which have had an effect upon the development of European history down to our own day.

Looked at from another point of view, the Kingdom of Bulgaria was another barbarian successor state, comparable to Merovingian Gaul, Visigothic Spain, or perhaps Anglo-Saxon England. Yet, quite apart from its later reabsorption into the empire, Bulgaria differed in a number of important respects from most of the western successor states. There was far less continuity than in Gaul or Spain, as witnessed by the fact that Slavonic and not Greek or Latin became the current speech of the people and the language of state and church. It may be that the most valid comparison is with Anglo-Saxon England. But the differences are many. Bulgaria was always a single, centralised state, not a group of principalities and ephemeral kingdoms. And Bulgaria was not remote from the ancient centre of the empire, like England, but right on its threshold, so that Bulgarian armies could again and again threaten Constantinople itself.

There are thus a number of considerations which might make a comparative study of Bulgaria and Byzantium in the ninth and tenth centuries of more than narrow specialist interest. One is bound next to ask whether there is enough evidence to permit a valid comparison. There are certainly great gaps in the evidence available to us. Neither for Byzantium nor, still less, for Bulgaria, have we the kind of detailed economic documentation that exists, for instance, for contemporary China of the late T'ang period. Can we say anything useful about such matters as taxation, trade, or distribution of wealth? In the present writer's view we can, by seeing which of a limited number of possible models fit the known facts. This is indeed the only way in which the economic history of any but a few recent and favoured ages can be studied. In fact the historian of ninth-century Bulgaria is no worse off in this respect than the student of ninth-century England.

The archaeologist can provide useful material for the historian in this field. But there are certain snags. Byzantine archaeology has traditionally tended to concern itself above all with churches and their decorations. This is not unexpected, as until recently most Byzantine archaeologists were by training art historians. It has the unfortunate result that we know very little about the material background to everyday life. In a few special cases there has been complete and thorough excavation and recording of large inhabited areas. Examples are the American excavation of Corinth and of the Athenian Agora, or the Soviet excavation of Cherson. But much of the medieval material from these admirable excavations is still unpublished. From Constantinople and its vicinity nothing comparable is available. Bulgarian archaeology is in many ways more highly developed. The Hungarian Kanitz and the Czech Jireček provided reliable descriptions of ancient remains even before Bulgaria obtained its independence from the Ottoman empire. After independence patriotic feeling provided a stimulus to the investigation of the country's past. Another stimulus was provided by Russian interest in a country which had contributed so much to Russian civilisation and which lay on the direct route to the

Bosphorus. The Russian Archaeological Institute in Constantinople carried out major excavations in a number of Bulgarian sites, and in particular at Aboba, which is generally identified with the ancient Bulgar capital of Pliska. The Czech scholar Karel Škorpil played an important part both in this work and in the training of Bulgarian archaeologists. In fact few Bulgarian ancient or medieval historians had not some archaeological training and experience. Since the Second World War and the establishment of the People's Republic of Bulgaria the scale and quality of Bulgarian archaeological work has increased still further. And apart from the continuing excavation at Preslav and other major medieval sites there have been several interesting studies of the humble settlements of the Slavs and Proto-Bulgars. Most of this material is published rapidly. The important epigraphic monuments of the Bulgarian Kingdom have been edited in exemplary fashion by V. Beševliev. There is as yet no corpus of Byzantine inscriptions. However there are some difficulties. The most important is that scarcely any site or monument from the early medieval period has so far been reliably dated. Thus all dates established by archaeological evidence must be regarded with some scepticism. And in particular the attribution of one monument to the late Roman period and of another to the Bulgarian period is often dependent on subjective considerations. We cannot yet distinguish with any sureness between the handiwork of provincial Roman architects of the age of Justinian and that of Bulgarians—or Byzantines—working for King Boris.

Another shortcoming of our evidence is that we see Bulgaria almost exclusively through Byzantine eyes. The period under study is covered by a series of Byzantine historians and chroniclers whose narratives survive—Theophanes the Confessor, George the Monk, Genesius, the Continuators of Theophanes—as well as by contemporary Byzantine official writings such as the legal enactments of Basil I and Leo VI and the treatises on foreign policy—*De Administrando Imperio*—and on palace ceremonies of Constantine VII Porphryogenitus, and by the letters and occasional compositions of several of the principal participants in the events—Photius, Arethas, Nicolaus Mysticus, Leo Choirosphaktes. From Bulgaria we have no historical narrative, no administrative texts, no personal documents, apart from some diplomatic correspondence of King Symeon in Greek. What survives in Old Slavonic is mainly translations or adaptations of religious works. But the prefaces to these often contain information on contemporary Bulgarian life. There is also a Bulgarian law code in Slavonic.

From western Europe we have odds and ends of minor observations on Bulgaria and the Bulgarians, and the very important but scrappy and disconnected *Responsa* of Pope Nicholas I to the queries addressed to him by King Boris shortly after his conversion. There is consequently a great deal that we do not know about Bulgaria. Apart from its rulers, few men or women emerge as credible, rounded personalities. The floodlight of history did not play on Bulgaria as it often did on Byzantium.

> Denn die einen sind im Dunkeln
> Und die andern sind im Licht;
> Und man siehet die im Lichte,
> Die im Dunkeln sieht man nicht.

The treatment which follows is determined largely by the availability of evidence. Many important topics are passed over in silence or only touched upon. The need to make, not a static comparison of two societies at a moment of time, or during a brief period, but an examination of the changing relations between two communities during a long period, has also affected the form of the treatment. The changing fortunes of the Balkan peninsula in late antiquity and the early Middle Ages are described in an initial chapter, with special attention to ethnic changes and changing settlement patterns. In the following chapter an account is given of the course of Byzantine-Bulgarian relations in the ninth and tenth centuries. These two chapters are diachronic in their treatment rather than synchronic. There follows a series of chapters in which a comparative study is made of aspects of the two societies, beginning with the land and ending with culture and the patterns of everyday life. A brief final chapter takes up again some of the wider questions raised in the introduction.

Source references have not generally been given for most of the events recounted in the narrative portions of the book. They would have enormously increased the bulk of the work, and they are already available in standard works on the history of Byzantium and of Bulgaria. More frequent reference is made both to the sources and secondary works in the comparative chapters, though here again no attempt is made to quote all the evidence for everything that is said. In the critical bibliography at the end of the book I have tried to provide a guide to the formidable literature on the subject rather than to list every book used or quoted. The non-specialist wants to know where to turn for a balanced and authoritative account of this or that topic. The specialist will already have compiled his own bibliography. And he will certainly have to read Bulgarian and Russian.

In transliterating foreign names I have aimed at ready intelligibility rather than complete consistency. Greek names, whether of persons or places, are rendered by English equivalents, by Latinised forms, or by transcription, in the way most likely to be familiar to English readers: thus *John, Athens; Photius, Aetolia; Choirosphaktes, Serrai*. Old Slavonic names are transliterated with *ch, sh, zh* rather than *č, š, ž;* the *yers* (very short vowels) are rendered by *ŭ* and *ĭ* except at the end of words, where they are omitted, thus *Boris* and not *Borisŭ; yat* (a variety of long *e*) is rendered by *ě*. Modern Bulgarian names are transcribed according to the same system, and follow the post-1945 orthography; in particular the dull vowel represented in Cyrillic by *yer* is rendered by *ŭ* and not by *ǎ*. Any departures from these principles are the result of oversight.

2   The Balkans in Late Antiquity and the Origin of Bulgaria

It is necessary to follow the history of the Balkan area in some detail during the period from the fourth century A.D. to the middle of the ninth for several reasons. First, the gradual appearance in the area of the Roman empire of the Slavs and the Bulgars, the two basic ethnic elements in the medieval Bulgarian state, and their changing relations with each other and with the surviving remnants of earlier populations can only be traced if we begin our story in late antiquity. Second, the reasons for the peculiar ethnic mosaic, the cultural collapse, and the demographic decline which characterise the northern Balkans in the early days of the Bulgarian state are buried deep in the earlier history of the region. Third, the political, religious and strategic choices open to Byzantines and Bulgarians in the ninth and tenth centuries become much clearer if we examine their earlier relations, and the gradual development of the confrontation between them in its peculiar configuration.

The account must necessarily be a complex one, in which narrative and analysis are closely interwoven, and in which the main line of the narrative is from time to time interrupted to pick up the distant beginnings of a train of events which later becomes of crucial importance. In particular the early history of the Slav peoples and of the Bulgars calls for such 'flashback' treatment.

I have preferred to err by giving too much detail rather than too little. Partly this arises from the conviction that a knowledge of the past of any society is essential for the understanding of its present — the shibboleth which distinguishes the historian from the sociologist. Partly it is doubtless due to an irrepressible interest in the subject.

The Background

By the fourth century of our era the whole of the Balkan peninsula had formed a part of the Roman empire for three hundred years. From the point of view of population and history it fell into two main zones. In the south, in the area roughly corresponding to modern Greece, the inhabitants were uniformly Greek-speaking and the city, with its surrounding dependent territory, was virtually the only political organisation. The few non-Greek communities planted there, such as Roman colonies in Corinth, Megara, Patrae, Dyme in Achaea, Cassandreia in the Pallene peninsula, Philippi and Pella and the Italian merchant groups in such cities as Corinth had long ago been Hellenised. The same is true of the Macedonians, the people of southern Epirus, whose claim to be regarded as Greek had in earlier centuries not been universally recognised. This region—peninsular Greece and the islands—was one of ancient civilisation. Most of its political communities long antedated the conquest which brought them under Roman control. On the whole Roman power had meant stagnation, dwindling population and crumbling economy in Greece. There were exceptions. Athens drew students from the upper classes of the whole Roman empire because of the fame of its schools of rhetoric and philosophy. The transfer of the central administration of the empire by Constantine to his new capital at Constantinople gradually stimulated the economic life of the eastern European provinces.[1] But by and large Greece was an economic and political backwater in the fourth century, and probably underpopulated in comparison with earlier ages. It is significant, for instance, that after the Gothic raid of 267, most of the area inside the walls of Themistocles at Athens was abandoned, and a new wall was constructed surrounding the Acropolis and a small area to the north, within which settlement was concentrated.[2]

To the north of Greece lay a geographically and ethnically much more diversified area. The line of separation of the two corresponds closely, though not exactly, with that marking the northern limit of the cultivation of the olive. Though generally mountainous, the northern Balkans also comprised extensive plains, often watered by perennial rivers, some of which were navigable, as well as extensive areas of rolling hill country. The mountain belt running behind the Adriatic coast—the Dinaric Alps—was barren and treeless in ancient times as today. But the Balkan chain, running across the eastern part of the peninsula from east to west, south of the Danube, the Rhodope mountains, the mountains of western Macedonia and Albania were wooded, and often provided high summer pastures above the forest line. The main ethnic groups in the north Balkan area had been Illyrians in the west, Thracians in the east, and Daco-Moesians between the Balkan range and the Danube.[3] All groups had been subjected for centuries to influences from the Mediterranean world. Greek cities had been founded along the southern and eastern coasts of Thrace. The native Thracian political organisations, which had the form of confederacies or short-lived empires rather than lasting centralised states, had been subjected first by Macedonia, then by Rome (though a client Kingdom of Thrace was permitted to exist until 46 A.D.). The Thracian ruling class had been thoroughly Hellenised south of the Balkan chain. Between the mountains and the Danube Greek penetration had been much less intense. Political independence lasted much longer. It was not till early in the first century of our era that Moesia, as this region was called, became a Roman province. Roman garrisons were established along the Danube, and colonies of veterans were settled at a number of points. The Thracian upper class here became Romanised rather than Hellenised. By the fourth century both parts of the Thracian area were studded with cities, each with its dependent territory. But there were still large areas which did not belong to any city, but were administered directly by imperial officials. Most of the population south of the Balkans spoke Greek, those north of the Balkans and those west of a line running roughly from Sofia to Durazzo, spoke Latin. Thracian continued to be spoken in the countryside though we cannot estimate the extent of its survival, any more than we can estimate how much Gaulish was spoken in Gaul at the same period. And some sense of Thracian ethnic unity survived. We hear of the suppressing of cult sites of Thracian gods about 400;[4] the Bessae, a Thracian tribe, are alleged to have been converted to Christianity by Nicetas of Remesiana in 396;[5] we hear of Thracian monasteries in Palestine and in Constantinople as late as the sixth century.[6] Thrace served as a reservoir of military manpower in late antiquity, and men with Thracian names, practising Thracian religious cults, are found all over the empire.[7] On the survival of Thracian speech and ethnic consciousness in the fourth century and later cf. V. Beševliev, *Personennamen bei den Thrakern,* 1970, pp. 69-137, a valuable collection of material which must however be used with some caution.

In the western section the situation was similar. There had been in the course of the centuries considerable Roman settlement among the Illyrian population. Cities had grown up, not only on the Adriatic coast, where they sometimes occupied the site of Illyrian tribal capitals or of Greek colonies, but also in the interior, particularly along the major river valleys. By the fourth century the bulk of the population had been Romanised in the sense that they spoke Latin in public. But the continuing survival of the Illyrian language, probably in the mountainous area of northern Albania and the neighbouring region of Yugoslavia, is proved by the existence today of the Albanian language, the core of which is Illyrian.

Throughout the northern Balkans there was already great ethnical diversity, pockets of Goths, Bastarnae (probably a Celtic-speaking people), Carpi, Sarmatians, Scythians, Alans (probably all Iranian-speaking) and others being found among the Thracians or Illyrians. This state of affairs was the result of centuries of the establishment of conquered or refugee communities in these territories by the Romans, and of the settlement of bodies of Roman veterans, as well as of individual migration. It is hard to determine the extent to which these enclaves preserved their language and way of life. Many were certainly absorbed into the basic population of Romanised or Hellenised Illyrians and Thracians. Yet they must have made some contribution to the common culture of the area. And they certainly contributed to the extinction of old tribal and ethnic traditions.

Through the Balkan provinces of the Roman empire ran a number of roads of strategic significance. They generally followed the line of earlier roads or lines of communication. The most important was that which ran south-eastwards from Aquileia via Emona (Ljubljana), Siscia (Sisak), Singidunum (Belgrade), Naissus (Nish), Remesiana (Bela Palanka), Serdica (Sofia), Philippopolis (Plovdiv), and Hadrianopolis (Adrianople) to Constantinople. Cutting through the peninsula from west to east ran a Roman military road, the via Egnatia which, starting from Dyrrhachium (Durazzo) on the Adriatic ran through central Albania, rounded lake Ohrid on the north, passing through Lychnis (Ohrid), and Edessa to Thessalonika, then following the low ground between the mountains and the sea to Constantinople. These two main roads were linked by another which, leaving the Belgrade-Constantinople road at Naissus followed the valley of the Morava, passed over the easy col to join the Axius (Vardar) at Scupi (Skopje), and follow its valley via Stobi (near Veles) to Thessalonika. A less important link road left the main diagonal road at Serdica, proceeded up the valley of the Oescus (Iskar), over the col to the headwaters of the Strymon (Struma), and thence down the river valley to join the via Egnatia a little to the north-east of Thessalonika. Another road ran along the south bank of the Danube from Singidunum to Durostorum and on to the Black Sea at Tomis. It was linked to the diagonal road by secondary roads following the passes through the Balkan chain, of which the most important were those running from Serdica down the valley of the Oescus to Oescus (Gigen) and from Philippopolis via Nicopolis (Nikyup) down the Iantrus (Yantra) to the Danube. Finally, a road followed the coast of the Black Sea from the mouth of the Danube via Odessus (Varna), Mesembria (Nesebŭr), Develtos (near Burgaz), and Salmydessus (Kiyikoy) to Constantinople.

These Roman roads were protected by a system of military posts and forts, particularly when they passed through defiles. Some of these had gathered a population of veterans and traders around them and become veritable cities. Long after the last Roman soldier had left great areas of the Balkans, the Roman roads and their supporting works continued to exist, and to determine the routes of movement and the zones of settlement of the various peoples who entered the Balkans. Those who held the roads could move more or less freely along them. But they often had no control of the areas between the roads, except in so far as they patrolled them in strength.

In the fourth century the Danube was the frontier of the Roman empire. On one side lay Roman provinces, paying taxes to the Roman government and subject to Roman law. On the other lay a patchwork of client states, tribes and ephemeral political groupings over which Roman control was at best indirect, by means of treaties and subsidies, and at times non-existent. For a time, from the beginning of the second century A.D. to late in the third, direct Roman control had been extended north of the Danube into Dacia (Transylvania and western Wallachia) and Latin-speakers from various parts of the Roman world had settled there as soldiers or traders. But the growing pressure of peoples on the move north of the Danube forced the partial abandonment of the new province under Gallienus in 256 and its total evacuation under Aurelian in 274.

The Danube frontier was garrisoned in the fourth century by a large army based upon a system of fortifications in depth and supported by a strategic reserve which could be moved from region to region as the situation demanded. The distinction between the *limitanei*, based on strong points in the frontier zone and maintained by land-holdings, and the *comitatenses*, the mobile field army under direct command of a general attached to the imperial court, had already begun to be blurred by the transference of units from one category to the other, but the principle upon which it was based still held. Among both categories of troops there were many soldiers recruited as individuals from territories beyond the frontier, as well as bodies of foreign mercenaries serving under their own officers—the *foederati*. The bulk of the army was probably recruited from the Balkan area, though there would from time to time be units of Asian, African or other origin to be found along the Danube frontier. The permanent garrison on the Danube frontier in the middle of the fourth century has been calculated to have been about 145,000 strong—64,000 on the lower Danube, and 81,000 in the upper Danubian provinces, which do not directly concern us here (cf. A.H.M. Jones, *The Later Roman Empire*, 1964, 682-3). There were also several flotillas based on harbours on the south bank and patrolling the river during the nine months of the year when it was open for navigation.

This formidable defence system, which was naturally complemented by diplomatic activity, distribution of subsidies etc. north of the river, had scarcely ever been penetrated, apart from raiding operations of purely local significance. The only exception was during the period of political instability and protracted civil war in the middle of the third century, when a force of Goths from the middle Dniester area had crossed the Danube and marched through the Balkan provinces collecting booty until they reached Athens, where they sacked the lower city but were unable to take the Acropolis. But these invaders withdrew at once beyond the Danube. Though ready to break through the frontier of the empire when they could, the barbarians took its existence for granted.

The Barbarian Invasions of the Fourth and Fifth Centuries

Such was the situation when in 376 the Alans, an Iranian-speaking nomadic people moving westward through the steppe zone, overwhelmed the kingdom of the Ostrogoths in the Eastern Ukraine and drove their kinsmen, the Visigoths, from their home on Dniester. The Visigoths fled to the Danube and asked the Roman authorities to enrol them as *foederati* and to grant them land in Moesia south of the Danube. There were probably already some small Gothic communities settled between the river and the Balkan mountains, among whom Christianity had made some progress. After much negotiation, the Visigoths were ferried across the Danube at Durostorum. They numbered several tens of thousands of adult males, together with their families. Once in Roman territory they were treated by local officials with a combination of dishonesty and inefficiency which both aroused their resentment and reduced them to the verge of starvation. In 378 they turned against the Romans, and were joined by a number of Gothic slaves from the cities and estates of the Balkans as well as by men condemned to penal servitude in the mines in various parts of Thrace, who brought with them valuable technical skills. The Gothic army, mainly a cavalry force, swept through Thrace and on 9 August 378 defeated the Roman field army at Adrianople, killing the emperor Valens.

The Goths, now joined by groups of Alans and Huns from beyond the Danube, who scented booty, advanced on Constantinople, but were unable to take the city. The new eastern emperor, Theodosius, by a combination of diplomacy and force, and by taking on large bodies of Goths as *foederati*, succeeded in averting the most acute danger. But a substantial rump of armed Goths remained at large for a generation in the Balkan provinces, living off the land, destroying the economic infrastructure, and disrupting the established patterns of life. Unlike previous raiders, they were present in force and they meant to stay. After protracted negotiations and a series of abortive campaigns the Visigothic force was finally diverted into Italy, where in 410 it captured and sacked Rome, and thence to southern Gaul and ultimately to Spain. There a Visigothic kingdom was set up which survived until it was destroyed by the Arabs in the early eighth century.

Though no independent Gothic force remained in the Balkans, a great many Goths were settled on the land there as Roman soldiers, adding a new element to the population. We do not know where the main areas of settlement were. More important, a very long period of security had come to an end. The Turkic Huns, who followed upon the heels of the Alans across the steppe zone, invaded Thrace in 408-9, again in 422, and almost every year thereafter until after the middle of the fifth century. The details of their invasions are of little importance, but they continued to undermine the social and economic balance of life in the northern Balkans. Unlike the Visigoths, they made no serious penetration of peninsular Greece. It was not merely a matter of physical damage, which could always be made good: the expectation each year of further invasions in succeeding years made men loth to repair damage as it occurred. The future was heavily discounted. Small holdings thus fell into disrepair and were often in the end abandoned as the cultivator or his heir left to swell the growing numbers of landless men in regions of the empire less exposed to attack. Patterns of trade were broken and never restored, industrial installations destroyed and never replaced. The troops sent by the government in Constantinople, with their demands for supplies at fixed prices, for quarters and for forced labour, were sometimes no less of a scourge than the invading Huns. And the tax-collector, who might be tolerated when taxes bought security, became the most unwelcome of visitors when they no longer did so. Some men decided to quit the empire altogether and throw in their lot with the barbarians, among whom both the rate of taxation and the efficiency with which taxes were collected were less than in the Roman empire. The Huns, whose own way of life was highly specialised for mobility, had need of craftsmen, merchants and men with elementary administrative skills, and they often welcomed Roman defectors'. Priscus of Panium, who accompanied a Roman embassy to the court of Attila in 448 or 449, reports a highly revealing interview with such a defector, who was certainly not the only one of his kind. Finally, some of the inhabitants of the northern Balkan provinces were carried off as captives by the Huns and either kept by their new masters or sold back as slaves to the Romans. So the first half of the fifth century must have seen demographic changes in the area the extent of which it is impossible to estimate, as well as extensive destruction of agricultural and industrial installations and a disastrous fall in public confidence.

Throughout this time, and indeed for a century and a half later, the frontier was still held in a military sense. The chain of forts along the Danube was still garrisoned. Strong points which were taken by raiders were soon rebuilt. Indeed there was a good deal of new military building, repair and strengthening of city walls and so on. But it was clear that the army which for four centuries had protected the peaceful life of the Balkan provinces was now no longer able to do so. It could neither keep invaders out, nor prevent them getting back to their bases north of the Danube, laden with booty. It continued to be an ethnically mixed force. And to the mixture there was added in the second half of the fifth century a new element, the scarcely Hellenised Isaurian mountaineers of the Taurus range in Asia Minor.

The second half of the fifth century saw less frequent and less disastrous raids than the first half. But there was no long period of peace and security during which the damage of the two preceding generations could be repaired. Attila died in 453, and the Hun state, which had depended largely on his personality, broke up. The resulting splinter groups continued to raid the Balkan provinces, though they did not usually penetrate very deep. The Ostrogoths, formerly in subjection to the Huns, were settled in Pannonia and paid by the Romans to act as a buffer against other peoples on the move. When the emperor Leo I tried to reduce the subvention paid to them they invaded the western Balkans and got as far as Dyrrhachium in 461. A truce was negotiated and some years of peace ensued. But from about 470 they began systematic invasions of Illyricum, and were later settled, as unwelcome and uneasy *foederati*, in Lower Moesia—between the Danube and the Balkan chain—and in the Dobrudja, while another group of Ostrogoths moved about the northern Balkans. Both groups needed land above all, and until they could get it they used their military strength to blackmail their titular commander, the East Roman Emperor. In fact those who most suffered were the inhabitants of Thrace, Moesia and the Illyrian provinces. Not only was the countryside devastated, the Ostrogoths, no doubt with the aid of Roman engineers in the first place, soon learned how to take cities. In the late seventies or early eighties of the century they captured and destroyed Stobi and Heraclea Lyncestis (Bitola) in western Macedonia. The former city was abandoned by its surviving inhabitants and never rebuilt. Other Ostrogothic raids penetrated as far as Thessaly and to the walls of Constantinople. The Ostrogoths, having no lands of their own to cultivate, could live only by depredation at the expense of the agricultural population of the Balkan provinces. That after so many years of war and devastation and the accompanying depopulation the provinces could still maintain such a formidable body of unwelcome guests for nearly a generation is a measure of how great their productivity must have been a century earlier.

In 488 the Roman government managed to get rid of the Ostrogoths from the Balkans by sending them under their king Theodoric, who had spent many years of his youth as a hostage in Constantinople, into Italy to expel the usurper Odoacer. Ostensibly an officer of the East Roman empire, Theodoric set up what was in reality an independent kingdom of Italy. The departure of the Ostrogoths gave only temporary relief to the hard-pressed inhabitants of the northern Balkan provinces. In 493 the Bulgars, a Turkic people who had been useful allies of the empire in the reign of Zeno, and who had earlier probably formed part of the Hun confederation, crossed the Danube, advanced into Thrace and killed a Roman general in battle. This raid was followed by others by the Bulgars and by other peoples from north of the frontier. In 499 a Bulgar raiding force in Thrace destroyed two thirds of a Roman army of 15,000 which had been sent to halt them. In 502 Thrace was once more invaded, and great quantities of booty and prisoners were taken across the Danube without any attempt at resistance by the field army; the frontier army was usually helpless once the frontier had been penetrated. It is significant of the new military situation in the second half of the fifth century that by 469 a new wall was built reaching from the Black Sea to the Sea of Marmara about forty miles from Constantinople, following the same line as the present-day Çatalca fortifications. The capital was no longer protected by the army on the Danube, and the territory between the Danube and the new Long Walls was regarded as expendable if the worst came to the worst. In the meantime the short-term danger represented by the Bulgars was evaded by the customary method of enrolling some of them as *foederati* in the Roman army and paying the others to make war on a people living to the east of them in Bessarabia or the nearby Ukraine, the Antae. Though the Antae may have owed much of their political organisation and some of their ruling class to the Iranian Sarmatians, who had long lived north of the steppe zone in eastern Europe, the testimony of contemporary witnesses and the evidence of personal names make it clear that actors now appear upon the Balkan scene who will play the principal part in subsequent events there. A brief digression on their previous history may therefore be appropriate.

The Advent of the Slavs

The speakers of Slavonic had been settled in the area of the upper Vistula and middle Dnieper since the fourth millennium before our era. In this region, where forest and steppe mix, they slowly developed their peculiar culture. The use of bronze was gradually adopted during the second millennium by diffusion from their southern neighbours. They practised a mixture of stock-breeding and agriculture adapted to the conditions of their homeland, which provided little surplus to be accumulated in the hands of a ruling class. Their settlements were small, often on river terraces, their humble houses were often partly sunk in the ground for warmth in the long cold winter. From the beginning of the first millennium B.C. the Slavs were in contact with Iranian-speaking peoples of the steppe zone, who may have exercised some kind of overlordship over them, first the Cimmerians, and later the Scythians. They are probably to be identified with the 'Scythian ploughmen' of whom Herodotus speaks (4.17). It was during the period of Scythian predominance, about the middle of the first millennium B.C. that the Slavs appear to have learnt the use of iron. After this long period of contact with Cimmerians and Scythians, to which are to be attributed a number of Iranian loanwords in common Slavonic, there followed a period during which the Slavs were subject to penetration and displacement by invaders.

First came the Iranian-speaking Sarmatians, who unlike their Scythian predecessors left the steppe and entered the forest and steppe zone, where they exchanged their pastoral way of life for agriculture, which they probably learned from their Slav subjects. There was probably a good deal of intermingling of Slavs and Sarmatians. Large villages are found, with buildings adapted to different economic purposes. The presence of uniform wheel-made pottery throughout the Ukraine, Moldavia, Wallachia and Transylvania in this period indicates that the craftsman was beginning to be differentiated from the peasant. The existence of both cremation and inhumation all over the area suggests some mingling of religious beliefs. By about 200 A.D. new invaders appeared on the scene, the Germanic-speaking Goths advancing up the Vistula. They probably subjected at least some of the Slavs to their dominion. Their influence is attested by a stratum of very old Germanic loanwords in common Slavonic. The disturbance caused in the peaceful and rather static life of the Slav peasants by these successive penetrations and by their close symbiosis with Sarmatian and Goth may have led to the beginning of an eastward and southward spread of the Slavonic tribes. It probably had much to do with the establishment of the mysterious state of the Antae between the Don and the Volga, and later west of the Don, in which there was at least a strong Slavonic element.

The advent of the Huns towards the end of the fourth century A.D. shattered the uniform Slavo-Gothic culture of the forest-steppe zone and drove the Goths towards the Danube. The break-up of Gothic power led to a slow spread of Slavonic farmers and stock-breeders outwards from their original area of settlement towards the east, the south and the west. The dense forest zone, to which the Slavs' way of life was ill-adapted, was left to the Baltic and Finno-Ugrian tribes who had lived there for millennia. The penetration of the forest by the eastern Slavs belongs to a later period. The reasons for this Slavonic expansion are obscure. The population was evidently increasing. But this could only occur if more food could be produced. Perhaps improvements in agricultural technique, new breeds of animals, new varieties of crops, enabled these peasant communities to bring into cultivation land which would previously have been left wild. In any case the expansion is a fact, though we know scarcely anything of the way in which it took place. It was not an invasion. The Slavs were not swiftly-moving armed horsemen, like the nomads of the steppes or the Goths. They formed no large political units, had no kings. They spread by walking, or by sailing on the great rivers, for they were superb boatmen. They must have taken over much land which had been left untilled after the devastations of the Huns. Where they evicted the

previous cultivators, it was after hostilities on a small scale—scuffles
rather than battles.

By the end of the fifth century Byzantine sources report the presence
of this new people, whom they call Sklavenoi, all along the Danube
frontier. At the same time a recognisable cultural profile emerges
over an area extending from the Elbe in the west to the Dnieper in the
east, from the Baltic Sea and the forest zone in the north to the Danube
in the south. It is characterised by small, unfortified villages of square
wooden houses, partly sunk into the ground and with a stone stove
in one corner. Near the villages are burial grounds containing cremation burials either in urns or in pits. Hand-made pottery of a greyish
clay mixed with sand or crushed sherds has rounded shoulders and
often a slightly out-turned rim. The distinction between craftsman
and peasant, which began to develop in the homeland, was given up
by the Slavs in their period of migration. Byzantine contemporaries
tell us something about this people, whose humble remains have only
recently been clearly distinguished by the archaeologist. They had
no political organisation higher than the tribe, and even the power
of the tribal chief was very limited. There was little social differentiation among them. They moved on foot, or in the dug-out boats, which
they built and handled expertly. They swam well, and could swim un-
detected under water, breathing through a reed as through a snorkel.
They wore no body-armour, but carried shields and spears, or bows
with which they shot poisoned arrows. In warfare they avoided open
plains and stuck to hilly wooded land, in which they ambushed their
enemies with great skill. They were specialists in night attacks. Their
pale complexion and reddish-blond hair attracted the attention of
Mediterranean observers, Greek and Arab alike. They were of course
pagans, and more will be said about the religion of the Slavs later. What
struck the Byzantines who first came into contact with them—and
who saw non-Christian religions in the light of Hellenic paganism—
was the existence of one god among others who was lord of the thunder
and to whom animal sacrifices were offered at special shrines;
the worship of a number of female deities connected with vegetation
and the countryside; and the absence of any belief in destiny.

Following their usual practice, the Byzantines soon began enrolling
Slav detachments as auxiliary forces in their army, and we hear of such
Slavonic troops taking part in Justinian's campaigns in Italy and on
the Persian front. In this way the Slavs would first be brought into
direct contact with the civilisation of the late Roman empire and with

the Christian religion, and would learn something of the topography of the land facing them across the Danube, where they were prevented from settling by the Roman garrisons of the frontier defences.

We may now return to our narrative of events in the Balkans in the sixth century. Two new peoples are recorded by our sources north of the lower Danube, the Kotrigurs and the Utigurs. They appear to be Turkic speakers, part of the debris left by the dissolution of the Hun empire. Whether, as seems probable, they are to be identified with the Bulgars whose raids into Roman territory have recently been mentioned cannot now be determined. Still less certain is their identification with the Bulgars who a little later appear north of the Danube delta and in Pannonia, and with whose fortunes this book will largely be concerned. It is well to bear in mind that the pastoralists of the steppe moved quickly over large distances; that in the absence of a powerful state like that of the Huns, the Khazars or the Mongols, clans and tribes are continually making alliances and subjecting their neighbours, thus forming ephemeral quasi-states often known by the name of the tribe in a position of leadership at the time, and that Greek writers are generally extremely vague in their identification of the steppe peoples, often calling them by the name of their distant predecessors, which had become part of the literary tradition. Be that as it may, the first half of the sixth century is marked by raids of growing severity made into Roman territory by these peoples, and we hear of Slavs both accompanying them—perhaps providing supporting infantry to the steppe people's cavalry—and fighting against them. It is generally useless to try to determine exactly who was involved in each raid. In 517 Macedonia and Thessaly were ravaged as far as Thermopylae, presumably by raiders following the Morava-Vardar route. A thousand pounds of gold did not suffice to ransom the prisoners, many of whom were taken back north of the Danube by their captors. Shortly afterwards Germanus, nephew of the emperor Justin I, inflicted a crushing defeat on a Slav force, and peace was restored south of the Danube for a number of years.

In 528 the Bulgars raided Thrace, in 529 we hear of Slav invaders. The probability is that in both cases the two peoples were acting in concert. Such invasions continued in succeeding years. In 533 the Roman commander-in-chief in Thrace, Chilbudius, himself allegedly a Slav, was killed by a Slav raiding force. Once again the Byzantine authorities took strong action. There was a major defeat of the Bulgars somewhere between the Balkan chain and the Danube. At the same

time Sirmium (Sremska Mitrovica) was recaptured from the Ostrogoths. In a law promulgated in 535 Justinian boasts of the restoration
of peace on the Danube (*Novel* 11 pr.). It did not last long: Sirmium
was lost to the Germanic Gepids of Pannonia in the next year and in
540 there was a major invasion by the Bulgars or Kotrigurs, accompanied by Slavs. Justinian's concentration of units of the field army
in Africa and Italy in the course of his reconquest of these territories
had probably led to some weakening of the defence in depth on the
Danube frontier. One invading force reached the walls of Thessalonika, then turned eastwards along the Via Egnatia, forced the Long
Walls and appeared outside the walls of Constantinople itself. Unable
to take the city, they withdrew to the Danube taking with them
100,000 prisoners. The second invading force entered peninsular
Greece and got as far as the Isthmus of Corinth before returning to
the Danube laden with prisoners and booty. No invasion on this scale
had been seen since the operations of the Ostrogoths two generations
earlier.

From 540 on there was little peace in the northern Balkans, despite
the extensive programme of military works to protect the main Roman
lines of communication, the strengthening of the huge military bases
on the Danube itself, the reinforcement of the Danube flotillas, for
which all invaders had a healthy respect, and the efforts of the diplo-
matists of Constantinople to persuade more distant peoples of the
steppe zone to fall on the rear of the Bulgars (or Kotrigurs) and Slavs.
But the frontier itself was held, and the pressure of the invaders seems
to have slackened after 551, thanks to an alliance between the Romans
and the Utigurs, who lived east of the Kotrigurs. There was no settlement by peoples from north of the Danube in the Balkans except for
limited settlement of *foederati* by the Romans themselves. In 558-9
major invasions began again. The Kotrigurs, with the Slavs in their
train, crossed the frozen Danube at the beginning of 559 and fanned
out in three directions: through Macedonia and Greece as far as
Thermopylae, into the Gallipoli peninsula, and towards the Long Walls
which protected Constantinople. Only the threatened cutting off of
their retreat by the fleet on the Danube forced them to return, once
again with many prisoners and much booty. There was a fresh invasion
of Thrace on a smaller scale in 562. What strikes the reader of contemporary accounts of these massive invasions of the mid-sixth century
is the virtual absence of any mention of the countless strong points
and fortified positions occupied by the Romans. The invaders seem

simply to have bypassed them. They certainly did not stop to assault them. And once they have passed through the defensive zone, they seem to have no difficulty in going where they like until they reach the fortifications of one of the great cities of the empire. When they fight a regular battle in open ground they are generally defeated. And they keep well out of the way of the Roman fleet. The immediate motive of the invasions is to take booty and prisoners. But behind this there probably lay the need to get land to settle on. They are constantly being pushed on from behind, both by the continuing demographic expansion of the Slavs and by the movement from east to west of yet further pastoralists of the steppe. But the Roman authorities have learnt from their experience with the Visigoths and the Ostrogoths, to say nothing of what had happened in the western empire, where the *foederati* had ultimately taken over province after province from them. Only small numbers from beyond the Danube were allowed to settle, and then under strict Roman control. So long as the Romans hold the fortified cities and the strong points which guard the main roads, the invaders cannot take over the land, even if it is lying un-cultivated as a result of devastation. And they cannot take fortified cities and strong points; their technology is not up to the task. This was the situation of stalemate which existed in the closing years of the reign of Justinian.

In 558 a new people appeared on the frontier of the empire in the Caucasus. The Avars had previously established their domination over a large area north and west of China. Overthrown by the revolt of their Turkic subjects, many were put to the sword. The rest swept across the steppe zone of Eurasia with incredible rapidity, and now demanded land in the Roman empire for settlement. The government in Constantinople, first under Justinian then under his nephew and successor Justin II, temporised. The Avars were given a subsidy and asked to deal with certain enemies of the empire north of the Black Sea. This they did with such cold-blooded efficiency that they were soon on the Danube, demanding land once more. The Byzantines drew out the negotiations as long as possible. For a time the Avars were put off with an offer of land north of the Sava, if only they would expel the Herules who were then occupying it. Justin II suspended payment of subsidies to them without provoking any hostile reaction. The Avars seem to have been at first very unsure of themselves in their new environment. They even allowed themselves to be attacked and defeat-ed by a Byzantine army. But the news of Byzantine defeats on the

Persian front in 573 or 574 changed the situation. The Avars crossed the Danube, eluding the Byzantine navy, and defeated a Byzantine army. The emperor Tiberius, his hands tied in Persia, signed a treaty ceding to them the region of Sirmium, but not the city itself. The chronology of events in the next few years is very uncertain. The Avars seem to have turned against the Slavs north of the Danube, perhaps acting ostensibly as allies of the empire, and to have subdued them. They then may have urged the Slavs to raid Byzantine territory south of the river; we hear of a major offensive about 580. The Avars asked the emperor Tiberius II for permission to cross the Danube and 'punish' the Slavs, but the emperor saw the trick and refused. But soon the Avars no longer needed his permission. In 582 they besieged and took Sirmium, the key to the Balkans, and in the next few years Slavs and Avars poured into the peninsula, meeting with scarcely any resistance. The Avar crossing of the Danube was carried out on boats built by their Slav subjects or allies. cf. Theophylact Simocatta *Hist.* 6.3.

The problem of the relation of the Avars and the Slavs is a difficult one. Now we hear of Avar invasions, now of Slav invasions, again of Avaro-Slav invasions; the earliest express mention of Slavs as allies of the Avars is in raids on Roman territory in 576-7. Let us get some points clear. First, the Avars, who had long been in the sphere of influence of both Chinese and Sasanian culture, were at a much higher level of political development than the Bulgars, Kotrigurs and Onogurs, and *a fortiori* than the Slavs. The Avar community was a state, with institutions, an organised army, and a king or khagan. The powerful personality of the khagan Baian emerges from the Byzantine and western sources. They conducted diplomatic negotiations and signed treaties not only with the Byzantines, but with the Lombards, the Franks and other peoples. They had long given up the relatively unprofitable business of herding animals for that of herding men. The Slavs had no political cohesion; each little community seems to have acted for itself, and we never hear of diplomatic negotiations or treaties. The Avars were not numerous, though whether they were more or less than 100,000 strong we do not know; the Slavs were to be counted in millions. The Avars did not cultivate the soil; the Slavs were excellent farmers. The Avars were uninterested in settlement outside of the steppe zone, in which they knew how to live; the Slavs needed the agricultural land of the Balkans. It was in the interest of the Avars to cream off the agricultural surplus of the Slavs, and the more land they cultivated the more there would be to cream off; it was in the interest of the Slav communities to attach themselves to the Avar armies, whose military technology was superior to their own. This is probably the basis of their uneasy collaboration. And the Slavs doubtless did not confine themselves to following in the wake of Avar armies, but moved forward into unoccupied or poorly defended territory whenever they could. In 582 Slavs and Avars reached Anchialos, on the Black Sea. A few years later they were pouring into Greece, and it may be that they besieged Thessalonika in 586. So long as the Byzantines were occupied in war with Persia, Slavs and Avars could go almost anywhere they liked in the Balkans. And when the Avars withdrew, as they did on several occasions, the Slav peasants stayed.

The emperor Maurice forced the Persians to concede victory in 591, and turned his attention to the reconquest of the Balkans. Ten years of hard-fought war ensued, punctuated by a short peace with the Avars. Many of the new settlers were driven back north of the Danube, but many no doubt stayed on in the more remote areas. In 602 the Byzantine army was ordered to winter north of the Danube in order to keep up the pressure on the retreating enemy. This order provoked a military revolt, which soon spread to the capital. Maurice was murdered, and Phocas, the leader of the revolt, proclaimed emperor. Phocas had his hands full dealing with his own subjects, and the Persians seized the opportunity to reopen hostilities. The Danube frontier was left without a garrison, and Avars and Slavs once more poured unhindered across the river and spread through Illyria, Moesia, western Thrace and peninsular Greece.

Both had learned a great deal from the Romans. The Avars were keen students of siegecraft, and we hear of a Roman defector, no doubt a military engineer, acting as their instructor. The Slavs too had learned how to take fortified positions. They had long had in their midst numerous captives and defectors from Roman territory, including craftsmen of every kind. A contemporary military handbook records the interesting fact that the Slavs did not keep their captives in permanent slavery, as did other peoples, but after a fixed interval allowed them either to return home or to remain as free men with their former captors. In this way Roman technicians of all kinds must have settled among the Slavs and passed on their skill. And the Slavs themselves were apt pupils. Their expertise in making boats, which is often commented on, implies widespread acquaintance with wood-working and the use of tools. The details of this process of acculturation remain unclear. What is clear is that between the middle of Justinian's reign and the end of the sixth century the Slavs had learned siegecraft and acquired or constructed the necessary engines. When they invaded the Balkans in the eighties of the sixth century and again after 602 they took city after city. They were thus in a position to settle permanently and till the land. During some thirty years the ethnic composition of the Balkan population was completely changed.

Although it is evident that a radical transformation took place, it is difficult to establish with any clarity exactly what happened. In the west virtually all territory north of the present Greco-Yugoslav frontier with the exception of the coastal cities seems to have passed out of Byzantine control. Kastoria remained in Byzantine hands, though the surrounding countryside was largely occupied by Slavs. The great city and port of Thessalonika was never lost by the Byzantines in spite of a series of sieges, some by Slavs alone, others by Slavs and Avars acting in concert. The first of these may have been in 586, but was more likely in 597, and another probably took place during the reign of Phocas (602-610). Shortly before 626 there was an attack in force on the city by a number of Slav tribes acting in common under a leader called Chatzon, and operating by sea in their dug-out boats as well as on land: this seems to have formed part of a general thrust into the Aegean area by the Slavs. A storm destroyed the Slav fleet and the city was saved. Its hinterland, however, was in Slav hands, and a kind of symbiosis between the Byzantine city and the surrounding Slav peasants began quite early. In the eastern part of the Balkan peninsula the area north of the Balkan chain was completely lost to the Byzantines, except for some strong points in the Dobrudja. The cities along the Black Sea coast were in general held, since the Byzantine fleet had control of the sea, but individual cities from time to time fell temporarily to the Avars or Slavs. South of the Balkan chain the situation is less clear. Naissus fell shortly before the great siege of Thessalonika by Chatzon, and Serdica appears to have fallen at the same time. But it was soon recaptured and remained in Byzantine hands, though dwindling from a great city to a garrison-town clustered round the sixth century church of the Holy Wisdom, and the surrounding territory became entirely Slav.

In 626 the Avars under the khagan Baian, supported by a large contingent of Slavonic troops, besieged Constantinople. They were equipped with a variety of sophisticated siege engines, and accompanied by a fleet of dug-out boats manned and presumably built by Slav sailors. Their attack coincided with an advance by the Persians under Chosroes

II to the Asiatic shore opposite Constantinople, and it was generally
believed that the Avars were acting in concert with the Persians. In
the outcome the siege was unsuccessful, and both Avars and Persians
had to withdraw. This defeat marked a turning-point in the fortunes
of the Avars, whose interest in the Balkans diminished as they were
faced with revolts of their subjects and pressure from the Franks in
Pannonia. The Byzantine government had to deal henceforth with the
Slavs on their own. No doubt the long-term perspective was their absorption into the empire as tax-paying Christians. In the meantime
Constantinople itself and its Thracian hinterland had to be held. The
latter became particularly important when Egypt fell, first to the Persians and then to the Arabs, and Egyptian corn no longer reached the
city. Hence Byzantine policy was to hold on to a series of fortresses
protecting eastern Thrace—Develtos, Adrianople, Traianopolis (today
Alexandroupolis)—to retain control of the coast road along the Black
Sea shore and of the Via Egnatia as far as Thessalonika, and to try to
establish a Byzantine presence in as much of the diagonal road as was
feasible. On the whole this policy was realised. The Via Egnatia could
only be kept open by patrolling in force, and land communications
with Thessalonika were never secure. But the ring of inner fortresses
was held, Philippopolis remained Byzantine, Serdica was recaptured,
from the Slavs or Avars, though we do not know when. And the
coastal cities of the Black Sea remained Byzantine possessions.

   Further south, in peninsular Greece, there was extensive Slav settlement in the last decades of the sixth and the early decades of the seventh
century. Its extent is very hard to estimate. Fallmerayer's thesis, recently revived by Jenkins, that the original population of Greece was wiped
out or expelled by the invading Slavs, and that the present Greeks are
the descendants of Hellenised Slavs, has bedevilled discussion of the
problem for more than a century. It is based essentially on a series of
lapidary statements by sources who, if contemporary with the events,
were far removed geographically, like Isidore of Seville and Willibald
of Mainz, or who wrote many generations later, like the epitomator
of Strabo's *Geography*, the emperor Constantine VII, the patriarch
Nicholas III and the Chronicle of Monemvasia. We have to check
the sweeping statements of these authorities against surviving
narrative and hagiographical sources, episcopal lists, known changes
in the administrative structure of the area, the evidence of place-names
and the like. From these it is clear that certain of the major cities remained in Byzantine hands: Athens and Patrae certainly, Corinth

except for one possible brief occupation, Thebes almost certainly. We hear of Greek inhabitants of areas seized by the Slavs taking refuge in various strong points on the coast and elsewhere, or emigrating to Byzantine southern Italy. In the eighth century there was a Slavonic *archon* in Thessaly who conspired with one of the sons of the empress Irene against his mother. The Peloponnese was heavily settled by Slav peasants, and centuries later mount Taygetus was still inhabited by Slavs who lived under a special régime. Place-names of probable Slavonic origin—and it must be emphasised that there is a great deal of uncertainty in some of the etymologies—are dense in Epirus and Thessaly and in the western Peloponnese, much less dense in central Greece, and hardly existent in Attica and some other regions of eastern Greece.

All in all we can legitimately conclude that there was extensive displacement of the original population, that much of western Greece and the Peloponnese passed out of Byzantine control for a time, but that the Aegean coast and parts of central Greece, together with coastal cities elsewhere, were never overrun. The areas of Slav settlement in peninsular Greece were probably more broken up than in the northern Balkans. None of them was far from a Byzantine city or from the sea in which the Byzantine fleet could cruise at will. And we must be careful not to assume that because an area was effectively out of the range of the Byzantine government all its inhabitants were of foreign stock. Many Greek-speaking peasants probably remained on their land off the main routes of Slavonic advance, only too glad to be protected from the Byzantine tax-collector by the new invaders. There is a further factor relevant to the Slav settlements in Greece, to which little attention has been paid in the past. The agricultural technique of the Slavs, developed over several millennia in the forest-steppe zone of central Europe, was relatively well adapted to areas with heavy soil, perennial rivers, moderately warm summers, forests to conserve the water, etc. In the strange Mediterranean world of olive and vine, bare limestone hills, light soil, and long, hot, dry summers the invaders must have been at a disadvantage. In particular their pattern of settlement along river banks was impossible in peninsular Greece, where the larger intermittent rivers with their changing course turn the lower part of their valleys into uninhabitable malarial swamps, and the smaller rivers are dry for most of the year. They would, where they could, settle in areas most adapted to their own pattern of agriculture. One such was the plain of Thessaly, another the plain of Laconia.

Epirus, with its relatively heavy precipitation and its background of snow-capped mountains, suited them better than arid Attica. They would also avoid the high mountain pastures characteristic of some parts of Greece, for they were essentially farmers, not transhumant stock-breeders. So it is likely that Greece after the Slavonic settlement was ethnically a rather complex mosaic, with Slav and Greek in contact along a number of lines.

The long-term Byzantine reaction to the occupation of so much territory within the historical frontiers of the empire was to seek to bring the newcomers under imperial control bit by bit. We hear of settlement of Slavs from areas in Thrace which the Byzantines reconquered as soldiers in Asia Minor. The experiment was not a complete success. Many of the new soldiers deserted to the Arabs. There are traces of ad hoc administrative arrangements to deal with Slav areas over which Byzantine control had been successfully reasserted. An active policy of conversion of Slav communities to Christianity was begun by church and state. And conversion to Christianity at this time implied the use of Greek as a liturgical language. Patterns of trade developed between the various *Sklaviniai*, as the Byzantines called areas inhabited by Slavs on theoretically imperial territory, and the cities held by the imperial authorities. At the same time, the tribal nobility of the various Slav communities felt the pull of Byzantine culture and Byzantine ways of life. We hear of the prince of one of the Slav tribes near Thessalonika, Perbund, who was accustomed to live in the city, dress like a Greek, and speak Greek. When he was arrested and taken to Constantinople on suspicion of plotting revolt, a joint mission of Slavs and citizens of Thessalonika went to the capital to intercede in his favour. The case was probably quite typical. The main effort in this process of absorbing the Slavs was probably made in Thrace, near Thessalonika, and along the line of the diagonal road. Peninsular Greece could wait, and in any case the *Sklaviniai* were less favourably situated there than further north. The re-establishment of Byzantine control can be traced by the setting up of *themes* — provinces under a regular government, with a locally raised army, taxes, courts etc. The theme of Thrace, comprising the immediate hinterland of Constantinople, was set up between 680 and 685, that of Hellas in central Greece before 695. The next group of themes was established about a century later, that of Macedonia (in fact western Thrace) towards 800, that of Thessalonika early in the ninth century, that of Strymon later in the century, that of the Peloponnese some time before 812 and perhaps already in the eighth century, that of Dyrrhachium early in the ninth century and that of Nicopolis in Epirus a little later.

But before these themes were set up, marking the gradual restoration of Byzantine administration and influence in the areas occupied by the Slavs, a new development had taken place which was to change for ever the face of the northern Balkans, namely the establishment of the Bulgars south of the lower Danube. This will be the next main topic in our survey of the history of the Balkans in the Dark Ages. But before turning to discuss this topic it would be well to glance at the problem of what happened to the original inhabitants of the areas occupied by the Slavs. First, it is likely that many areas, especially in the northern Balkans, were thinly populated and uncultivated when the Slavs arrived, as a result of the two centuries of warfare and invasion which had gone before. In many cases there was no one for the newcomers to displace. Then we hear of refugees moving to areas nearer Constantinople, or to the islands, or to Byzantine southern Italy. A third situation, and one arising particularly when the Avars were in command of operations, was that of the wholesale evacuation of the inhabitants of a newly-conquered area to some other region under the invaders' control. For instance we hear of a large body of Greek or Latin speakers removed from Illyria and Thrace during the first Avar advance into the Balkans and transported to the neighbourhood of Sirmium, where they retained their language, their ethnic identity, and their Christian religion for sixty years. Later they took part in a revolt against the Avars, were granted land somewhere in Macedonia by the leader of the revolt, and finally made their way to Constantinople. There must have been many such cases of mass deportation, most of which would end in the absorption of the deportees into their new milieu.

Lastly, it is clear that some of the original inhabitants took up ecological niches unattractive to the Slavs, and in this way played their part in the new economy of the Balkans. This is particularly true of transhumant stock-breeding. Leaving out of account the Rumanians north of the Danube, who may or may not be descendants of Latin-speaking inhabitants of the Balkans, there were until recently all over the Balkans wherever there are high mountain pastures groups of sheep and goat breeders practising transhumance and speaking a language related closely to Danubian Rumanian. Sometimes they were based on villages in the valleys and went up in summer to their mountain pastures. Sometimes their base was in the high ground and they had no permanent dwellings in the valleys. These Macedo-Rumanians, Meglenites and Istro-Rumanians are presumably descendants of Latin-speaking inhabitants of the Balkans, mainly Romanised Thracians and Illyrians, who took to this specialised way of life when driven off their agricultural land by the incoming Slavs, and they were without doubt more extensively settled in the past than in recent years.[8] Another group which may have originated at the same time and in the same way are the Greek-speaking transhumants of Epirus and elsewhere, the Saracatsani, whose way of life and system of values is almost identical with that of the Romance-speaking transhumants, and who are probably in the main the descendants of Hellenised Thracians. Almost confined to Epirus today, the Saracatsani once spread over a wider area. There are Greek-speaking Saracatsan communities who have long given up the transhumant way of life in various parts of present-day Bulgaria.[9] Lastly, the ancestors of the Albanians seem to have been specialist stock-breeders, who only later, and in specially favourable circumstances, took up agriculture. They are generally thought to have been descendants of unromanised Illyrians who held out in the high mountains of northern Albania and the neighbouring regions of Yugoslavia. But V. Georgiev has recently argued, with some plausibility, that they are descendants of the Daco-Moesian speakers from north of the Balkan chain. The question is as yet unresolved and of little importance for the theme of this book.

In general, then, even after the great Slav invasions of the late sixth and early seventh century the Balkans must have been an ethnic mosaic. Eastern Thrace and the Black Sea coast, as well as Thessalonika and parts of peninsular Greece remained solidly Greek, their population strengthened by refugees. Elsewhere there survived pockets of Greeks, Latins, and no doubt unromanised Thracians, Illyrians, Daco-Moesians and Dalmatians. Some kind of Byzantine presence was maintained along the great diagonal road probably as far as the defile of Dragoman. Cities and city life did not survive in the conquered areas. The Slavs learned in time how to take cities, but they were not interested in living in them. The Avars were capable of using cities—there is a story of the khagan Baian forbidding the demolition of the baths in captured Anchialus. But the Avars did not settle in the Balkans, and by the middle of the seventh century their influence there was at an end. So the ruined cities dotted the landscape, uninhabited except by occasional squatters, serving as quarries for

stone, while the Slav peasants built their settlements some distance
away from them.

This formulation requires some qualification, as conditions varied
from region to region. There is possible evidence of continuity of occupation at Bononia (Vidin) and Durostorum (Silistra) on the Danube;
Nicopolis ad Istrum (Nikjup), which was off the main invasion routes
of the Avars, may have been in continuous occupation until the end
of the Middle Ages; in southern Bulgaria there was more continuity
of occupation, even in the territories long lost to the Byzantine empire.
But what did not continue was the antique pattern of city life, by which
an urban population of rentiers, merchants and craftsmen was maintained by the surplus produce of the surrounding countryside, and
which found its expression in a whole structure of institutions, from
city councils and bishoprics to theatres and baths. If some of the buildings continued to be occupied, it was by squatters rather than citizens.
However, these squatters are likely to have been survivors from among
the original inhabitants rather than Slav immigrants. So far as the
evidence goes, early Slav settlements were always made at some distance from Greco-Roman cities, whose towering walls and massive
buildings were useless and perhaps disquieting to the newcomers.[10]

Immediately after his decisive victory over the Persians in 626 the
emperor Heraclius turned his attention to the former Balkan provinces
of the empire. Certain of the measures then taken had a lasting effect
upon the history of the north-western Balkans. The Croats, a people
probably of Sarmatian origin and living among Slavonic tribes in Bohemia and Silesia, were encouraged by the Byzantines to revolt against
the Avars and to settle in the region south of the Save and behind
the Dinaric Alps, where they speedily established themselves as the
dominant power. Their rulers accepted Christianity from Byzantium,
though they later lapsed, and it was from Rome, via the surviving Dalmatian cities, that the later conversion of the Croat people proceeded.
Another half-Slavicised Sarmatian people, the Serbs, also revolted
against the Avars, left their home somewhere in Saxony and were
settled by Heraclius in the neighbourhood of Thessalonika, which
was being threatened by the neighbouring Slav tribes. They were later,
perhaps at their own request, moved to the area south of Singidunum
and settled among the Slav tribes there as allies of Byzantium. In this
way a large part of the north-western Balkans was brought under the
control of powers loosely allied with the empire, a fact which in
Byzantium political thinking was interpreted as the restoration of

Byzantine sovereignty. That this Byzantine counter-attack took place so far from Constantinople is to be explained by the consideration that in Heraclius' eyes the enemy was the Avars, whose army was able to defeat Byzantine forces, and whom he saw as master-minding the invasion and occupation of imperial territory. The far more numerous Slavs were a nuisance, but not a mortal danger. They could be absorbed or dispersed later. So the emperor was bent on settling allies on whom he could rely as close to Pannonia, the centre of Avar power, as possible, while large parts of the eastern Balkans and peninsular Greece were left in the hands of the Slav invaders. Had Heraclius in his last years not directed his attention entirely to resisting the advance of the Arabs in Syria, Palestine and Egypt, the policy of settling a *cordon sanitaire* of allies on the Avar frontier might well have been successfully continued.

The Origin of the Bulgarian State

The Bulgars have appeared already in our survey of the fortunes of south-eastern Europe in the Dark Ages. They were a Turkic people, who first emerge as an identifiable group after the collapse of the Hun empire. They were probably related to the Kutrigurs and Utigurs who occupied much of the steppe zone north of the Danube delta and the Black Sea in the sixth century, and indeed may be mainly their descendants. This is the common view. Beshevliev has recently argued with some plausibility that they are to be distinguished from the Kutrigurs and Utigurs, and that it was only when they appeared north of the Danube that they absorbed these remnants of the Huns, probably few in number by this time, and with them some of their traditions, including the memory of Attila and his son Irnak. [11] The matter is of little importance for the subject of this book. The main body of the Bulgars probably spent some time living as pastoralists in the steppe north of the Caspian Sea. Some of them appear on the left bank of the lower Danube in the last decades of the fifth century, either as raiders or as mercenaries in the Roman service. The sixth century seems to have been one of relative calm for the Bulgars—unless they are to be identified with the Kutrigurs and Utigurs, who engaged in one another's mutual destruction at this time. In spite of the military weakness of the Roman empire in the latter part of the sixth century, Roman influence upon this people settled beyond the frontiers of the empire was considerable. We hear of a Bulgar prince coming to Constantinople for baptism about 600, no doubt as a result of Byzantine diplomatic reaction to the threat of the Avars and their Slav subjects. The establishment of the Avars in Pannonia apparently changed the balance of power in the steppe zone in such a way as to permit — or oblige — the Bulgars to expand. About 600 they seem to have split into several groups. One went to the Kuban steppes; another migrated far to the north-east and settled on the banks of the lower Kama, before its confluence with the Volga, where they played a part in the ethnogenesis of the Chuvash people, a third group attached themselves to the Lombards, took part in their invasion of Italy, and ended up near Benevento. But the largest group resettled or remained in the lower Danube area, from which they took up their old habit of raiding the Roman provinces to the south. There were apparently Bulgar contingents along with the Avars and Slavs at the sieges of Thessalonika and Constantinople. One of their leaders, Kubrat, seems to have broken with the Avars and formed an alliance with the local Slavs.

The history of the Bulgars in this period is extremely obscure, the names of their leaders are badly transmitted in our scanty sources, and any reconstruction of the course of events is hypothetical. The mysterious Kuver, a high officer under the Avars who, with the aid of a body of Romans who had been settled for two generations north of the Danube and of some Slav tribes, rebelled against the khagan, moved south into former Roman territory and gave siege to Thessalonika, has been thought by some to be a son of this Kubrat; his date is about the third quarter of the seventh century. The mention in the rock inscription at Madara, probably dating from the reign of Khan Tervel, of 'my uncle in Thessalonika' suggests that Kuver was indeed a Bulgarian and a son of Kubrat. If so, his establishment in former Roman territory overrun by the Slavs is a close parallel to what happened in the north-east Balkans. It was there that Asparukh, according to tradition another son of Kubrat, ruled over the main body of the Bulgars just north of the Danube delta. Pressed by the growing power of the Khazars to the east, he and his people were forced to take refuge in an island in the delta. The emperor Constantine IV saw in this move a threat to the Black Sea coastal strip still held by the Byzantines, and perhaps to Thrace. A campaign was mounted, perhaps in concert with the Khazars, to oust the Bulgars from their refuge. The campaign was bungled, the emperor withdrew to Mesembria with gout, the army broke up in disorder, and the Bulgars were able to break out of the delta and establish themselves in eastern Moesia. A late source puts their numbers at 10,000 fighting men.[12] There they subjected the Slav tribes of the area, obliging them to pay tribute and settling them on the frontiers of the territory which they controlled.[13] The Byzantines were in no position to do anything about this new invader of what had been their territory. They may indeed have welcomed the Bulgars as a counterpoise to the Avars, much as Heraclius had welcomed the Croats and the Serbs. At any rate they came to terms with the Bulgars, and signed a treaty granting to Asparukh all the land between the Danube, the Balkan range and the sea, as well as an annual subsidy. This treaty, probably signed in 680, marks the first formal recognition by the Byzantine government of the existence of a foreign state on what had been imperial territory, but perhaps too much should not be made of this. It is likely that the organisation of the first European theme, that of Thrace, was a reaction to the new situation created by the arrival of the Bulgars in the Balkans.

The Bulgars seem to have inherited from their nomad past a complex and stable social and military hierarchy, recalling that of the Orkhon Turks at the same period. They were organised into tribes, and the hereditary chief of one of the tribes, that of Dulo, acted as leader of the whole confederacy. Under the leader or Khan were a number of ministers belonging to the tribal nobility bearing different titles and with more or less clearly defined responsibilities. There were two classes of nobles, though the precise distinction between them escapes us. The army was the whole Bulgar male population, presumably organised in tribal contingents, and supported by the forces of the Slav tribes which the Bulgars controlled and with whom they were very closely linked from the start. For their strong sense of ethnic unity did not prevent them mingling with the Slav communities, with whom in any case they must have been in contact since the early sixth century. It is possible to distinguish Slav and Bulgar sites from the Dark Ages. The Bulgars seem to have lived in round, yurt-like houses inherited from their steppe past, and to have inhumed their dead, while the Slavs lived in square, half-underground houses with a stove in one corner, and cremated their dead. Different types of pottery are associated with the two peoples. But we soon find evidence of mixed settlements; as none of these settlements can be dated with any certainty, too much importance should perhaps not be attached to this archaeological evidence, but it should not be altogether neglected.[14]

The Bulgars established their capital at Pliska, between the Danube and the Balkan chain, where the ruins of a late Roman city provided building material. There they built a complex of public buildings for the Khan and his court, surrounded by an earthwork perimeter wall within which the whole Bulgar people could probably find shelter. They no doubt used the forced labour of Byzantine captives and of the surviving Roman population, especially to construct the heavy stone buildings. The original Bulgar state was confined to a corner of the north-eastern Balkans, from the Danube to the Balkan chain, and from the Black Sea to the Avar frontier, which may have followed the line of the Iskŭr. It is not known how much territory Asparukh controlled to the north of the Danube but it may have been quite extensive.

Asparukh's son and successor Tervel formed an alliance with the exiled Byzantine emperor Justinian II in 705 and helped to restore him to Constantinople. This was a gamble, but one which came off, and it increased the power and influence of the Bulgar state. Tervel was welcomed to Constantinople and given the rank of Caesar, a title which only recently had marked out its bearer as heir apparent to the reigning emperor. It still implied a close relationship with the emperor: Tervel was no doubt baptised, but there was no wholesale conversion of his people. More important, Tervel was given the area of Zagoria, probably the region between the Balkan range and the Gulf of Burgas. But the coastal cities of Mesembria, Develtos and Anchialos remained in Byzantine hands. So the situation remained throughout most of the eighth century. The iconoclast emperor Constantine V fought a series of campaigns against the Bulgars without dislodging them from their land, though he may have recaptured part of the territory ceded by Justinian II. In 784 the empress Irene was able to make a peaceful progress from the Byzantine naval base at Anchialos to Berrhoea (Stara Zagora), without provoking any hostile reaction from Bulgaria. In the west Bulgar expansion was firmly blocked by the Avars. But they did make tentative moves south-westwards, towards Macedonia, where Kuver had tried to establish himself in the previous century, and where the Slav population was relatively independent of Byzantine and Avar power alike. In 789 a Byzantine general was killed by the Bulgars while reconnoitring disputed territory in the Struma valley. However, in the early years of the ninth century two events took place which transformed the situation of the Bulgar state. The crushing defeat of the Avars in Pannonia in 796 by Charlemagne's son Pippin led to the speedy disintegration of the Avar state, and opened the way to westward expansion for the Bulgars. And the old royal house of Dulo was replaced, we do not know exactly how, by a new dynasty, that of the Pannonian Bulgars, who had revolted against their Avar lords after 796. The new ruler, Krum, succeeded Khan Kardam in 802 or 803.

Bulgaria and Byzantium in the Early Ninth Century

The immediate effect of the collapse of Avar power was the extension of Bulgarian territory far to the west, as far as the Theiss, where it marched with the land of the Franks. Most of this new territory was inhabited principally by Slavs, over some of whom the Pannonian Bulgars had established overlordship. Frightened by this increase in Bulgarian power, and perhaps hoping by a show of strength to divert Bulgaria westwards, the Byzantine emperor Nicephorus set out in 807 to invade Bulgaria. A further motive for the Byzantine resumption of hostilities was probably fear of Bulgar influence on the Slav populations of peninsular Greece and Macedonia. There had recently been a revolt by some of the Slav tribes of the Peloponnese which had been put down with great severity. However Nicephorus got no further than Adrianople before he had to return to the capital to deal with a plot against him. Krum, whether he had harboured aggressive intentions previously or not, realised that he had better strike first. Rather than throw himself against the ring of fortresses protecting eastern Thrace, he moved against Macedonia, where he could probably count on the support of much of the Slav population. In 808 he swept down the Struma valley, defeated a Byzantine army, and took 1,100 pounds of gold intended as army pay. But the way to Macedonia was blocked by a series of Byzantine strong points in western Thrace, of which Serdica was the principal. In 809 Krum captured Serdica, killed its garrison of 6000 and demolished its walls. As yet the Bulgars were not interested in holding fortified positions themselves. Nicephorus' reaction was to march through the mountains and sack and burn Krum's capital of Pliska in the autumn of the same year. The main theatre of operations was transferred to Thrace. In 811 Nicephorus again captured Pliska, destroying the royal palace, which was probably of wood, and making a display of barbarity—we hear of Bulgarian babies being thrown into threshing machines. Krum apparently made overtures for peace, but Nicephorus was obdurate in the euphoria of victory.

However, the Bulgarian army had not been destroyed. As Nicephorus and the Byzantines, laden with booty, wound their way through the mountains on their return journey they were caught in an ambush and the whole army, with its commander, perished. It was the first time for nearly six hundred years that a Roman emperor had been killed in battle. The Byzantines had not only lost their best fighting men, they were utterly demoralised and could not understand what had gone wrong. The Bulgars did not waste time. Krum attacked the key Byzantine cities around the Gulf of Burgas. Develtos was taken, the inhabitants of Anchialus fled. Panic spread into Thrace, where there was wholesale flight from the fortress city of Philippopolis. Krum, anxious not to overstretch his resources, proposed peace. It is interesting to note that his envoy, Dargomer, bore a Slavonic name. The emperor asked for the restoration of the *status quo ante bellum*. Krum pressed on, and by autumn 812 had taken Mesembria, the major port on the west coast of the Black Sea, with magnificent natural and artificial defences. He did not remain there, but dismantled the walls and retired to Pliska for the winter. In the next year he defeated the main Byzantine field army, and by July was at the walls of Constantinople. Though the Bulgars had made great progress in siegecraft, they were unable to tackle the superb fortifications constructed by Theodosius II four centuries earlier. And as they had no fleet, they could not hope to starve the city to surrender. Nevertheless Krum maintained the siege for nearly two years. It may be that he did not realise the impasse into which he had got himself. But it is possible that he hoped to profit by a *coup d'état* within the beleaguered city which would bring to power an emperor willing to make concessions to the Bulgars. He seems to have been well aware of the disaffection of some units of the army, and may have had contacts within the walls. What is clear is that he had no intention of taking over Constantinople. There were abortive negotiations, ending in an attempt by the Byzantines to assassinate Krum. More important, while the Khan besieged Constantinople, his generals were mopping up the remaining Byzantine cities of Thrace. Adrianople surrendered in autumn 813, Arcadiopolis (Lüle Burgaz) in the ensuing winter. How events might have turned out we shall never know, for Krum died suddenly in April 814 while preparing a new attack on Constantinople, and the Bulgarian army withdrew.

Krum was succeeded by his son, Omurtag, but apparently only after quelling a revolt of the old Bulgar nobility. The details escape us. It is this which explains Omurtag's failure to press home the favourable military position established by his father. In the winter of 815-16 he concluded a treaty with the emperor Leo, valid for thirty years, which arranged the exchange of prisoners—in particular those taken from the Thracian cities and transported to Bulgaria—and fixed the frontier, which was more or less that determined by Justinian II and Tervel a century earlier. Incidentally this treaty is hardly mentioned by the Byzantine historians and chroniclers, but is imperfectly preserved on a stele which probably stood originally in the palace at Pliska, and is now in the Archaeological Museum in Sofia.[15]

In the main the Thirty Years Peace was maintained. The Bulgars did not seek to expand into eastern Thrace, which would inevitably bring them up against the problem of the capital and its impregnable fortifications. They dug a great ditch and rampart along the frontier from Develtos to the Maritsa near Simeonovgrad, which they kept permanently manned. The cities which Krum had taken from the Byzantines—Serdica, Philippopolis, Develtos, Anchialos etc.—were left deserted, in a kind of no-man's-land. Only Mesembria and Adrianople were rebuilt by the emperor. Presumably this reflects a lost clause of the treaty. In the meantime the Bulgars directed their attention westward, into territory not covered by the treaty, and to building a great new royal residence at Preslav in the years following 821. Omurtag concerned himself principally with the northern part of his kingdom, which lay north of the Danube, and with his relations with the Franks. In his reign, a modern Bulgarian historian has written, Bulgaria became one of the Great Powers of Europe.

Omurtag's successor, his youngest son Malamir, took up hostilities against the empire, provoked by a Byzantine plan to sail up the Danube and remove a community of Greek prisoners settled north of the river. In 836 he annexed the unfortified city of Serdica and put in a Bulgarian garrison. He was clearly establishing himself on the road to Macedonia. On the termination of the Thirty Years Peace he sent troops into the Struma valley at a time when the Byzantines were hampered by a revolt by the Slavs of the Peloponnese. There seems to have been a large-scale westward expansion into the largely ungoverned country of northern Macedonia, which led to a war with Serbia in 839-42, but the details are inaccessible to us. In Thrace itself Philippopolis and Philippi were annexed by the Bulgars, and the surrounding Slav populations absorbed into the Bulgarian state. There seems to have been a truce which probably granted to the Bulgars the right to expand into Macedonia, an expansion which the Byzantines could not in any case hinder. Khan Malamir died in 852 and was succeeded by his nephew Boris, the son of his elder brother. With the accession of Boris begins the century which forms the subject of the present comparative study. Before closing this historical introduction we must glance again at the situation in the southern part of the Balkans, peninsular Greece.

In the seventh century the Byzantines were in no position to devote attention to Greece, which lay off the main lines of communication of the empire. We hear of *Sklaviniai* in various parts. The effective range of Byzantine control was confined to a zone in central Greece around Thebes, Athens and Corinth, and to a series of ports with their immediate hinterland—Thessalonika, Nauplia, Monemvasia, Patras. The islands of the Aegean and the Ionian islands also remained firmly in Byzantine hands, at any rate until the loss of Crete to the Arabs in about 826. Areas outside Byzantine control were not necessarily inhabited entirely by Slavs, as has been remarked. The Slav communities in Greece neither established a political unity of their own nor had one superimposed upon them from outside, as happened to those of the northern Balkans under the Avars and Bulgars. They lived in tribal units, each governed by its council, and forming ephemeral alliances among themselves for particular purposes. Within this tribal society the beginnings of a military aristocracy were forming, and this new ruling class was often strongly attracted by the prestige of the Greek way of life. Even for the ordinary tribesman, contact with Greeks must often have been close. The needs of trade brought Slav peasants to the Greek cities and Greek merchants to the Slav villages. And there were certainly Greek peasant communities surviving in various parts of Greece out of the reach of Byzantine state power. So a gradual process of Hellenisation and naturally of Christianisation, whose steps we cannot trace, began early and continued uninterrupted. Byzantine society was not racist. A Slav who spoke Greek and was an orthodox Christian found few doors closed to him. Thomas, a member of one of the Slav communities settled by the Byzantines in Asia Minor, became a leading officer under Leo, and led a revolt against his successor Michael II, in the course of which he was himself proclaimed rival emperor. The revolt was unsuccessful. The Patriarch Nicetas (766-80) is said to have been a Slav, but the evidence is uncertain. We hear of missionaries working among the Slavs of Greece during the seventh century. The liturgical language used was Greek, and Christianisation must have soon brought Hellenisation in its wake. Nevertheless the bulk of the Slavs in Greece were at the beginning of the eighth century both pagan and independent of the Byzantine government. There was a major attack by the Peloponnesian Slavs on Patras in about 807. Its defeat was followed by punitive expeditions and a serious effort to bring the Peloponnese once again under Byzantine control. At the same time the Slavs near the mouth of the Vardar were still pagan and practised piracy. But in the early years of the ninth century the area under Byzantine control round Thessalonika was extended, and by the middle of the century a group of new *themes* had been organised in this region. New episcopal sees make their appearance, particularly in the Peloponnese, testifying to the absorption of the Slav settlements into the Byzantine community.

By the middle of the ninth century, then, the Slavs of peninsular Greece and southern Macedonia had formed no political society of their own, and were well on the way to absorption into the life of the Byzantine world, which soon led to loss of their national identity and their language, except for a small pocket in the mountains of the southern Peloponnese. In the northern Balkans the situation was very different. There the Slav settlers had been united under the power of the Bulgar state, a state in which from the beginning the Slavs had played a major role, and in which by the middle of the ninth century the fusion of the Bulgar and Slav ruling groups had made considerable progress; the Bulgars had partly forgotten their original Turkic language and had adopted that of their Slav fellow-citizens. It is probably more than accidental that the line dividing the two regions of the Balkan peninsula coincides closely with that marking the northern limit of the cultivation of the olive. It is a line which separates two very different styles of life, the Mediterranean and the central European.

3 Bulgaro-Byzantine Relations in the Ninth and Tenth Centuries

When Boris succeeded to the throne of Bulgaria in 852 he found on his southern frontier a Byzantine empire which was rapidly recovering from the long eclipse following on the Arab conquests and the Slav and Avar occupation of the Balkans. There was an economic recovery which filled its treasury with gold. A new interest among the ruling class in its own past led to an educational and cultural renaissance. New public buildings, in a style which combined motifs from late antiquity with innovations, some probably of oriental origin, were constructed everywhere. And the Byzantine army turned from a defensive to an aggressive role. Recovery and restoration were the watchwords. Boris must have viewed with disquiet the growing military strength of his powerful southern neighbour. Fortunately for him the first priority for the Byzantines was to win and hold the strategic passes through which the Arabs had made their regular raids into Asia Minor. Asia Minor, not Thrace, was the economic and demographic centre of the empire.

To enable it to concentrate its forces in the east the Byzantine government of the empress-regent Theodora and the logothete Theoctistus was prepared to make concessions to the Bulgarians. Shortly after Boris' accession the Byzantines ceded to Bulgaria a belt of territory some 25 miles wide south of the old frontier in Thrace, and including the now ruined fortresses of Develtos and Anchialos. Encouraged by this apparent weakness Boris concentrated his military effort in the far west, pushing through Macedonia to reach the mountains of Albania and the northernmost peaks of Pindus. This was all territory to which Byzantium laid claim, but in which there had been no effective Byzantine authority for two and a half centuries. There was little the Byzantines could do to stop Boris if they would.

In 856 Michael III and Bardas replaced Theodora and Theoctistus at the head of affairs in Constantinople. The new ruler pursued a vigorous policy of aggression in the east, against both the Arabs and the Paulicians. But in the far west he was unable to stem the Arab advance in Sicily and southern Italy. At the end of his reign only Syracuse and Taormina remained in Byzantine hands in Sicily. Michael had therefore an interest in continuing his mother's policy of peace with Bulgaria. The unexpected Russian attack on Constantinople itself in 860 directed Byzantine attention to the danger from this new state emerging far away in the heart of north-eastern Europe, and made friendly relations with Bulgaria all the more desirable. Nevertheless when Boris, anxious to build up Bulgaria into a great power, formed a military alliance with the Franks, the Byzantine reaction was swift and sharp. A Byzantine army invaded Bulgaria, supported by the fleet in the Black Sea, and no doubt in the Danube delta. Boris was caught at a disadvantage. In any case he wanted at all costs to avoid a full-scale military confrontation with the empire, particularly since a series of striking victories by the general Petronas on the eastern frontier had enabled troops to be transferred from there to Thrace. He at once accepted Byzantine terms. These were not onerous from the military point of view. But they required that Boris and his people should accept the Christian faith and that the Bulgarian church be subordinate to that of Constantinople. For a further analysis of the implications of this for Bulgaria, see Chapter Eight. For some years before, the Byzantine authorities had been deeply interested in conversion as a means of extending Byzantine influence. The concept arises naturally out of the Byzantine idea of the empire as a unique instrument of God's plan for the salvation of mankind, destined to last until the Second Coming. Acceptance of the spiritual authority of the church implied in principle acceptance of the temporal authority of the emperor and vice versa. It may have been brought to the forefront by recent Byzantine experience in the east, where mass conversion of Moslems, Paulicians or Monophysites often followed on Byzantine conquest. Missions had recently been sent to the Khazars, to Russia and to Moravia. As it turned out, none of these produced lasting results. But in 864 this was not evident. Bulgaria could not be allowed to remain in pagan independence. So Byzantine insistence on its conversion as a condition of withdrawal of its invading army was only to be expected. It is a neat example of the intimate collaboration of Church and state in the Byzantine empire. As a counterpart to the conversion the Bulgarians probably received some territory in Thrace. And the frontier was left vague in the west, where Bulgarian expansion continued unchecked.

The ensuing rebellion of boyars hostile to a *rapprochement* with Byzantium nearly cost Boris his life. But it was suppressed, and the opportunity taken of replacing many of the traditionalist Bulgar and Slav clan-leaders by men sympathetic to Boris' plans and dependent on his patronage. Boris himself realised the danger of becoming a

Byzantine satellite, and for a time flirted with the church of Rome, which was at that moment anxious to assert its power in the Balkans. The Byzantine clergy were expelled from Bulgaria for some years. But in the end the realities of power told. Bulgaria returned in 870 to the Byzantine obedience but with a degree of internal autonomy in church affairs which was the price paid by the Byzantines for the abandonment by Bulgaria of its connection with the church of Rome and its search for allies in western Europe.

A new spirit of cooperation prevailed between Bulgaria and Byzantium. Young Bulgarians were sent to Constantinople for education. Byzantine craftsmen were sent to Bulgaria to build churches and palaces. But Boris and his colleagues were well aware that Byzantine ideas could be as dangerous as Byzantine arms. A Greek-speaking church whose clergy in the last resort owed allegiance to the emperor in Constantinople could in a short time sap the self-confidence of the Bulgarian people and alienate those very groups in Bulgarian society whose support was essential. When in 885-6 a group of pupils of Cyril and Methodius, who had been sent by the Byzantine church to evangelise Moravia, arrived in Bulgaria with liturgical books in Slavonic, Boris welcomed the opportunity to form in his kingdom a Slavonic church, whose clergy would be native Bulgarians, who would preach in the language of the people, and who would neither feel in themselves nor inspire in others an overriding loyalty to the Byzantine empire. Slavonic clergy were trained by Naum in north-eastern Bulgaria and above all by Clement in Macedonia, and liturgical and other works were translated into Slavonic under Boris' patronage.

Meanwhile the death of Basil I in 886 and the consequent deposition of Photius and restoration of Ignatius to the Patriarchate reduced the immediate likelihood of direct Byzantine intervention in Bulgaria. In 889 Boris, who must by now have been in his sixties, abdicated in favour of his eldest son Vladimir or Rasate and entered a monastery. Vladimir, who had probably been kept too long in the background, was closely linked with those backward-looking elements in the Bulgarian ruling class who had revolted against Boris in 864. There was a violent swing against Boris' policy of building up an independent church without provoking the Byzantines and against the austerity which he had imposed upon the Bulgarian court. Some sort of steps seem to have been taken towards the formal restoration of paganism. There may also have been overtures made to the Pope. The whole policy which had avoided open war with Byzantium for nearly sixty years, while

Bulgaria transformed itself from a federation of tribes and clans into a centralised feudal state was in danger of being frustrated. The Byzantines could not have stood by while an anti-Christian and anti-imperial régime was installed at Pliska. Boris, who may have tried to exercise some kind of control over Vladimir from his monastery, emerged from his cell in 893, rallied his old guard and, making the most of his immense personal moral authority ousted his son from power and had him blinded. In the delicate situation in which he found himself he convened a council of boyars, attended by provincial governors and high officers of state as well as by Bulgar and Slav tribal leaders. He justified his action to them and obtained their agreement to accept his younger son Symeon as ruler. Symeon had received a Greek literary education in Constantinople and was at the time of his accession a monk in Bulgaria. He had probably been destined by his father for high ecclesiastical office. His education had given him an intimate knowledge of Byzantine life and a deep hatred of the Byzantine aristocracy who had treated him contemptuously as ἡμίαργος—half-Greek, '*métis*'. And his years of contemplation in the monastery had given him a taste for action. Two other matters settled at the council of boyars in 893 represented the fruition of much of Boris' work. The capital was transferred from Pliska, which had many pagan and Proto-Bulgar associations, to the new royal residence of Preslav. And Greek was replaced by Slavonic as the language of liturgy and teaching of the church and the language of internal administration of the state. At the same time a Slav archbishop was probably appointed.

The Byzantine government might have reacted sharply. But Leo VI and his advisers were probably glad to see the unpredictable Vladimir replaced by a brother whom they regarded as a Byzantine protégé. In any case Leo, though a learned man, prolific legislator and active reformer of Byzantine administration, had no taste for military matters, and worse still, no foreign policy. And he was under the influence of his father-in-law the *basileopator* Stylianos Zaoutzes, an able man who shared his lack of interest in foreign affairs and who was too ready to reward his supporters.

Symeon seems from the outset of his reign to have decided to reverse his father's policy of avoiding a confrontation with the Byzantine empire. He was aware of the opposition in many quarters in Bulgaria to what looked like weakness. And he calculated that unless the balance of power was changed, Bulgaria was bound to be brought into the political orbit of Constantinople and to lose her freedom of action, whether or not she succeeded in maintaining an independent Slavonic church.

Bulgaria's strength, he believed, lay in her army, a formidable force of peasant soldiers well equipped and led, while the Byzantine army was stretched by its commitments in the east and weakened by the collapse of the system of military land holdings. Boris had sought to avoid a military conflict, Symeon awaited one eagerly. His long-term aims are not always easy to discern. At his accession he probably hoped to establish Bulgaria as a state equal in standing to the Byzantine empire, equal in military power and owing no debt of ultimate submission to the emperor at Constantinople. This was a direct challenge to the whole Byzantine concept of a unique oecumenical empire, destined to last until the end of the world. Symeon understood this concept very well, but he rejected it utterly.

The *casus belli* for which Symeon was waiting was not long in coming. Bulgarian merchants visiting Constantinople to sell their wares were housed in an official lodging, a *mitaton,* as were merchants from other foreign lands. Their stay in the capital was limited to three or six months at a time, and their goods had to be sold in their *mitaton,* not in the open markets of the city. It was in the *mitaton,* too, that the ten per cent tax was levied on the goods they brought, of which they had to pay one half while the other half was payed by the purchaser. In return for this limitation of their freedom they were guaranteed against harassment by Byzantine local authorities and exploitation by private merchants. These matters were settled in commercial treaties between the Byzantine and foreign governments, and were part of the system of international trade. A lively exchange of Bulgarian hides, wax, flax, honey and other goods for Byzantine products was conducted under these arrangements. In 894 two Greek merchants, Staurakios and Cosmas, used their influence with the all powerful Stylianos Zaoutzes to have this system set aside. The *mitaton* for Bulgarian merchants was suddenly transferred from Constantinople to Thessalonika and the collection of the taxes farmed out to Staurakios and Cosmas, who promptly raised the duty on Bulgarian goods. This was a step completely at variance with Byzantine practice at the time. According to our sources, which are all hostile to Zaoutzes, Leo VI later repented of his unwise decision and punished Staurakios and Cosmas severely, while only his impending death saved Zaoutzes from sharing their disgrace. The true motive of Leo in sanctioning such a departure from normal usage can never be discovered. It may be the mixture of corruption and muddle which the sources suggest. It could be a step taken for security reasons. Be that as it may, it was a severe blow to Bulgarian trade which followed the Belgrade-Constantinople road, the Via Egnatia or the Black Sea coastal road to Constantinople. Medieval sovereigns were not usually sensitive to mercantile interests. But Symeon reacted at once. A personal request to the emperor to annul the offending order met with refusal. Immediately the Bulgarian ruler—who only a year earlier had still been a monk—marched at the head of his army into the Byzantine theme of Macedonia, i.e. western Thrace. The main Byzantine forces were in Asia Minor. The troops sent out from Constantinople were crushingly defeated by Symeon and their commander Procopius Crenites killed, along with many of his officers. Symeon seized every opportunity to humiliate the Byzantine emperor in the eyes of his subjects, for example by cutting off the noses of soldiers of the imperial guard whom he captured and returning them to their master. This was the first battle between Bulgarian and Byzantine troops for more than half a century, and the outcome was a signal Bulgarian victory.

The Byzantines dared not disengage their main field army in the east to face the new threat in the west. But though they were militarily inferior their diplomatic possibilities were much greater. The patrician Nicetas Skleros was sent by sea with Byzantine gold to the Magyars, at that time settled north of the Danube delta, on the frontier of Bulgaria. He persuaded the Magyar leaders Árpád and Koursanis to attack the Bulgars in the rear. This was the classic move of Byzantine diplomacy, and one no doubt prepared in advance as a contingency plan.

While the Magyars attacked from the north, the Byzantine land army marched through Thrace under Nicephorus Phocas and the fleet sailed to the Danube mouth under the patrician Eustathios. Leo probably expected Symeon to yield to this threat without a battle, and even sent an envoy to his camp to offer peace terms. But he had misjudged his man. Symeon in vain tried to block the Danube crossings, but Eustathios' fleet helped the Magyars to cross the river. They swept through Bulgaria, pillaging and burning, and Symeon's army fled before them without offering combat. Symeon himself took refuge in the Danube fortress of Silistra while the Magyars went on to sack his capital of Preslav before withdrawing across the Danube. Symeon asked the Byzantines for peace terms, and Leo unwisely withdrew his forces from Bulgaria.

When Leo Choirosphaktes, the Byzantine ambassador, reached Symeon's court he was thrown into prison. Symeon had meanwhile followed the Byzantine example and was negotiating with the Pechenegs, a Turkic people then established in the steppes north of the

Black Sea. Bulgarians and Pechenegs fell on the Magyars from both sides, inflicting upon them a terrible defeat and ravaging their territory. The demoralised Magyars crossed the Carpathians into the plain of Hungary, where they soon became the terror of western Europe. Symeon now felt himself in a stronger position *vis-à-vis* the Byzantines, and refused to make peace unless the Bulgarian prisoners, whom the Byzantines had bought from the Magyars, were returned to him. The emperor Leo, who had signally failed to realise the radical change of Bulgarian policy since the accession of Symeon, agreed. The prisoners were returned and negotiations on peace terms begun. But Symeon, having recovered his lost subjects, broke off the negotiations and once again imprisoned the hapless Leo Choirosphaktes. The emperor decided at last to transfer troops from the east and sent a large army into Bulgaria. Symeon caught it in an ambush at Bulgarophygon near Adrianople and defeated it with crushing losses.

By now it was 896. It was the turn of the Byzantines to seek to ransom their prisoners. We have some of the correspondence between Symeon and Leo Choirosphaktes on this matter. Symeon, who had been educated in Constantinople, propounded to the Byzantine ambassador a problem well known to Greek logicians. He would return the prisoners if the emperor answered correctly one question. That question was: 'Did he intend to return them?' Leo recognised the trap and made a suitably ambiguous reply. For some time the exchange of letters went on, Symeon and the ambassador alike displaying their familiarity with the finer points of classical philosophy. The point of this curious correspondence was no doubt to give Symeon the pleasure of beating the Greeks at their own game and to gain time. He probably also hoped to impress the Byzantine dignitaries with his own sophistication. Bulgaria could no longer be treated as a land of barbarians. In the end terms were agreed upon: 120,000 Byzantine prisoners were returned, and the emperor agreed to pay an annual tribute to Bulgaria. There was also a territorial adjustment in Thrace in Bulgaria's favour. Symeon had succeeded in defeating the Byzantines in the field, and then humiliated them at the conference table. He was being treated by the Byzantine emperor as a near-equal, as the King of Persia had once been treated, or the Caliph of Islam. He was well pleased with his achievements, though they were bought at the cost of fearful devastation of much of his country. Whether old Boris in his monastery was equally pleased by the new turn in policy made by his bookish son, the erstwhile monk, is another matter.

The treaty of peace remained in effect until the death of Leo VI in 912. These were difficult years for the Byzantine empire. The war with Symeon had given a breathing space to the Arabs, and Armenia was at once lost to them. Taormina, the last Byzantine strong point in Sicily, fell in 902. And Arab naval strength in the Aegean grew until their fleets could sail where they wished. Demetrias in Thessaly was sacked in 902. In 904 a great Arab fleet under the command of Leo of Tripoli, a Greek renegade, entered the Aegean, captured Abydos, then turned west and seized Thessalonika, the second city of the empire. There was a massacre of the citizens, and measureless booty and countless prisoners were taken. Apart from these losses, Byzantine prestige suffered a serious blow. Symeon did not fail to profit by the empire's defeat. The western frontiers of Bulgaria were probably not defined by the treaty. At any rate Symeon pushed south and west in Macedonia. An inscribed stone dated 904 from Nea Philadelpheia 22 km north of Salonica marks the 'frontier between the Romans and the Bulgarians' (Beševliev No. 46). In the far west Bulgarian territory reached the Adriatic between Hagioi Saranta and Dyrrhachium, on the coast of present-day Albania. This extension of territory was obtained by a series of local advances, each of which the Byzantine authorities were prepared to ignore, since they were unwilling to face the possibility of open war with Bulgaria.

Leo VI's *laissez-faire* policy in regard to Bulgaria was not to the taste of all his subjects. When Leo died in 912 his successor, his brother Alexander, a man of little judgement or experience of affairs, decided to seek popularity by taking a strong line with Symeon. He peremptorily and insultingly cut off the tribute due to Preslav under the treaty signed by Leo. Symeon, who had consolidated his territorial gains and replaced the soldiers lost in the previous war, was waiting for just such an opportunity to be offered him. In 913 he marched the main body of the Bulgarian army right through Byzantine Thrace without opposition and encamped before the walls of Constantinople itself. Inside the city all was in disarray. Alexander had died in June, and a council of regency acted for the seven-year-old son of Leo VI, Constantine VII. Its leading members were the Patriarch Nicolaus Mysticus and the empress Zoe, widow of Leo VI. They had no concerted policy, and they were faced with an attempt at usurpation by Constantine Ducas, the commander-in-chief of the army, which they put down with difficulty.

Symeon was no longer bent on booty or the accretion of territory.

From aiming at establishing a Bulgarian state parallel to the Byzantine empire he had by now advanced to a new ambition, that of becoming himself ruler of an enlarged empire which would include Bulgaria, and of putting on his own shoulders the mantle of legitimacy of the Christian Roman emperors. It was not an absurd ambition. His ethnic origin might provoke a raised eyebrow or a curled lip in some Byzantine milieux, but Byzantine society was not racist. Men who were not Greek by descent had ruled the empire before. What was required was orthodox religious belief, Greek culture, and success. Symeon had the first two of these, and the third seemed within his grasp. The walls of Constantinople, however, proved impregnable from the land, and Symeon had no fleet. He was forced to negotiate, but he could at least negotiate from strength. He and his escort were received within the walls with every mark of respect by the regency council and the boy emperor. The concessions made to him were unprecedented. He was naturally given his arrears of tribute. The young emperor was betrothed to one of his daughters. And a coronation ceremony of some kind was held in the church of the Virgin at Blachernae, at which the Patriarch put upon Symeon's head not a diadem but some part of his own liturgical head-dress and declared him *Basileus*. The interpretation of this ceremony has been disputed ever since it took place. Some believed then, and believe now, that Nicolaus Mysticus crowned Symeon as co-emperor with Constantine VII. If he did so, it must have been without the agreement of the empress Zoe. Others believe that the whole ceremony was a meaningless sham designed to impress a gullible barbarian. But Symeon was far too well acquainted with Byzantine ways to be easily taken in, and far too dangerous to provoke. Some degree of ambiguity was essential to the Patriarch if he was to retain the confidence of his fellow regents; and it was acceptable to Symeon, who imagined he would only have to wait a little for his daughter to become empress and he himself the power behind the throne, and in due course for his grandson to become emperor. He probably accepted something which to Byzantine eyes could be represented as coronation of a *Basileus* of Bulgaria—and the Byzantines had recognised no other sovereign as *Basileus* since the Sassanid monarchy of Persia had been overthrown by the Arabs—and to Bulgarian eyes might be taken to imply partnership in the Byzantine empire. The whole matter is highly mysterious and already overlaid in our sources with much self-exculpation.[1]

However we are to interpret what took place, it appeared to put the mastery of the empire in Symeon's hands. He returned to Preslav in autumn 913 to await the full fruits of his victory. However he had misjudged the strength of the opposition to his plans in Byzantine ruling circles. The empress Zoe felt that she and her son had been betrayed, and many of the clergy regarded Nicolaus as uncanonically appointed, and remained loyal to the deposed Patriarch, Euthymius. As the attempted usurpation by Constantine Dukas had shown, Nicolaus could not count on the unconditional support of the army or its leaders. The concessions made to the Bulgarian ruler united the various elements hostile to Nicolaus. He was removed from the council of regency, and the dowager empress Zoe assumed charge of affairs. The projected marriage between Constantine VII and Symeon's daughter was cancelled and Symeon's coronation declared to be null and void. Success seemed to be slipping from Symeon's grasp. But his military power remained undiminished. In 914 his armies once again invaded Thrace, while Symeon demanded that the Byzantine population should recognise him as legitimate emperor. In the following campaigning seasons he made similar incursions into the regions near Dyrrhachium and Thessalonika, demonstrating the power of Bulgarian arms and doubtless demanding recognition of his coronation in 913.

The government of empress Zoe dared not continue to allow Symeon to march where he liked through Byzantine territory proclaiming himself to be a legitimate emperor. If it was to hold on to power it had to counter-attack. But recent experience had made Byzantine commanders cautious about challenging the Bulgarian army in the field. So a combined operation by land and sea was carefully planned. The land army, under Leo Phocas, was to march up the Black Sea coast road, while the fleet, under Romanus Lecapenus, was to go ahead of the army at sea, attack behind the enemy lines and cut his communications. The aim of the expedition was to strike into the centre of Bulgarian power in north-eastern Bulgaria, and if possible to capture Preslav, as Nicephorus I had captured Pliska a hundred years before. There were negotiations with the Pechenegs to induce them to attack Bulgaria from the north. In summer 917 the expedition moved off. Leo Phocas, however, was no match for Symeon. The Bulgarian army fell on the Byzantines by surprise by the river Achelous, near Anchialos on the Gulf of Burgas, on 20 August. The Byzantine army was utterly routed. Leo Phocas only just succeeded in fleeing to the well-defended city of Mesembria. The bones of the dead were still to be seen scattered on the ground fifty years later.

Byzantine plans were completely frustrated. When Romanus Lecapenus and his fleet reached the Danube mouth the Pechenegs refused to play their part. In Constantinople Nicolaus Mysticus came to the fore again. In a long letter to Symeon, written immediately after receiving the news of the defeat at the Achelous, he expatiates on human liability to error, declares the loss of life to be the fault of Byzantines and Bulgarians alike, points out that he himself had no hand in the military plans, argues that in any case the Byzantines had not seriously intended to attack Bulgaria, only to relieve the pressure round Thessalonika and Dyrrhachium, and conjures Symeon in the name of Father, Son and Holy Ghost not to pursue his military advantage. It is a curious letter, and no doubt Symeon took careful note of it when it was delivered to his camp by the abbot of a well-known monastery. But he continued to pursue the survivors of the Byzantine army down the coast road towards Constantinople, and inflicted a second crushing defeat on them in a night-attack at Catasyrtae not far north of the capital.

He realised that it was useless to sit down once again before the walls of Constantinople. Access to the city depended on political rather than military victory and the Patriarch was clearly hesitating. Symeon no doubt had adherents within the city, who could put pressure on him and on others in high places. In the meantime he withdrew with his army to Bulgaria, in part to deal with the situation in Serbia. Byzantine diplomacy had long been working there to create an anti-Bulgarian group among the various tribal princes, and had had some success. A Bulgarian punitive expedition broke up the hostile coalition. In 918 Symeon again allowed himself to be distracted from his principal objective, and invaded northern Greece, pushing south as far as the Gulf of Corinth. This seems the most probable date for his Greek campaign. It is said in the *Life of St Luke the Younger*[2] to have taken place 'ten years' before Symeon's death. This would put it in 917, an impossible year, as Symeon was then engaged in the Achelous campaign. Scholars have sought various ways out of the difficulty. At any rate the campaign must be dated some time between 917 and 921, not 916 as Runciman suggested. The question poses itself why Symeon allowed himself to be diverted from his main objective of keeping up the pressure on Constantinople. It may be the result merely of the restlessness of this man of action. He may have hoped to induce the Byzantines into transferring troops from the capital to peninsular Greece; if so he failed in his intention. The most fundamental explanation is probably to be sought in the essentially aggressive character of the Bulgarian state. The heavy cost of maintaining a large army in the field could not be met out of the economic surplus normally available within Bulgarian society. Booty and new territory to exploit were essential, particularly as more and more of the available economic surplus was taken by feudal proprietors instead of being at the disposal of the state.

Whatever the explanation of Symeon's deviation from his objective, it proved fatal to his success. In Constantinople the ineffectual regency council, dominated by priests and women, steadily lost the support of the ruling class. A strong man with a military background was what they wanted. The two principal candidates were Leo Phocas, son of the great commander Nicephorus Phocas and commander-in-chief of the army, and Romanus Lecapenus, commander of the imperial fleet. Phocas belonged to one of the most powerful families of territorial magnates and Lecapenus was the son of an Armenian peasant who had worked his way up in the imperial service. In the end it was Lecapenus who manoeuvred himself into power. Perhaps he was merely a better intriguer than the aristocratic Phocas; perhaps the series of defeats which the army had suffered at the hands of Symeon made its commander an implausible saviour of the state; perhaps men understood that what gave the empire a decisive advantage over Symeon's Bulgaria was its command of the sea, which must be held on to at any cost. Be that as it may, Romanus Lecapenus had himself appointed a member of the regency council and gradually ousted the dowager empress Zoe, who favoured Leo Phocas, and her friends and advisers from positions of power. In May 919 he consolidated his position by marrying his daughter Helena to the fourteen-year-old Constantine VII and by taking the title of *Basileopator*, formerly held by the all-powerful Stylianos Zaoutzes under Leo VI. In the next year he was raised by Constantine first to the rank of Caesar then to that of co-emperor, and effective ruler of the empire.

Symeon had lost the political battle that might have brought him to the head of a revitalised Roman empire of which Bulgaria would have been an essential part. A few years before he had hoped to be father-in-law of the emperor and the power behind the throne. Now Romanus Lecapenus was in that position, with the support of the mass of the citizens, even if many of the landed aristocracy were lukewarm or sullenly hostile. From 920 until his death Symeon continued military operations against Byzantium, using up more and more of Bulgaria's human and material resources in what was by now a vain endeavour. He could defeat Byzantine armies and take provincial cities. But without a fleet he could not bring Constantinople to capitulate. He could devastate the European provinces, but he could not carry the war into Asia Minor, the demographic and economic heartland of the empire. And he had not the charismatic prestige, the countless personal connections, and the reserves of gold and luxury artefacts which enabled the empire to build up a network of alliances surrounding its enemies. Symeon, unlike his father, thought in military rather than diplomatic terms.

In 920 the Bulgarian army was engaged in Serbia, where once again the Byzantines had succeeded in establishing an anti-Bulgarian coalition. At the same time an attempt was made to seize key positions in Thrace giving control of the Dardanelles. Symeon was evidently testing the possibility of taking the war into Asia Minor by by-passing Constantinople. In 921 the Bulgarians appeared once more before the walls of Constantinople, and again in 922. In 923 Adrianople, the key to Byzantine Thrace, fell to Symeon. Throughout these years he had been in correspondence with the Patriarch Nicolaus Mysticus, through whom he proposed that Romanus Lecapenus abdicate, that a marriage alliance be established between his own family and that of Constantine VII, and so on. Needless to say these overtures were rejected. With Adrianople in his hands, however, he was in a stronger negotiating position, for there was great fear in Constantinople. But Romanus Lecapenus counted on the walls of Constantinople and his own diplomacy to save him. He had been for some time negotiating with the Magyars, Pechenegs and Russians to create a grand alliance favourable to Byzantium on the northern frontier of Bulgaria. Symeon too had been negotiating with the Fatimid Caliph of Africa for naval support. This was an obvious step for him to take, and if successful it would have changed the situation radically in his favour. But it presented religious difficulties which might have seriously weakened the allegiance of many of his subjects. And above all Bulgaria had little to offer that the Caliph wanted. However an agreement was reached in 923–4 and in 924 Symeon led his army again to the walls of Constantinople to await the arrival of the ships of his Moslem ally. By September he realised that the Moslem fleet was not coming and that the Byzantines had outbid him at the Caliph's court. His hopes dashed, Symeon asked for a meeting with the emperor. For the last time he entered the city in which he had passed his youth. Byzantine chroniclers recount at length the meeting of the two monarchs, including the significant detail that Symeon was accompanied by a numerous suite of soldiers and civilians who constantly hailed him as *Basileus* in the Greek tongue. Romanus too did all possible to impress his guest and the bystanders with his power. The same chroniclers are curiously silent about the results of the meeting. Was any kind of truce arrived at? Probably not, though neither side pressed things to a definite rupture. For Symeon the meeting in September 924 marked the failure of his grand project. He had not succeeded in taking the city or in breaking through to Asia Minor. He had not won the adherence of a party in Constantinople. And now the ominous movements on his northern frontier required his immediate return to Preslav. He continued to style himself Emperor of the Romans and Bulgarians and to provoke diplomatic protests from Constantinople. In 926 he raised the archbishop of Bulgaria to the status of a patriarch, independent of and of equal rank with the Patriarch of Constantinople.

In the meantime Byzantine diplomacy, disappointed in the unstable Serbian principalities as instruments of its policy, had turned to the powerful Croatian Kingdom of King Tomislav to the north-west. An alliance was arranged. When Symeon marched through Serbia in 926, overthrowing hostile princes and massacring countless peasants in a show of strength, and then sent a major force into Croatia, it was annihilated by Tomislav's army. Only the intervention of the Pope, who was worried about Croatian intentions towards the cities of the Dalmatian coast, saved Bulgaria from an invasion by the victorious Croats. It can have been little consolation to Symeon that the Pope, in his correspondence, accorded to him the title of emperor. As he was planning a further campaign against Byzantium he died in his capital of Preslav on 27 May 927. Byzantine chroniclers recount that an astrologer identified a statue in the Xerolophos quarter of Constantinople, near the forum of Arcadius, as the *Stoicheion* of Symeon, the physical object to which his fate was mysteriously linked. Romanus Lecapenus sent men by night to cut off the head of the statue, and at the same moment Symeon died in Bulgaria. The story probably reflects official propaganda based upon popular superstition, and testifies to the impression which Symeon made on his contemporaries.

After Symeon's death a striking change takes place in Bulgaro-Byzantine relations. Thirty-three years of almost unbroken war are succeeded by forty years of peace. From challenging Byzantine power in the Balkans and seeking to take over the empire's role as the one fully legitimate Christian state, Bulgaria becomes a docile dependant of Byzantium. At the same time the Slavonic Christian culture initiated under Boris and encouraged by Symeon in spite of his overriding military preoccupations continues to develop and flourish. Bulgaria does not become a cultural province of Byzantium. The reasons for this sudden change are not easy to discern with precision. Personalities play some role. Symeon's successor, his second son Peter, was a colourless character unable to inspire either loyalty in his fellow-countrymen or fear in his enemies. The exhaustion caused by long years of war had certainly weakened Bulgaria militarily and economically. The losses in men of military age cannot be estimated, but they were certainly very high. Apart from the annual campaigns against Byzantium, Bulgaria had been repeatedly involved in hostilities in Serbia. There was also a running war with the Magyars after they settled in the Danubian plain; we have scarcely any information on its progress, but it doubtless contributed to the steady drain on Bulgarian manpower. Bulgaria proper had not been invaded since the Magyar invasions of the '90s, so there would have been little recent damage to the economic infrastructure. There must however have been considerable interruption to the international trade to and from Constantinople passing through Bulgaria. The Byzantines would suffer less from this interruption than the Bulgarians, since this trade formed a small part of their total international trade, and in any case some of it could be diverted to other routes, particularly sea routes. A factor often forgotten was the loss to the Magyars during Symeon's reign of Transylvania which Krum had won from the Avars in 805, leaving only the plain of Wallachia as a survival of the once vast Transdanubian Bulgaria. This loss must have reduced both the man-power available to the Bulgarian army and the revenues in kind accruing to the government from direct taxation of free peasants. We do not know whether the mines of Transylvania were exploited during the period of Bulgarian rule. If they were, this would aggravate the effects of the loss of most of Transdanubia.

Probably the most important factor of all in Bulgaria's decline was the growing power of the feudal aristocracy, who diverted into their own pockets resources previously available to the community. It is difficult to trace this growth, whose effects become obvious in the mid and later tenth century. The evidence, such as it is, is presented elsewhere. If this growing feudalisation took place at a time when Symeon's wars causing a temporary shortage of able-bodied men, landowners would do all in their power to keep the peasants tied to their estates. Furthermore the whole system of recruitment of the Bulgarian army, which was essentially based on tribal levies, must have been affected by this radical and rapid change in the relation between man and man, and man and the land.

All these, and possibly other, factors underlie the sudden defusing of the Bulgarian situation after Symeon's death in 927. His second son Peter succeeded him because his eldest son Michael was confined to a monastery for reasons which we cannot discern. This break with the long-standing Bulgar tradition of inheritance of the Khanate by primogeniture led to dissatisfaction among the boyars and magnates, culminating in the escape of Michael from his monastery in 930 to head a revolt in western Bulgaria.[3] For years he maintained his control of the western Macedonian mountains. Meanwhile Peter was married, within a few months of his father's death, to Maria Lecapena, daughter of Romanus Lecapenus' eldest son Christopher. His title of *Basileus Boulgarōn* was recognised, as was the independence of the Bulgarian patriarchate. The empire could afford concessions on points of protocol now that Bulgaria was no longer dangerous. An annual subsidy was promised to Peter, under the guise of maintenance for his Byzantine wife. The Bulgarian government was headed by George Sursubul, brother of Symeon's second wife, who assumed the guardianship of Symeon's younger sons, Ivan and Benjamin. Maria and her Byzantine entourage seem to have dominated the court, causing it to be distrusted by the mass of the people and by the territorial magnates.

There is no need to chronicle in detail the various exchanges of embassies between Preslav and Constantinople. They took place against a background of military defeat and political disintegration of the Bulgarian state. In 934 there was an invasion by the Magyars, which seems to have reached Develtos. They were probably aiming at Constantinople, but it was Bulgaria that was devastated. They repeated their raids in 943, 958 and 962. In 941 Prince Igor of Kiev led one of the great Russian attacks by sea against Constantinople. It was defeated. Igor then succeeded in negotiating an agreement with the Pechenegs, whose territory lay between Kievan Russia and Bulgaria, and whose friendship the Byzantines sought to maintain. The Pechenegs were to break their alliance with Byzantium and support a Russian land attack on Constantinople. The terrified King Peter of Bulgaria turned to Romanus Lecapenus for help. The emperor, by a lavish and judicious distribution of gifts, succeeded in dissuading Igor from pursuing his attack. The Pechenegs, disappointed of their expected booty, crossed the Danube and pillaged much of Bulgaria, while the

Byzantines did nothing to help. In Byzantine eyes Bulgarian losses did not count. It was not until 965 that Peter broke sufficiently free of Byzantine tutelage to negotiate an alliance with the German emperor Otto, directed particularly against the Magyars. But it seems to have been of little avail. In the face of this defencelessness local magnates became more and more independent of the government in Preslav and followed the example set by Prince Michael.

There was a wave of asceticism, as men sought refuge in monasteries and hermitages from a world which could not provide the minimal conditions of decent life. Peter himself was a devotee of holy men. The greatest of these was St John of Rila, a herdsman turned anchorite who lived for many years in a hollow oak, winning a reputation for sanctity that spread throughout Bulgaria. The monastery which he founded in the Rhodope mountains after his oak blew down flourishes to this day. He died in 946. Of more fundamental importance was the development among the mass of peasantry of a counter-church and counter-society, dualist in belief and irreconcilably hostile to Church, state and the established order of things. This drew substantial parts of the population into non-cooperation and civil disobedience against a society towards which they no longer felt any loyalty. These developments are analysed elswhere in this book.

In 965 Maria Lecapena, the Byzantine queen of Bulgaria, died, and Byzantine influence at the court of Preslav diminished. The more warlike among the boyars called for an independent stand. However Peter continued to send envoys to Constantinople to collect the subsidy to which he had been accustomed. By this time Romanus Lecapenus had long ago been ousted from power by a palace revolution. His son-in-law and erstwhile protégé, the scholarly and cautious Constantine VII, had at last enjoyed the imperial authority which he inherited and had died in his turn. His son Romanus II had followed him to the grave after a short reign, leaving two infant sons, Basil and Constantine. Their mother, the dowager empress Theophano, had taken as her second husband Nicephorus Phocas, the commander-in-chief of the army, a member of a great family of magnates, and nephew of Leo Phocas whom Symeon had defeated at the Achelous. Nicephorus soon had himself proclaimed co-emperor with his young stepsons, and was the real ruler of the Byzantine empire in 965. An able general, a representative of the new class of feudal lords, and a convinced believer in the special status of the Byzantine empire, whose territory he was augmenting by his victories in Crete and on the eastern frontier, he was not a man to be trifled with. Well aware that a party hostile to Byzantine interests was now in power in Preslav, he chose to strike a pre-emptive blow. Peter's ambassadors were greeted with gross insults, the King called a prince clad in skins and their fellow-countrymen filthy beggars, and the request for subsidy—or tribute, as it had been called—was unconditionally rejected.

Realising that Nicephorus was bent on war, the faint-hearted Peter withdrew his request for money and apologised humbly for ever having made it. Nicephorus was unmoved, and sent his forces to reconnoitre the Bulgarian frontier. He wanted not merely to humiliate Bulgaria, but to destroy it and incorporate its territory in the Roman empire to which it properly belonged. But he was not anxious to fight on Bulgarian soil, where the many defiles in the mountains lent themselves to ambush and where so many Byzantine armies had met with disaster in the recent past. Like most good soldiers he did not like battles; they were too chancy. Others would fight for the empire's interests. The patrician Kalokyras, a native of the Byzantine outpost of Cherson in the Crimea, was sent to the court of the pagan Prince Svjatoslav of Kiev with 1500 pounds of gold. Svjatoslav was easily persuaded to make war on Bulgaria though he had, as it turned out, other aims in mind than earning his bribe from the Byzantines.

In summer 967 Nicephorus accused Peter of having let the Magyars pass through his country to attack the empire—a transparent attempt to find a *casus belli*—and Svjatoslav crossed the Danube into Bulgaria with 16,000 men. Bulgarian resistance was crushed and the Russians swept through the country between the Danube and the Balkan mountains. During the winter Peter—or his boyars, since the old King had suffered a stroke at the news of the Russian invasion—made the only move open to them and called upon the Pechenegs, traditionally allies of Byzantium, to attack the Russians in the rear. This they did to such effect that Svjatoslav had to return in haste to save Kiev from capture. Then a dramatic change took place. Svjatoslav, incited by the treacherous patrician Kalokyras, conceived the project of attacking the empire itself through Bulgaria. He talked of establishing his capital at Little Preslav, the Bulgarian market town on the Danube, and extending his power as far south as he could. Much of this was idle dreaming. But Svjatoslav had immense resources of man-power and was a formidable enemy. Nicephorus realised at once that things were not going as he had planned. He hastily sent a high officer of state to Preslav to sign an alliance with Bulgaria against the Russians and to make arrangements for the common defence of the Balkans. While these negotiations were taking place King Peter died, on 30 January 969. He was succeeded by his elder son Boris, who had been retained long in Constantinople, partly as honoured guest, partly as hostage. In autumn 969 Svjatoslav crossed the Danube again with a Russian army supported by Pecheneg and Magyar mercenaries. The hastily-made defensive arrangements were of no avail. The Russian army swept through the northern provinces, took Preslav and captured the King and all his family, crossed the Balkan range into Thrace and took Philippopolis, where 20,000 citizens were impaled as a punishment for having defended their city.

In Constantinople consternation reigned. On 10 December 969 Theophano had Nicephorus Phocas murdered and her lover, the general John Tzimisces, proclaimed co-emperor and guardian of the young princes. Tzimisces, an experienced soldier, immediately took control of the situation. His first step was to exile the treacherous and impulsive dowager empress Theophano, who had raised him to the purple. Next he opened negotiations with Svjatoslav, offering him large subsidies if he would withdraw from what was rightfully the territory of the empire. The very existence of Bulgaria had been conveniently forgotten. Svjatoslav's reply was to order Tzimisces to withdraw into Asia, as he considered the whole European territory of the empire to be his. There was nothing for the Byzantines to do but settle down to a long war.

It began in 970 with the defeat at Arcadiopolis of a Russian invading force by Bardas Sclerus, the new emperor's brother-in-law, and its withdrawal into eastern Bulgaria. Tzimisces did not venture to pursue it, but waited until 971. In that year operations were further delayed by a revolt in Asia headed by Bardas Phocas, a kinsman of the murdered Nicephorus. Not until 972 did a well-prepared Byzantine army march into Bulgaria, while the fleet cruised along the Black Sea coast and up the Danube to cut off the Russians' retreat. The Russians had left the mountain passes insufficiently guarded. Probably their army was largely engaged in police operations against the Bulgarian population. At any rate Tzimisces reached Preslav without a major engagement. The city was strongly defended, and it took several days of bitter fighting before it finally fell. By this time the Bulgarian capital had been reduced to a heap of ruins, among which lay the corpses of many of its inhabitants. It was never rebuilt properly, though its fortifications were patched up and it was rechristened Ioannopolis, after the emperor who had destroyed it. A further series of battles and sieges, in which the fire-shooting ships of the fleet played a large part, forced the Russians to capitulate. Svjatoslav handed over all his prisoners, promised to leave Bulgaria for ever, and asked for the former treaties between Kiev and Constantinople to be brought into force again. Tzimisces, who had lost many men in the hard-fought battles, agreed to the terms proposed. The Bulgarian King Boris II was in the Byzantine camp. But neither he nor any other Bulgarian was consulted on the peace terms. The Bulgarian state was no longer recognised, and its former lands were treated as imperial territory. The Bulgarian royal treasure, including Symeon's crown, was taken to Constantinople, where Boris II formally abdicated. His abdication put an end to the treaty obligations between Byzantium and Bulgaria. The Bulgarian patriarchate was allowed to lapse, and the church hierarchy brought under the control of Constantinople. The territory of eastern Bulgaria, devastated and depopulated, was incorporated into the Byzantine administrative system.

This was not quite the end of the story. Western Bulgaria and Macedonia had been untouched by the Russian invasion and were not under Byzantine occupation. The sons of a boyar, governor of one of the Bulgarian provinces, proclaimed themselves the successors of the dynasty of Krum and Boris and Symeon, and established an independent Bulgarian state in the west. The details of its origin are extremely obscure.

The western Bulgarian kingdom resisted Byzantine pressure for another half century. The organisation and administration of the country followed the pattern established by Boris and Symeon. But everything seems to have been on a smaller, more provincial scale. And though many churches and other buildings were constructed, Samuel's court at Sofia, Vodena, Prespa or Ohrid was not a centre of Slavonic culture comparable to Preslav. For a time Samuel was able even to extend his territory at the expense of Byzantium. John Tzimisces made no further moves against Bulgaria before his death in 976. The army was probably too busy establishing and maintaining law and order in the newly-conquered provinces. His successor, the young emperor Basil II, now of age, was occupied for the first few years of his independent reign in dealing with the dangerous rebellion of Bardas Sclerus in Asia Minor. Samuel profited by making raids in all directions, and from 980 onwards drove southwards into the plain of Thessaly and besieged Larissa. In the end he captured it, helped by sympathisers within the city.

The shock produced by the fall of Larissa roused Basil II to action.

For the rest of his life he dedicated himself with almost paranoic single-mindedness to the conquest of the Bulgarian successor-state and the re-establishment of Byzantine power — and his own personal power — throughout the Balkan peninsula. There may have been deep psychological reasons for his sudden abandonment of the pleasures of Byzantine life to become a warrior-monk wholly devoted to the pursuit of power, but they were not the determining factor in the outcome. The Byzantine empire, prosperous and expanding, could not after all that had happened tolerate a Bulgarian state on its frontier. And a Bulgarian state based on the mountainous west of the country, far from the populous and fertile eastern provinces, a state which could only attack Constantinople and its neighbourhood by dangerously lengthening its lines of communication, could not hold out indefinitely against the full concentration of Byzantine military strength.

The war need not be recounted in all its picturesque detail. In any case gaps in our sources make it impossible to reconstruct all the campaigns. The Bulgarians had their victories. They caught Basil's army in a defile in 986 and nearly destroyed it. They even recaptured the old capitals of Preslav and Pliska during the following years. They took Dyrrhachium on the Adriatic coast and gained an outlet to the west. These were the result of skilful use of the formidable peasant army which the Bulgarians could put in the field, and of the sympathy which they enjoyed from the Slavonic inhabitants of many of the regions which they conquered. They were also attributable to Basil's preoccupation first with rebellion in the east, then with a threatened Russian attack. The former was crushed in the field of battle, the last evaded by diplomatic means, when Prince Vladimir was baptised and received as bride the emperor's sister Anna. By 990 Basil was ready to deal with Bulgaria. Slowly but surely during the years the Bulgarians were driven back towards the centre of their power in the high mountains of western Macedonia. Basil struck now from this direction, now from that. And he was successful in detaching from their allegiance several of the Bulgarian commanders opposing him. These he rewarded with high office and rich estates. Among them was the eunuch governor of Skopje, Romanus, son of King Peter, the last living descendant of the dynasty of Krum and Boris. He ended his days as a Byzantine patrician in command of the fortress of Abydos on the Dardanelles. These desertions became more and more frequent as Samuel lost control of strong point after strong point. Even his own daughter Miroslava went over to Byzantium with her Armenian husband Ashot of Taron.

Side by side with this welcome for high-born deserters went increasing Byzantine brutality towards rank and file prisoners, military or civilian. In 1014 some 15,000 Bulgarian soldiers were captured after a desperate engagement in the upper Struma valley. Basil blinded 99 out of every 100 and left the hundredth man with one eye to guide his companions back to their master. When this ghastly cortège reached Ohrid the shock killed King Samuel. In 1016 during a campaign in Macedonia Basil put out the eyes of every Bulgarian he found, soldier or civilian. Medieval warfare was a bloody business. But Byzantine rulers could take the long view and generally conducted their wars with an eye to the peace which would follow, when their erstwhile foes might become their friends. The 'frightfulness' of the last years of the Bulgarian war is an indication that no settlement was hoped for or wanted. Unconditional submission to the empire was to be the only outcome.

After Samuel's death the Bulgarian Kingdom began to disintegrate as its parts were cut off from one another by Byzantine advance and as various members of the royal family set themselves up as ephemeral local rulers. One after another they surrendered to Basil, to be rewarded with high office and grants of land. The last effective King of Bulgaria, John Vladislav, who proudly entitled himself 'Emperor of the Bulgarians', fought desperately until he was murdered by an unknown assailant before the walls of Dyrrachium early in 1018. By later in the same year all was over. Basil received the surrender of Ohrid from the dowager queen Maria, widow of King Samuel, and the last Bulgarian fortress of Pernik, west of Mount Vitosha, was delivered over by its courageous defender, the Bulgarian general Krakra. Isolated pockets of resistance probably held out in the mountains, necessitating operations by Basil in northern Greece, but the Bulgarian state no longer existed. Its territories had become Byzantine provinces, its citizens subjects of the emperor in Constantinople.

Yet this was not a return to the age of Justinian, before the Slav invasions of the Balkans. During the centuries of Bulgarian rule important changes had taken place. The Slavs in peninsular Greece lost their language and their ethnic patterns of behaviour. The period of most rapid Hellenisation was in the ninth century. After that we hear only of relatively small pockets of unhellenised Slavs in inaccessible areas such as Mount Taygetus in the Peloponnese. The same is true *a fortiori* of the large Slav communities settled in Asia Minor, which entirely lost their ethnic identity and became absorbed into the local population. This was what had been happening for centuries in the Roman empire and in its Byzantine successor, as tribal communities became absorbed into a common society of Hellenic culture.

In what had been Bulgarian territory, however, this process did not take place. For practical purposes we can take the southern frontier of Symeon's Bulgaria as the northern frontier of Hellenic speech and national consciousness. Though a Byzantine province from the end of the tenth or early eleventh century until the end of the twelfth, Bulgaria maintained its Slavonic speech, its literary culture based upon that speech, its peculiar stock of folk tales and legend, its poetry and song, and doubtless its dance, its mode of dress, its way of life and its consciousness of its own history. There was much inter-penetration of course. Many of the Bulgarian aristocratic families inter-married with similar Byzantine families and became virtually Hellenised. Greek was evidently widely known in the towns of Bulgaria during the two centuries of Byzantine rule. But no Byzantine Greek who went to Bulgaria was in any doubt that he was in a foreign land. As the Byzantine military and political power declined catastrophically in the late twelfth century one of the many Bulgarian revolts was successful and Bulgaria was restored to independent statehood. The administration and titulature in this second Bulgarian Kingdom owed much to Byzantine models. But it also perpetuated much that went back to the days of Boris and Symeon, whose heirs its rulers felt themselves to be. It was a land of Slavonic culture, though of course many of its churchmen and other intellectuals were equally at home in Greek. Tŭrnovo, the capital, was the centre of a vigorous school of writers and translators whose medium was Slavonic. Once again an independent church, using Slavonic liturgy and under its own patriarch, was set up. The second Bulgarian Kingdom maintained itself until the end of the fourteenth century, when it vanished as a political entity in the general conquest of the Balkan peninsula by the Ottoman Turks.

What had taken place was the formation of the Bulgarian nationality. Not of the Bulgarian nation, for this is a further development which requires many conditions not existing in the Middle Ages, such as a single economy, a common market, a single, sovereign state, and so on. Nations are largely the product of the modern industrial world. By nationality is meant an important and often long-lasting intermediate stage between the fragile unity of tribe or clan, based on real or imagined kinship and liable to be ruptured by membership of some other community, such as a city, a religious group, etc., and the unity of the modern nation-state. The formation of a nationality is a complex process and its details vary from case to case. What seem to be necessary—though not always sufficient—conditions are a common language, a common literature employing that language, a common territory of significant extent, a common historical tradition (of which we find a trace in the so-called *List of Princes,* probably a Slavonic translation of a Greek text, carved on stone at Pliska or Madara [4]), and no doubt common legends, songs, rituals, games, food habits, patterns of dress, and so on. There is frequently, but not always, a common religion. There is usually, but not always, a common state structure arising out of the pre-existing tribal and clan structures, sometimes under the catalyst of invasion or penetration from outside, but not imposed from outside as an act of policy by another state. It was on such a basis and in such ways that the English or French nationality developed out of the welter of Germanic and Romano-Celtic communities in the one case, and out of the semi-tribal Frankish monarchy and the surviving Gallo-Roman communities in the other. Similarly in Bulgaria during the existence of the Bulgarian state a common nationality was evolved out of the semi-pastoral Turkic Bulgar horde, the various tribal principalities and ephemeral unions of the Slavs, the Romanised or Hellenised Thracians and Daco-Moesians and doubtless other elements too. The leaders of the revolt which led to the revival of an independent Bulgarian state at the end of the twelfth century were probably of Vlach origin. Once formed, Bulgarian nationality was immensely tougher and more durable than the pre-existing communities. It is significant that John Vladislav, the last ruler of independent Bulgaria before the Byzantine conquest, emphasises in an inscription that he is 'Bulgarian by birth.' [5]   It was resistant to Byzantine absorption and later to Turkish conquest, and in the nineteenth century formed the foundation upon which the modern Bulgarian nation-state was built.

The Bulgarian nationality is one of the earliest discernable in medieval Europe, and certainly the earliest within the range of influence of the Byzantine empire. The empire was ordered upon quite different principles. It was certainly not based on ethnic unity, whether real or fictitious. It did not have a common language in the sense of a common mother-tongue for its citizens. They included not only Greek speakers, but Slavs, Armenians, Georgians, Abkhazians, Arabs, Syrians, Latins, Turks and many others, who lived intermingled with one another and were not territorially separated. Greek was the language of administration and culture. Use of it had no ethnic implications at all. Gregory Pakourianos, commander-in-chief of the army in the early years of Alexios I Comnenus, was a Georgian. No doubt he spoke Greek perfectly and transacted all the important business of his life in it. But in the monastery which he founded in 1083 at Bachkovo in former Bulgaria he insisted that Georgian be the language of liturgy and of everyday usage, and that no Greek be admitted as a member of the community.[6] The number of non-Greeks in the empire increased rapidly in the tenth century, as regions on the eastern frontier, where the mass of the population were Armenians, Kurds or Syrians, were subjected to Byzantine rule. The empire owed its unity—which was very real—to its obedience to a single ruler appointed by God, to its common administrative and legal system, to the ease of movement within it, and to many other factors. It had a common past to look back on, but much more important was the common future to which it looked forward, when God's design would be fulfilled. The whole structure and functioning of Byzantine society were unfavourable to the development of nationalities in the sense here discussed. It would certainly be wrong to speak of a Greek nationality in the ninth and tenth centuries, though Greek was doubtless the native tongue of the majority of the inhabitants of the empire. But those Greek speakers called themselves either Romans—a concept which included also non-Greek speakers—or Cretans, Peloponnesians, Bithynians etc.[7] In the course of time a Greek nationality did emerge. Perhaps the beginnings of it can be discerned in the twelfth century, and there is no doubt of its existence in the last centuries of the Byzantine empire. But it long post-dated the formation of Bulgarian nationality. And it did not until relatively recent times shake itself free from the ecumenicity and supra-national nuances which it had inherited from Byzantine political thought and practice. How far the existence of Bulgaria on the very doorstep, as it were, of regions with a fairly homogeneous Greek population contributed to the formation of Greek nationality by its example and its polarising effect is an interesting question which cannot be discussed here. What we are concerned with is Byzantine-Bulgarian relations in the ninth and tenth centuries. And we have seen that they are not a mere fortuitous succession of hostility and friendship, but that they embody a recognisable historical process, to which parallels can be found in western Europe at the same time and in other parts of the world in later ages.

4 The Land

Both Bulgaria and the Byzantine empire were agrarian countries, in the sense that by far the largest part of the population of both was directly engaged in the production of food and raw materials through agriculture and stock-breeding. This is true of all medieval societies. There were however significant differences between the agrarian processes of the two regions, which were partly the result of permanent geographical differences, and partly determined by the history of the societies which inhabited them.

The territory of the Byzantine empire in the ninth and tenth centuries belonged in the main to the Mediterranean world, characterised by mild, wet winters, long, hot, dry summers, the proximity of sea and mountains, rapid loss of surface water and absence of perennial rivers. Even the plateau of Asia Minor has Mediterranean features, and is sharply distinguished from the much more arid plateau of Iran, which favours nomadism. Anatolian agriculture was based upon the use of rain water and cultivation of fruit trees together with cereals, in the words of Xavier de Planhol 'une polyculture sèche méditerranéenne'.[1] It is probable that the warmer, moister conditions of antiquity had favoured the introduction into high Anatolia of crops which can no longer be cultivated there. For instance the extensive olive plantations at Synnada in Phrygia[2] have long ago disappeared, and may already have vanished by the tenth century.[3] At any rate the Mediterranean pattern of agriculture had imposed itself throughout the empire so far as natural conditions allowed. This essentially involved extensive olive cultivation, viniculture, winter-sown wheat or barley cultivated often between rows of olive trees, much miscellaneous fruit cultivation, including figs, cherries, plums, almonds, walnuts etc., quick-ripening crops of green vegetables harvested before the summer drought begins, and in particular pulses. Intensive cultivation, without fallow, was practised in a few favoured locations. Fodder crops, such as lucerne, formed a significant proportion of agricultural production. There was little artificial irrigation, other than the digging of wells. Even the terracing of hill sides was probably not much practised in the ninth and tenth centuries.

The history of Byzantine or Bulgarian agriculture remains still to be written. However we do possess two interesting texts which throw light on Byzantine agriculture, the *Farmer's Law,* which most but not all authorities now date about 700, and the *Geoponica*, an agricultural encyclopedia compiled in the middle of the tenth century but embodying much earlier material. The differences between the pictures which they paint are striking. They are only partly to be accounted for by the likelihood that the *Farmer's Law* deals with a commune settled on frontier or abandoned land, like the western mark, and practising extensive subsistence agriculture, while the *Geoponica* is written for the growing class of large landowners cultivating for the market. They also reflect the steady improvement in the techniques of Byzantine agriculture in the intervening centuries. Of particular note is the much greater variety of crop plants mentioned in the later text, and the frequent reference to the cultivation of leguminous crops to be ploughed in to increase the nitrogen content of the soil.[4]

On Bulgarian agriculture we are less well informed. Most of the territory of Bulgaria belongs to the world of central Europe, with its extensive plains and wide valleys among the mountains, its heavily wooded mountain-sides which helped to retain the ground water, its heavier soils, its perennial rivers, its less hot, dry summers and its cold, though fairly short winters. It is reasonable to suppose that regions which had for two centuries been outside the Byzantine empire were less affected by the technical improvements just mentioned than those regions which were all the time the object of Byzantine administration. This supposition is borne out by the statement in the *Life of Clement of Ohrid* that the saint brought to the land of the Bulgarians all kinds of fruit trees from the land of the Greeks in order to improve local cultivation.[5] We should therefore expect a less varied as well as a different agriculture in Bulgaria. The scanty historical sources reveal wheat and millet as the principal cereal crops, though barley and oats were known.[6] At the time of the Byzantine conquest of Bulgaria, at the beginning of the eleventh century, the land tax was paid in wheat, millet and wine, and there is no reason to suppose that this was not the practice in the tenth and probably in the ninth century too. Viniculture was general. The Slavs would not be familiar with it in their homeland on the Vistula, but may have come into contact with it on their way southwards through Transylvania. The Bulgars, a nomadic pastoral people, certainly did not cultivate the vine before their arrival in the Balkan peninsula. It seems most likely that the newcomers learned the complex and sophisticated technique from the earlier Romanised or Hellenised inhabitants. This is further evidence for some degree of continuity of settlement and cultivation in the northern Balkans.

The invaders did not find a *tabula rasa*. Fruit trees are often mentioned, but with no details. The olive does not seem to have been generally cultivated — as indeed it could not be in many parts of Bulgaria for climatic reasons. Where we do hear of it in the period after the Byzantine conquest, it is always in southern Macedonia or on the Black Sea coast, regions which both climatically and culturally had more in common with the southern Balkans than with their immediate hinterland. Flax was produced not only for local use, but also for export to Constantinople in the tenth century.[7] Among vegetables we hear of beans, cabbage, garlic and melons. Stock-breeding played a greater role in Bulgaria than in the European provinces of the Byzantine empire. In the kitchen middens of Pliska pig bones predominate. At Popina near Silistra, dating from the eleventh and twelfth centuries, those of large cattle are much more numerous. This may be an accident. But Bulgarian archaeologists in recent years have adduced further evidence for the growing importance of large cattle in the Bulgarian economy between the eighth and the twelfth century.[8] This would indicate a growth of cleared pasture land at the expense of forest, and suggests an increase in the rural population, and a growth in the area brought under cultivation, since much of the pasture would be fallow land. Sheep were bred everywhere in the mountains, and sheepskin rugs from Bulgaria were much appreciated in Constantinople. Horses are rarely mentioned, and horse bones are infrequent at Pliska and other sites. Some scholars argued that the horse was scarcely used, in spite of the suitability of certain regions of Bulgaria for horse-breeding and the presence of imperial stud-farms there in the twelfth century. This view is perhaps exaggerated. After all the Proto-Bulgars were horsemen, and in their assimilation by their Slav subjects they are unlikely to have lost all their inherited skill and values. Yet Bulgaria in the ninth and tenth centuries was not a land of horsemen. The Bulgarian army was mainly an infantry force, while the Byzantine army depended upon a core of cavalry partly maintained by land grants. Bee-keeping was extensively practised in Bulgaria, and we hear of honey from the Struma valley being sold in the market at Constantinople in the tenth century. In a world where sugar cane is unknown — except in remote areas where it had been introduced by the Arabs — honey is the main source of sugar. But it may be that bees were kept in Bulgaria partly for their wax, which for certain purposes, such as lamp fuel, replaced the olive oil used in Byzantine territory.

Iron agricultural implements were widely used by the Byzantine peasantry, and scythes, iron axes and the like are mentioned both in the *Farmer's Law* and in hagiographical texts. The use of iron in the countryside was probably more widespread than in the contemporary west.[9] In Bulgaria village smiths were common. One is mentioned in the *Miracle of St George*,[10] and John the Exarch includes smiths in his list of artisans.[11]

Iron plough-shares, sickles and hoes have been found at Pliska and other Bulgarian sites. There is no doubt that much skilled iron-work was carried out in Bulgaria, though the difficulty of dating finds makes it hard to distinguish the period of independence from that of Byzantine occupation. It is likely, however, that the wooden plough was commoner than the iron-shod plough, as it was in Bulgaria at later periods. Recent study has suggested that different types of plough were used in different regions of Bulgaria, perhaps reflecting the different ethnic origins of the population.[12] The variety of plough patterns is clear; the explanation remains uncertain. They are all essentially scratch-ploughs. The plough was normally drawn by a pair of oxen. Indeed the pair of oxen forms the unit of tax-assessment at the end of Bulgarian independence, and no doubt much earlier too. There is no sign of the type of heavy wheeled plough with a mould-board, which requires a team of four or more oxen. There is little evidence for more sophisticated tools such as scythes.

The ninth and tenth centuries were a period of rapid and decisive transformation in the relations between men and the land in the Byzantine empire. The seventh and early eighth centuries had seen the development of a fairly uniform early Byzantine agrarian society. The great estates of late antiquity had largely vanished during the long years of Persian, Arab, Slav, Avar and Lombard invasions. The pandemic of bubonic plague in the middle of the sixth century may have set off a demographic chain reaction resulting in a marked fall in the population. At any rate there is plenty of evidence for the abandonment of cultivable land. And large numbers of 'barbarians' were settled, mostly in Asia Minor, as cultivators and sometimes as soldiers, presumably on land which had been neglected.

At the same time the loss of the corn supply from Egypt, first temporarily interrupted in 608, then again in 619 after Egypt fell to the Persians, and finally terminated in 641, led first to a chronic shortage of cereals in Constantinople and in army establishments, and then to the development of cereal production in regions near the capital where more lucrative cash crops had been produced before, or which had lain uncultivated.

The great estate, with its slaves and *coloni*, vanished, and its place was taken by communes of free peasants—free in the sense that they owed no dues or services except to the central government. In such a village commune the cultivated land was individually owned, the often extensive wasteland communally owned, and user rights regularly redistributed. There were various possible vestiges of an earlier communal ownership of the cultivated land, such as the right to pick fruit to eat from another man's trees, but in general this was a society of individual landowners. What made it a commune was not so much its internal organisation as its relation to the state. For the members were jointly responsible for the payment of taxes to the imperial government. As a consequence they had a prior right of purchase should a fellow-member wish to sell his holding, and the right to occupy and cultivate land which for any reason was left uncultivated. This is the agrarian society revealed by the *Farmer's Law*. Its resemblances to the western mark are striking, but its differences are also worthy of note.

Side by side with these peasant communes there were probably larger holdings of a different character, held by soldiers. Unfortunately the origin of these *stratiōtika ktēmata* is a matter of some obscurity. It seems most likely that it is connected with the origin of the theme system, whereby the ancient provinces were replaced as administrative units by military areas, each with its own army formation permanently based in its territory. But the matter cannot be proved. And the origin and development of the theme system is the subject of debate, which need not concern us here. The *stratiōtika ktēmata* are first encountered unequivocally in the legislation of the Macedonian emperors of the tenth century. They certainly existed much earlier. There is a clear reference to a military holding in the *Life of St Philaretos*. It seems most likely that during the seventh century, and probably as early as Heraclius, the custom grew up of distributing land holdings conditional upon military service. These were heritable, and their owners enjoyed immunity from certain taxes and all *corvées* due to the state. Their obligation was to provide a soldier, properly equipped. He might or might not be the owner of the holding; often he was the owner's son. The holding of a cavalryman, for example, would be considerable; it had to provide two horses, and no doubt a groom, as well as the soldier himself. Such land-holders were, in terms of a later social system, small gentry, not peasants. Infantry holdings, of which we hear much less in the sources, would be substantially smaller, but still bigger than the average holding of a member of a peasant commune.

By the second half of the eighth century, then, the Byzantine empire consisted largely of a mosaic of free peasant communes and military estates. There were some surviving larger estates, worked by tenants, slaves or wage-labourers, and of course there were extensive monastic estates, though their extent had been reduced by the Iconoclast emperors. Early in the ninth century a process begins which does not reach its climax until the eleventh. Successful military leaders and civil functionaries invest their gains in land, establish large estates, and gradually oust the peasant communes and the military proprietors. The factors favouring this were several: the relatively advanced state of Byzantine agriculture, which permitted large profits on the investment of capital, the ease with which individual holdings could be established by enterprising—and lucky—peasants on former wasteland or land not belonging to a commune, the relative freedom from invasion and war in most regions of the empire, the absence of any other possibility of placing capital. The process in the end went far beyond questions of land-tenure and led to the development of a hereditary feudal aristocracy, creaming off the surplus production of the primary producers and eventually taking over the central state apparatus. In this context 'feudalism' does not imply a complex system of mutual obligations between superior and inferior, as in the classical feudalism of parts of western Europe. It is used in a much more general sense of a society in which the land belongs to a class of magnates and they extract part of the farmer's surplus production from him in the form of rents in money, kind and services. The legal form in which this basic economic relation manifests itself depends upon the structure and history of the society in question, the strength or weakness—or even total absence—of a central government, and so on.

In the sphere which we are immediately considering, we find a concentration of land in the hands of certain wealthy families and monasteries acquired in a variety of ways, legal and illegal. The new landowner collects the taxes due to the state on these lands, but does not necessarily pay them over in their entirety. In course of time he acquires in various ways fiscal immunity, and also steps up the amount extracted from his tenants. In addition he imposes on them various kinds of *corvées* and sometimes exercises minor judicial rights over them. Though, owing to the strength of the central state apparatus, the kind of elaborate hierarchical structure characteristic of the feudal West never developed in Byzantium, those historians are right who describe the pattern evolving in the ninth and tenth centuries as Byzantine feudalism. But the dependent peasantry of the later Byzantine period are not the direct continuation of the *coloni* of the later Roman empire. There was a long intervening period when free peasant proprietors prevailed.[13]

The successive stages of 'Byzantine feudalism' are difficult to trace. No doubt their rapidity and their form varied much from region to region. Yet on the main line of the process there is no longer any dispute. In the European provinces there are probably three zones to be distinguished: Eastern Thrace, the hinterland of the capital; Western Thrace, Macedonia and Epirus; and peninsular Greece. The first was a zone of relatively intensive cultivation, in which peasant communes, if they ever existed, were early ousted by civil and military officials, whose quite small estates—*proasteia*—formed a tight mosaic. These landowners were, at this stage, generally able to protect themselves from the rapacity of the nascent feudal magnates. The second was an area only gradually brought under firm Byzantine control after being overrun by the Slavs in the sixth and early seventh centuries, and largely lost once again to the Bulgars in the reign of Krum. It was essentially a region of free peasant proprietors, with strong traces of an earlier tribal organisation. The third, always something of a backwater in Byzantine life, offered a mosaic of partly or wholly Hellenised Slav communes; surviving medium estates of the ancient type, monastic estates, and large feudal estates of the new type, particularly on land recently regained from the Slavs. We need not believe everything which the Continuator of Theophanes writes about the widow Danielis (Theoph. Cont. 226 ff., 316 ff.). But she is clearly a type-specimen of the new variety of landowner, except that she probably made more use of slave labour than would have been possible, say, in Asia Minor. By the middle of the eleventh century the Theban tax-roll—whatever the precise status of the document published by Svoronos—shows a large part of central Greece in the hands of absentee landlords, many of whom hold posts in the provincial administration.[14] The situation in Asia Minor at the end of the eighth century is depicted in the *Life of St Philaretos;*[15] Philaretos was probably an enterprising peasant— a *kulak*—rather than a dignitary.

The problem of the concentration of property in the hands of the *dynatoi* attracted the attention of the Macedonian emperors, who saw in it a threat both to the revenues of the state and to its military power. In a series of legislative acts they, as well as the usurper Romanos Lekapenos, sought to combat the acquisition of village commune lands and military holdings by grandees, whether by purchase or by fictitious adoption, testamentary disposition or other means. Their measures seem to have been of little avail. In the first place Leo VI may have already revoked the right of pre-emption in a Novel,[16] if indeed it is genuine. Secondly, the execution of these measures was in the hands of the very class who stood to profit most by the acquisition of peasant holdings, the high military and civil officials.[17]

We are less well informed on Bulgarian agrarian relations. Some probable hypotheses can be formed on the basis of the Responsa of Pope Nicholas I to Boris and of the *Zakon Sudnyj Ljud'ïm*. The Proto-Bulgars did not at first cultivate the land, but they did practise stock-breeding. Whether flocks were individually owned, or belonged to clans or tribes, we do not know. But it is likely that the great Bulgarian officers of state — the boyars — who were the descendants of the former tribal nobility, possessed large flocks with grazing rights over great areas. However they readily took to agriculture of the feudal type, though probably without the technical skill and scientific interest which many Byzantine landlords displayed. By the early ninth century they had ceased to be primarily pastoralists.

The main agricultural labour force was provided by the Slavs. Originally organised in communes based on kinship, with a fairly egali-tarian system, they were early forced to pay a part of their surplus to the Bulgar state, which also transported and settled them, in tribal units, in new areas. Over and above the tribute which they paid to the state, many of them were quasi-feudal dependants of members of the nobility. The stages by which they reached this state of dependence are not recorded, but can well be imagined: the tribal leaders become owners of the tribal land, and then become themselves fused with the Proto-Bulgar aristocracy. Ninth- and tenth-century sources show peas-ants falling into groups: free peasants, *epoikoi*, Slavonic *epigi*, owing dues to the state; peasants dependent on a lord, *paroikoi*, Slavonic *paritsi;* a third class, in some way less free than the *paritsi* were the *otrotsi*, whose status resembled that of a slave. At the lowest level of the nobility we find the *Kmet*, probably in origin the head of a free com-mune, now turned into an instrument of state or landlord. The *Zhupan*, originally a Slavonic tribal leader, had become absorbed into the Bulgar ruling class and probably retained only a tenuous connection with the kinship community which was his original *raison d'être*.

The *Zakon Sudnyj Ljud'im* (the legal code promulgated under Boris or Symeon) rules that if a *ljudin* flees from his *knez* to another *knez* he is to be beaten and returned. This has been taken as an indication that some Bulgarian peasants were tied to the soil as early as the end of the ninth century. But *knezhenie* is a territorial division in Old Slavonic texts, and the *knez* may be some kind of regional governor. The prohibition may refer to soldiers leaving the military district in which they are enrolled. The Bulgarian archbishopric at the beginning of the eleventh century possessed estates comprising not only land but a fixed number of cultivators. Its ownership of these estates, together with the men on them, was recognised by Basil II after the destruction of the Bulgarian state.[18] These cultivators appear to have been attached to the soil, though when or how they became so is uncertain. About the same date we meet a certain Glad, governor of a region between the Danube and the Maros in south-eastern Hungary. He had been sent from Vidin by the Bulgarian king as governor — it is not clear by what king — and left undisturbed by King Stephen I of Hungary. He and his son Octhum had 'a countless multitude of unbroken horses' as well as *'pecora infinita'* landed estates (*allodia*) and manors (*curiae*), and the right to collect taxes on salt coming down the Maros. But these two picturesque characters are probably not typical Bulgarian aristocrats. One of them had seven wives, *'quod in religione Christiana non perfectus erat'.* [19]

At first sight the situation in Bulgaria is similar to that in contemporary Byzantium. But there are differences. First, the formation of large estates begins later and advances more slowly in Bulgaria. There were certainly many free peasants still on the land when Basil II put an end to Bulgarian independence. Second, there seem to have been no military holdings in Bulgaria. The Bulgarian army was raised by a kind of *levée en masse* carried out by the local authorities, and was less of a professional élite than the army of Byzantium. Third, the effect of the destruction of free communes was probably more drastic in Bulgarian society. Men weeded out by one process or another from the wasteful subsistence agriculture could not so readily find other employment, thanks to the backwardness of Bulgarian industry, and they easily fell into debt bondage. The *Zakon Sudnyj Ljud'im* constantly speaks of paupers, thieves and bandits. This is evidence of the impoverishment of the peasantry as men lost their original connection with their commune and their land. There is no evidence for any attempt by the Bulgarian rulers to restrain the concentration of land in the hands of the boyars.

The same forces, then, were at work in Byzantium and Bulgaria, but they operated at different speeds, and their starting points were not the same.

5 Cities

The southern part of the Balkan peninsula was a region of ancient city life. In the northern part the cities were mostly established during the period of the Roman empire, though there were a number of earlier foundations along the west coast of the Black Sea. However, by the end of antiquity there was little difference between the cities of Greece and those of Illyricum, Thrace and Moesia, except that the former were more numerous and comprised practically the whole territory of the provinces, while the latter were fewer in number and were separated by imperial estates, tribal lands and other non-city territories.

The ancient city was in principle internally self-administering. Hellenistic or Roman governors were concerned with maintaining peace and if necessary arbitrating between cities. Roman procurators were concerned with fiscal relations between the imperial government and individual citizens or the civic collectivity. Otherwise the city ran its own affairs by means of an assembly of the citizens—which in most instances soon lost its legislative power, though it might long continue to function as an electoral body—a council, and magistrates. In practice this state of affairs was often modified. As early as the second century A. D. imperial officials took charge of the internal affairs of cities, first as an emergency measure, later on a more permanent basis. But the power of the *curiales,* those families whose wealth entitled them to membership of the council, remained real enough until the fourth century, especially in the larger cities. And in these there emerged within the *curiales* a smaller group—the *principales*—who formed a self-perpetuating oligarchy of local notables in whose hands lay whatever remained of the city's autonomy, plus a number of fiscal functions delegated to the city authorities by the imperial government. It was not until the fifth century that the system of self-administration began to break down, being taken over in part by officials appointed by the central government, in part by the bishop and his clergy. The process of decline is admirably summarised by Justinian in the Proem to his *Novel* 38 (536 A. D.). By this time, and probably already a generation earlier, the city councils had ceased to exist, their functions being taken over by an imperial official, the *vindex.* But the *ordo curialis* remained both as a legal entity and as a social group, contriving to share power with the state and the church. They are found effectively running cities under various names—*protiktores* is one—

as late as the end of the sixth century. It is not until the reign of Leo VI (886-912) that city councils were legally abolished, 'since civil affairs have been transformed, and everything now depends on imperial providence and administration' (Leo VI, *Novel* 46).[1]

This ruling oligarchy was made up of the owners of substantial estates within the city territory. For the cities of antiquity were not essentially centres of industry and trade, but agrarian centres, '*Landstädte*'. Each lived mainly from the produce of its own territory. Its governing class consisted of landlords, not of merchants or industrialists. The city provided facilities for the distribution of agricultural produce and offered to the landlords and their families and dependants a style of life impossible in the surrounding countryside, symbolised by the baths and the theatre which, along with temples and other public buildings, were to be found in the humblest of cities. A few cities, Athens, Corinth and Syracuse in the fifth century B.C., Alexandria, Antioch and Thessalonika in Hellenistic times, developed further into centres of manufacture and long-distance trade, less dependent on their immediate surroundings than the majority of cities. But these great cities were always few in number, and when circumstances became unfavourable they regressed to the status of agrarian cities.

Such were the cities of antiquity. The *Synecdemus* of Hierocles, a sixth century document, lists 265 cities in the Balkan provinces and their offshore islands. Most of these were very small places indeed, but they had the attributes of a city, not a village. And most of them were in the southern part of the peninsula: Macedonia, Thessaly, Achaea, Epirus and Crete between them account for 179 of the 265.

In the series of invasions from the late fourth century onwards, many of the cities of the Balkan provinces were captured and sacked. Some were rebuilt and resettled at once, others left as a heap of ruins. By the mid sixth century peace appeared to have been long re-established in the Balkans. Many cities repaired their walls and there was much public building, but it was the result of imperial munificence, not of local initiative. Some cities had already ceased to exist. Most, in spite of their outward façade, had lost many of their wealthiest and most influential citizens, particularly in the regions near the Danube frontier. But the cities were still there, living off the peasants and slaves who cultivated their land. Few of them now had theatres, but they all had churches of greater or lesser magnificence. And they represented the ideal of civilised life. The inroads of the Slavs and Avars put an end to city life in the northern

Balkans except along the sea coast. Cities were systematically destroyed and their inhabitants either fled or were taken prisoner or killed. The Avars had some interest in the use of city amenities but the Slavonic peasants had no use for cities, which were for them mere encumbrances upon the soil.

The narrative historians tell us very little about the fate of the cities in the Dark Age—approximately 600-800 A.D. Here and there the archaeologist now begins to shed a little light on the problem, but his evidence is often extremely difficult to interpret. However, many of the great coastal cities of Greece present no problem: Thessalonika, Chalkis, Athens and Corinth continued not only to be inhabited, but to function as cities throughout the Dark Age, though they might be again and again besieged, and sometimes temporarily captured by the invaders. The same is true of Thebes, and very likely of other cities in east central Greece. Patras was in all probability also in continuous occupation, though there is a tantalising story about the evacuation of its inhabitants to southern Italy. Many of the smaller inland cities in Hierocles' list were probably abandoned by their inhabitants and their walls allowed to fall into ruin. But others may well have continued as Greek islands in a Slavonic sea. Further north-east Constantinople remained the imperial capital throughout, though on occasion besieged by Persians, Avars and Arabs. The coastal cities of the Sea of Marmara and of the western shore of the Black Sea held out too, though some of them were temporarily captured by the Avars. The great fortress-cities protecting Thrace, Develtos, Adrianople and Philippopolis also remained in continuous Byzantine occupation, as did Serdica (with only a brief interruption) right up to its capture by the Bulgarian Krum in 809. Of the cities of Moesia, western Thrace and Macedonia we know little, and all the evidence is against continuity of occupation. The fact that some of them reappear as cities in the later Middle Ages is to be explained partly by the convenience of their situation, and most of all by the supply of building material which they provided ready to hand. We must not imagine the city notables and the bishop fleeing before an advancing horde of Slavs and Avars. Most of them had already left, when the security which permitted them to exploit the city lands could no longer be guaranteed. The cities of the north ceased to function as cities before they were captured; sometimes the Slavs even found the city sites abandoned.

The Slavs and the Bulgars in time, as their tribal structure broke down and as they became drawn into the network of long-distance trade which linked Constantinople with northern and western Europe, established their own urban settlements. These were often in the vicinity of a Greco-Roman city for convenience in the supply of building material, but rarely on the same site. Thus Serdica was not destroyed, but was replaced by a Slav settlement a short distance away, while the old centre was not reoccupied until much later. Slavonic/Bulgar Dristŭr was built near ancient Durostorum (which may never have been sacked). As we shall see, these new cities were of a different type, fulfilling a different function in society.[2]

If the ancient city was the centre of an agrarian community, enjoying internal self-government and providing the essentials of the good life for its citizens, or at any rate for some of them, the early medieval city in the Byzantine empire was often primarily of military significance—a *kastron* rather than a *polis*. Small in size, militarily defensible, it housed a garrison and its dependants in time of peace, and served as a refuge for the surrounding population in time of war. It did not aim to provide the amenities of the ancient city—though it might well have had baths. And its affairs were controlled by the garrison commander, not by magistrates chosen from among the citizens. Such a *kastron* might occupy the site of an ancient city, if it had a steep acropolis or other easily defensible feature, as at Philippi, Amphipolis (renamed Chrysopolis), Neapolis (renamed Christopolis, now Kavalla), Demetrias, Lamia, Corinth, Argos, Naupaktos. In some cities a much lower and less fortress-like acropolis had to suffice, *faute de mieux,* as at Thebes, Athens, Chalkis, Adrianople. Sometimes only a part of the area within the old city walls was fortified, as at Theveste in Africa, where one corner of the old city was surrounded by a wall and ditch, or at Athens. Sometimes the *kastron* occupied, not the site of the classical city but a nearby hill-top or projecting cliff, often the very spot from which the earlier inhabitants had descended to establish their city in the plain. Such was the case at Chonai in Phrygia, successor to Kolossai, and at a number of sites round the margin of the Thessalian plain and in Arcadia. This often involved a change of name.[3] Some *kastra* bear no relation to classical cities, but were built in response to Byzantine military problems. The best example is Monemvasia; others are Kastron Maina, Ioannina, and the old fort at Corfu. Many of the Dalmatian coastal cities are of this kind, for example Kotor, Dubrovnik, Split, Trogir. On the Black Sea coast, on the other hand, the major cities founded in antiquity remained firmly in Byzantine hands, serving as military bases and entrepôts, until the Bulgarian expansion under Krum early in the ninth century.

Only a few great cities retained the physical pattern of the ancient city, with a long perimeter-wall fully maintained. In the first place the capital, which was in any case exceptional. Then Thessalonika, the second city of the empire, which had a heavily fortified citadel within its perimeter-wall; Naples, which was similarly structured, with a citadel built by Belisarios within the ancient city walls; Nicaea, and a few other places.

In all these cities of the new type there was some population other than soldiers and their direct dependants. Peasants cultivated the fields within easy reach of the shelter of the walls. They no longer paid taxes through the city authorities, as members of a civic community, but directly to an imperial official, as individuals or as a village commune. In addition artisans, traders and others might gather round the fortress walls. Thus in favourable circumstances we find the medieval pattern of inner and outer city developing. In the heavily fortified inner city lived the ruling classes—army commanders, landowners who had migrated from the countryside, and so on; the outer city, lightly fortified if at all, was the dwelling place of craftsmen, merchants, and the peasants who cultivated the fields nearby. The inner city served as a refuge for the inhabitants of the outer city in time of war. The two formed a single social and economic complex.

In due course a new patriciate began to emerge in some of these double cities, especially those prominent in trade. Whether they are original inhabitants of the *kastron*, landed proprietors from the surrounding country, or successful citizens of the outer city is not clear. Thus we hear of *prouchontes* in Sparta in 998, of *archontes* in Athens in the twelfth century. A city nobility is found choosing magistrates at Edessa in 1098, and at Dubrovnik in 1192. There was a local nobility and local magistrates at Cherson, whose defection from allegiance to the imperial governor is envisaged by Constantine VII. It is unlikely that in any of these cases we have a survival of the civic institutions of late antiquity. They are rather the result of social differentiation within early medieval cities, in some cases combined with the relative weakness of the central government. This process was no doubt under way in the ninth and tenth centuries, though we do not generally see its results until much later.

Such was the general situation in the ninth and tenth centuries in the Balkan peninsula and nearby. It must be remembered that until the Seljuk conquests at the end of the eleventh century the main economic and demographic weight of the Byzantine empire lay in Asia Minor, and that, the capital and Thessalonika apart, the European provinces were relatively backward and neglected, with fewer and smaller cities. It is significant that in the first half of the tenth century there were about 371 bishoprics in Asia Minor as against 99 in mainland Europe, 18 in the Aegean islands, and 16 in Byzantine south Italy.[4] The cities of Asia Minor were involved not only in production and commercial exchange with one another, but also in long-distance trade with Russia and the Crimea, the Caucasus, central Asia, China, the Caliphate and India.[5]

It is time to examine more closely the differences between the Byzantine provinces and Bulgaria. First, cities were far more numerous in Byzantine territory. Not all the civic communities listed by Hierocles survived, but a surprising number did, and one or two new ones had been added. Apart from the special cases of Constantinople and Thessalonika, there were flourishing cities on the coasts of the Black Sea, the Sea of Marmara and the Aegean, and in peninsular Greece. Inland Thrace seems to have been fairly thinly populated, and to have had few cities other than the chain of frontier fortresses. Macedonia was largely outside Byzantine control. It is sometimes very difficult to distinguish between genuine medieval cities and mere fortresses—episcopal lists are not always as helpful as they should be. However, the following is a list of cities in the Byzantine provinces of the Balkans which are described by twelfth-century sources (generally Arab geographers) as 'populous', 'wealthy', 'prosperous', 'megalopolis' and similar terms: Corinth, Athens, Thebes, Larissa, Kitros, Ioannina, Kastoria, Thessalonika, Serres, Zichna, Philippi, Melnik, Rodosto, Nauplia, Mossynopolis. Demotika, Adrianople, Philippopolis, Sparta, Levadeia, Demetrias, Armyros, Karystos, Christopolis (Kavalla), Drama, Selymbria, Herakleia, Kallipolis, Panados.[6] Not all these cities were flourishing two centuries earlier. The building record in Athens, for instance, suggests that the eleventh and twelfth centuries were a period of enrichment and expansion. Yet many clearly were cities in the medieval sense as early as the ninth century. And the list given above is not exhaustive.

In Bulgaria the picture is very different. The coastal cities of Mesembria, Develtos and Anchialos were captured from the Byzantines by Krum in the second decade of the ninth century, and later returned to the Byzantines. There is no reason to suppose that their predominantly Greek population withdrew entirely, or that they lost their importance as entrepots. Odessos (=Varna) had fallen to the Bulgarians earlier, we do not know when. Serdica was captured by

Krum in 809: a place of some importance in late antiquity and the seat of an archbishop, it had its water supply and aqueducts restored by Tiberius II at the end of the sixth century. But it seems to have dwindled in size and importance and was little more than a garrison town at the beginning of the ninth century. The Byzantine soldiers were no doubt taken prisoner or sent home. But the Bulgarians themselves do not seem to have settled in the city at once.

There were the two successive Bulgarian royal capitals of Pliska and Preslav, both in north-eastern Bulgaria, in the region where the Bulgar state was first established on former Byzantine territory. Pliska has generally been identified with the extensive ruins at Aboba, though there are still scholars who argue against the identification.[7] Accepting provisionally that Aboba is indeed Pliska, two points must be made at the outset: (i) The site was that of a late Roman city, though which it was we do not know; (ii) The excavations of Škorpil and Uspensky in 1899-1900 were not carried out in such a way as to enable relative dates, let alone absolute dates, to be established with any certainty.

It is therefore difficult to distinguish between what the Bulgars found there and what they may have added later. There is an inner city, enclosed by a rectangular stone wall, of about 0.5 square kilometres. Surrounding this is a vast earth wall, in places still 10 metres high, enclosing an area generally rectangular in pattern of 23 square kilometres, most of which does not seem to have been built over. Neither the stone inner wall nor the earthen outer wall has been dated, so any hypothesis concerning their relation is possible. In the inner city are baths, large buildings heated by hypocausts etc., which may well belong to the original Roman city, as well as several monumental buildings of massive construction thought to have been palaces. Much of the space within the stone wall is not built over. Beneath the massive stone buildings archaeologists have traced the outlines of an immense building of square or rectangular form, apparently mainly constructed of wood. The outer city contains a number of churches, including a large Basilica 99 by 29.5 metres, with three aisles and a single apse. This has been taken to be a court church built by Boris immediately after his conversion. But it remains to be shown conclusively that it is not a church of late antiquity. There are also a number of substantial dwellings, a large building used as a pottery workshop, many small, square, half-subterranean dwelling houses, and several burial mounds, including one with a cremation, burial and remains of horses, doubtless the tomb of a pagan Khan or tribal leader. A number of inscriptions in Greek were found in the city, recording victories, deaths of boyars, treaties, construction of buildings, inventories of military stores, etc.

The simplest set of hypotheses to explain all this is that the Bulgar Khan, established his fixed residence on the site of a small late Roman city, which supplied convenient building material, and surrounded it with an immense earthwork rampart within which he, his men and his flocks could shelter in time of danger. His great throne room, not unlike the banqueting hall of Attila described by the historian Priscus, was of wood, as were the dwellings of his boyars and their retinues. Some of the installations of the late Roman city, such as the baths, may have been put into working order by captive or fugitive Byzantine craftsmen. These wooden buildings were destroyed by fire when Nicephorus captured and burned Pliska in 811.[8] The capital was rebuilt partly in stone by Krum and Omurtag and perhaps above all by Malamir, who was a great builder to judge by his inscriptions. The Bulgarians by this time had many Byzantine artisans in their service from the newly-conquered territories. Masonry from the pre-existing late Roman city was used, and probably from other sites as well, and decorative tiles may have been brought from all over Moesia, particularly from the ruined Danube forts. The architects who constructed these rather heavy, massive buildings were not master-craftsmen from Constantinople but builders from provincial cities now in Bulgar territory, and the models they followed were surviving late Roman buildings in the northern Balkans rather than the latest fashions in metropolitan architecture.

Preslav, some distance south-west of Pliska, had an outer wall of stone, following the contours of the irregular terrain, and enclosing an area of 3.5 square kilometres, and a rectangular inner wall, also of stone, enclosing an area of about 0.25 square kilometres. It too was built on the site of a small late Roman city, but the orientation and outline of its buildings is independent of any earlier construction. Fortunately it was not excavated with the techniques of the late nineteenth century; indeed relatively little excavation has yet been done there. The excavations at present being carried out by the Bulgarian Academy of Science, under Professor S. Stanchev and others, should in due course provide solutions to many problems, and give us much information on life in ninth- and tenth-century Bulgaria. In the outer city is a square building with a stone pylon, later converted by the addition of an apse. It has been suggested that this is a pagan cult site adapted to Christian use. There is also a well-preserved round church with a rectangular atrium containing a font. Its sophisticated construction, the finely-carved capitals, the niches with ceramic plaques and other features make it unique in old Bulgarian architecture. Opinion is divided as to when and by whom it was built, some holding it to be a late Roman church. This and other problems connected with the round church will be solved only by further excavation at Preslav. Six or seven probable monasteries have been wholly or partially excavated, including one with a wooden church on stone foundations. Unlike Pliska, Preslav has much decorative sculpture, evidently carried out by local craftsmen and incorporating animal-motifs unusual in Byzantine art. Within the outer wall are remains of smithies, and goldsmith's and jewellers' workshops. It was long believed, on the basis of an inscription, that Khan Omurtag built a palace at Preslav, but this view is now generally rejected.[9] It did not become the royal capital until the beginning of the reign of Symeon in 893, and most surviving structures, apart from the possible converted pagan site and the enigmatic round church, date from Symeon's time or later.

Pliska and Preslav are the two most prominent Bulgarian cities. Both are in origin and function quite unlike medieval Byzantine cities. Pliska was essentially a military camp which only gradually took on some of the aspects of a city, as artisans settled there—whether willingly or not we can scarcely guess—to serve the needs of army and court. After the conversion of the country to Christianity churches were built, doubtless on the initiative of Boris or some of his boyars. It does not seem to have been a significant centre of trade. The principal industries were those connected with the army and the court—iron-working and fine metal work—and those who carried them on are likely to have been Greeks from the cities captured by the Bulgarians. As well as a few Greek inscriptions there are many Slavonic inscriptions and graffiti in the Cyrillic alphabet and one brief inscription in Glagolitic.

John the Exarch in the Preface to his *Shestodnev* describes the magnificence of the Palace at Preslav.[10] And indeed art and technology are far more developed at Preslav than at Pliska. Archaeological evidence and that of early Bulgarian literature point to varied and developed industry, particularly metallurgy, ceramics and glass, and textiles. But Preslav was none the less a royal foundation and a royal residence, and the activities of most of its citizens were connected directly or indirectly with the court and the church. It does not seem to have been a centre of long-distance trade. Many of its craftsmen were in some kind of dependence upon the king or boyars. It was in a sense an artificial creation, rendered possible and desirable by the concentration in the hands of the ruler and his boyars of much of the surplus produced by the Bulgarian peasants. Though an administrative and military centre as was Constantinople, Preslav did not play the major role which Constantinople played in industry and trade. The absence of coined money restricted internal trade between city and countryside. We must not imagine at Preslav the complex and sophisticated control of supply and prices of essentials and key luxuries for which the Book of the Prefect is evidence at Constantinople.

So much for the two principal cities of Bulgaria, which had an unusual character of their own. There is less to be said concerning the other cities of ninth- and tenth-century Bulgaria. The Black Sea cities, Mesembria, Develtos and Anchialos, although captured by Krum, were only intermittently in Bulgarian hands. The Thirty Years Peace signed between Leo V and Khan Omurtag gave these former naval and military bases to the Byzantines,[11] and in Byzantine hands they remained until Symeon took them at the end of the ninth century. After Symeon's death they appear to have been returned to the Byzantines. Though there was some church building at Mesembria in the tenth century, and it served on occasion as a meeting-point for Bulgarian and Byzantine diplomats, it seems to have lost much of its earlier importance. The series of seals of *Kommerkiarioi* of Mesembria in the seventh and eighth centuries does not continue. Trade between Bulgaria and the empire seems to have been mainly routed through Constantinople or Thessalonika. Odessos (Varna) may have remained for some time in Byzantine hands after the foundation of the Bulgarian state, but by the middle of the eighth century it was a Bulgarian possession. It seems to have been a place of little account, in spite of its excellent harbour. The same is true of Dionysiopolis (Balčik) to the north. The Bulgarians never built a fleet and were not interested in naval bases.

Of the Danube cities Singidunum (Belgrade) may have been considerable — it was the seat of a bishop in the ninth century — but as a frontier post it was mainly of military importance. Bononia (Vidin) had its fortifications repaired, probably after the loss to Bulgaria of the territories north of the Danube in the reign of Symeon.

Destroyed by the Magyars, it was rebuilt by Symeon. Like Singidunum
it was primarily a military base. Červen was also the seat of a bishop
and appears to have been the principal Bulgarian city on the lower
Danube, overshadowing the Slavo-Bulgar settlement near the former
Roman town of Sexanta Prista, out of which the city of Ruse later
grew. Silistra, a major city in late Roman times, whose fourth-century
bishop Auxentius was a pupil of Ulfila and a writer, declined during
the sixth-century invasions. Its last recorded bishop, Dulcissimus,
fled before the Avars to the safety of Odessos. Neglected for a time,
the fortifications were apparently repaired by the Bulgarians at the
end of the seventh century. The city held out against the Magyars
in the reign of Symeon, but was captured by Svyatoslav in 969.
Several Proto-Bulgarian inscriptions testify to its importance.[12]

Cities in the interior of Bulgaria were few and of little importance.
In the far west Ohrid owed its importance to its choice by Clement
as his missionary centre. Church building began in the lifetime of
Clement, and by the end of the tenth century Ohrid must have had
a considerable population. The great fortress which dominates the
lower town was built by King Samuel at the end of the tenth century.
We know virtually nothing of the economic and social organisation
of the city. Skopje is scarcely mentioned until the final battles between
Basil II and King Samuel of Bulgaria. It was then a fortress of great
strategic importance, whose governor and commander of troops
was no less a person than Roman-Symeon, son of King Peter and
Maria Lekapena. He eventually betrayed the stronghold to the Byzantines. There is no evidence that Skopje was a significant centre of
trade or industry. Serdica was another matter. There a Slavonic
settlement grew up beside the late Roman fortress, which was long
abandoned after its capture by Krum in 809. It must have been a
considerable place, as it became the seat of a bishop in 864, when a
church hierarchy was established in Bulgaria. Later it was able to
hold out against Basil II himself, and was not finally captured until
1016, after a siege which lasted 88 days. Through these bare facts
we dimly see a city of some size, both a fortress and an industrial,
commercial and ecclesiastical centre. Philippopolis was also the
centre of a bishopric. We know very little of its size or importance
in the ninth and tenth centuries, and it would be unjustified to
suppose that the large and flourishing city described by Idrisi
and the historians of the Crusades in the twelfth century existed
two and a half centuries earlier. The original inhabitants were taken

prisoner when the city was captured by Malamir, and there is no evidence of their ever returning. Finally 'little Preslav', Preslavets, situated somewhere in the Danube delta, probably near Cernavoda, and possibly the site of the Bulgar court before Asparuch entered Roman territory. When Svyatoslav captured it in 968 he was overwhelmed by its riches, reports the Russian Primary Chronicle. The passage is worth quoting:— Svyatoslav said to his mother and his boyars:

> It is not agreeable to me to dwell in Kiev. I wish to live in Preslavets on the Danube, for there is the centre of my lands, for thither all good things converge—from the Greeks gold and textiles, wines and a variety of fruits, from the Czechs and the Hungarians silver and horses, from Russia hides and wax and honey and slaves.

Preslavets was evidently a centre of international trade between Byzantium, Russia and Central Europe, to which merchants from many lands resorted. But in the absence of other evidence it would be unwise to credit Preslavets with a large settled population on the basis of a single anecdote.

In our period, then, the European provinces of the Byzantine empire, like the rest of the empire, were a land of cities, most of which were continuations of ancient cities, though their structure and function had often been considerably modified. Bulgaria was a land from which most ancient cities had vanished, and where the largest and most flourishing urban communities were those gathered round a royal court—military-administrative cities. This, however, is too static a view of the matter. The relative stability which Bulgarian rule gave to a region where for two centuries no state had been able to exercise effective power favoured urban development. Archaeological evidence from medieval Bulgaria is usually difficult to interpret. But it would be abundantly clear, even without John the Exarch's account, that Preslav was far more of a city than Pliska. And the emergence in the period of Byzantine rule in Bulgaria in the eleventh and twelfth centuries of a number of substantial cities, described in glowing terms by Idrisi or by the Crusader historians, is evidence for the formation in the ninth and tenth centuries of urban nuclei where before there had only been settlements of Slav peasants in the shadow of the crumbling ruins of a late Roman city or fortress. We cannot follow this process in detail, but there can be no doubt of its reality. The heritage of classical urban life had been more definitively broken in Bulgaria than in Thrace and peninsular Greece, to say nothing of Asia Minor. The new cities were less linked geographically and historically with those of late antiquity than was the case in Byzantium, and they began their development in a centralised territorial state which had no ancient tradition of civic autonomy. In this way the Bulgarian cities differed from those of the Byzantine empire, though both belonged to a common genus. The massive fortifications still surviving not only at Pliska and Preslav, but at Vidin, Ohrid and elsewhere, underline the military character of the early Bulgarian cities, with their heavily defended inner citadels, surrounded by or adjacent to an outer city inhabited by farmers and artisans. These latter primarily served the needs of the feudal upper classes of the inner city, and were in the period we are studying only beginning to develop an economic life of their own.

6   Industry and Trade

The Byzantine empire was in general an area of advanced technology, with a stable monetary system, a large internal market in medieval terms, and extensive trade with distant lands. The eastern provinces of the Roman empire had been the most industrially developed. In spite of the loss of Syria, Palestine and Egypt in the seventh century this superior technology was maintained, and its level even raised by the new contacts with the Fertile Crescent, the Iranian world, and regions further east which developed through the spread of Islam.

One must beware in this connection of being misled by modern analogies. Industrial society of today makes most of its ultimate products available to all its members or most of them: this is a necessary condition of its existence. In the medieval world this is not so. A very high degree of sophistication and specialisation in the production of articles consumed by a small minority of the population may coincide with primitive methods in the production of articles for mass use. This was certainly the case in the Byzantine empire. Manufacture of silk textiles, jewellery, perfume etc. involved complex division of labour, though these products were not widely consumed. At the same time such articles as shoes or agricultural implements were produced by simple methods involving little division of labour.

There were certain industrial differences between the Byzantine empire and the rest of Europe which immediately affected the life of the ordinary man. First, iron was much more widely used and smiths were commoner. Second, because of more developed trade a variety of raw materials was available which was not found in the rest of Europe. Third, the existence of a stable monetary system and of regular exchange between country and town based upon it meant that manufactured articles were more widely used in Byzantine society than in most regions of Europe.

This brings us to the question of trade, which cannot in the Byzantine context be separated from industry. Hagiographical and other texts make it clear that merchants who sold goods which they did not manufacture were an everyday feature of Byzantine society, at any rate in the towns.[1] Such merchants often bought up agricultural produce from the peasants in the country and brought it to the towns to be sold. Fairs and markets were found everywhere; the smaller

ones served as points of exchange between local producers and con-
sumers, and in particular between urban craftsmen and the surrounding peasants. An example is the Paphlagonian fair described
in the Synaxary of Constantinople pp. 721-2 (ed. Delehaye). Larger
fairs attracted merchants from all over the Byzantine empire and
beyond it. The best-known example is the fair at Thessalonika described in the twelfth-century *Timarion*, but certainly originating
several centuries earlier, at which merchants selling goods from all
over the Mediterranean world and as far afield as Germany, Portugal
and Georgia gathered together annually on the feast of St Demetrius
in October. An intermediate case is the annual fair at Ephesus at
which, we are told, a hundred pounds of gold were collected in taxes
(Theoph. p. 728).

Lastly there was long-distance trade. Merchants specialised in
importing goods from the Moslem world, from Iberia, from the
Khazars, from Russia, from central Europe, and so on. Many of
these were Armenians, Jews, and Syrians who, being to some extent
outsiders everywhere, could easily move between different societies.
Much was brought to Constantinople by foreign merchants, whose
rights and privileges were minutely regulated in commercial treaties.
This extensive trade, in which Byzantine manufactured goods were
usually exchanged for raw materials from lands outside the empire,
was controlled by government officials—*Kommerkiarioi*—at points
on the main trade routes, who both collected taxes on goods passing
through and prevented the export of forbidden goods. This regulated
system of trade was rendered possible by the stable conditions over
a large area which the empire guaranteed, and the special terms
of trade which it was able to negotiate with foreign governments,
thus creating an area of trade far more extensive and homogeneous
than any existing elsewhere in Europe.[2]

It is against this background of widespread commercial exchange,
local, regional and international, that the state of Byzantine industry
and trade in the ninth and tenth centuries can be understood. Evidence on the goods actually produced depends mainly on the work
of the archaeologist. Until recently Byzantine archaeology was treated
in a somewhat stepmotherly fashion by classical archaeologists.
There are however published reports from the Great Palace at
Constantinople, from Athens, from Corinth, from Cherson, from
Pergamum, from Sardis and from Ephesus which provide much
information on Byzantine artefacts. As can be seen, we are desperately

short of material from Constantinople outside the Great Palace area, and from most regions of Asia Minor. Any conclusions reached must therefore be provisional. One of the best surveys of the archaeological evidence for Byzantine industrial production during the ninth and tenth centuries is to be found in A. P. Kazhdan, *Derevnja i gorod v Vizantii, ix-x vv.,* 1960, 190-249.

The ninth century seems to have been a period of rapid growth and improvement in Byzantine handicrafts, after a century and a half of stagnation. This applies not only to the luxury crafts, producing jewellery, high quality silk garments, enamels, icons, reliquaries and other ecclesiastical furniture, but also to those catering for the modest demands of the ordinary citizen. In pottery, for instance, we find side by side with traditional red clay-ware, undecorated or decorated by stamp or applique, a variety of new types—polychrome-ware decorated in slip or underglaze painting, white clay-ware with yellow-green slip, red clay-ware covered with slip and decorated with incised designs, and so on. There is evidence for the large-scale importation of certain wares from other parts of the empire, for example from Constantinople to Cherson, from Thessalonika to Corinth, etc. And the quality of the best pottery steadily improves, the walls become thinner and more uniform, the firing more regular. An Italian observer, whose date is unfortunately uncertain—he may have written as late as the twelfth century—comments on the novelty of Byzantine polychrome pottery.[3]

Byzantine glass-ware is well represented in the Corinth finds. The glass workshop excavated there, however, belongs to the eleventh to thirteenth century and is of doubtful relevance for the period under study. Techniques combining blowing and moulding were in use, and the better wares were decorated with zoomorphic and anthropomorphic motifs in gold, colour, or by incision. Coloured as well as plain glass was produced. Byzantine glass-ware was highly prized abroad, and glass vessels were among the gifts sent by emperors to foreign rulers. Theophilus Presbyter was struck by the technical process employed by the Greeks in the manufacture of coloured glass.[4]

Textiles in the ninth and tenth centuries were woven from wool, flax and silk. There was much home production, particularly of woollen garments. But articles of everyday use such as linen sheets were also produced as commodities for the market in many cities of the empire. Very fine linen sheets were among the articles brought by the widow Danielis from her workshops at Patrae to Constantinople in the middle of the ninth century, and there was clearly much importation and exportation of the finer grades of linen. Silk spinning and weaving and the making up of silk garments and other objects was a virtual Byzantine monopoly in the early middle ages. It was based on local silk production in areas where the mulberry was cultivated as well as on imported raw silk, and on a succession of specialist skills — spinning, dyeing, weaving etc. — which required long study and practice. The highest quality silk of all was not produced for sale by commercial entrepreneurs. It was made in the imperial factories situated within the perimeter of the Great Palace at Constantinople by specialist workers whose posts were hereditary, and was for distribution by the emperor to Byzantine dignitaries and foreign monarchs. Great care was taken to prevent these products coming on to the market or the secrets of the technique by which they were made being divulged. There was a much higher degree of division of labour in these imperial factories than in ordinary commercial workshops, because large numbers of people worked together under the same roof and were subject to a common direction. In spite of the precautions taken there must have been some spillover of technique from the imperial silk factories to private workshops.

Private silk production was probably confined to Constantinople until the ninth century, and then slowly spread to Corinth, Thebes, Thessalonika and other cities suitably placed. We hear of Jewish silk-weavers in Sparta in the tenth century. All its products were relative luxuries, and were widely exported.

Leather-working is often mentioned. A quarter of Constantinople was known as 'The Shoemakers'. Metal-working of all kinds, woodwork, ship-building, candle-making, soap-making, baking, perfumery etc. are mentioned frequently in sources of the period, though few of their products survive. The products of another group of crafts do survive in the form of Byzantine buildings. New styles, new solutions to technical problems, and new aesthetic ideals marked the renaissance which began in the ninth century. Few datable buildings other than churches remain, but they are numerous — the Church of the Virgin of the Pharos, the Attik-Camii, the Kalender-Hane, the Fenari-Issa in Constantinople, the Skripu church in Euboea, St Nicholas in Sparta, the earliest buildings erected by St Athanasius on Mount Athos, the Nea Mone in Chios and many others.

Compared with western Europe at this time, the Byzantine empire was a region of technological innovation, of increasing division of labour, and of commodity production of luxury goods for an extensive market, which might extend far beyond the confines of the empire.

Broadly speaking, three types of organisation of production and sale can be distinguished. First, that of imperial factories. Here there is no market; producer and consumer are in a sense the same. The craftsman is protected against economic disaster, and is usually in return restricted in his freedom to some extent. Apart from the manufacture of the highest quality of silk goods, which has been discussed, imperial factories produced jewellery and cult objects of various kinds, gold and silver plate and other luxury items for use or distribution by the imperial household. But the sphere par excellence of the imperial factories was the production of armaments. There was a great arsenal in the Mangana quarter of Constantinople, where military equipment of all kinds was made and stored in conditions of tight security. Some products, such as Greek fire and the 'siphons' through which it was discharged, were made only in the capital. Other articles such as arrow heads, swords and so on were manufactured elsewhere. At Corinth, for instance there seems to have been a workshop producing such articles. It is not clear whether this was under imperial or private control. The workers in imperial factories might be free or slaves, men or women. Women were employed particularly in textile production, and slaves probably performed tasks calling for less skill. The most skilled workers were mainly free men, but their occupation was often hereditary, and they were forbidden to leave it. This is a pattern of 'palace industry' which can be traced back through the Hellenistic world and ultimately to the great Bronze Age civilisations of the Near East. It permitted far-reaching division of labour and the development and conservation of very great skill. But concentration of production in large units of this kind was not generally economically viable in a society in which transport costs were relatively high. So imperial factories did not normally compete in an external market with smaller local producers. They were limited to the production of goods for which the state was the only or the principal customer.

Private producers and distributors of a great many commodities were organised at Constantinople in guilds—*somata*—whose activities are minutely regulated by the provisions of the *Book of the Prefect* issued by Leo VI. The literature on this text is immense, and the present writer has no desire to add to it. It appears that the many regulations of the *Book of the Prefect* are best explained by a compromise between two purposes. The emperor and the government wanted to keep supplies of essential food, clothing and other commodities flowing regularly and at stable prices. Their motive was primarily political, to prevent mass disaffection among the citizens of the capital, which could weaken the position of the ruler and might be exploited by a rival. This is a continuation of a policy observed by rulers of great states and by the ruling oligarchies of cities in the ancient world, which found its expression in the distribution of food free or at reduced price to citizens, and in other measures of social security. The aim was to smooth out the inevitable fluctuations in the price of basic foodstuffs and articles of mass consumption arising out of variations in supply, and above all to prevent price rises stimulated or aggravated by hoarding. There can often be a conflict of interest between the ruling class as a whole and individual members of it in this connection. One of the purposes of such regulations both in the ancient world and in the Byzantine empire was to ensure that the interest of the ruling class as a whole prevailed.

The second purpose discernable behind the regulations is to safeguard the interests of the producers themselves — to distribute work between all members of the guild, to prevent competition in prices, to prevent concentration of production, and to prevent the growth of vertical monopoly. In these ways the steady livelihood of each member of the guild would be best assured. These were on the whole the purposes which medieval craft guilds in the West pursued. The difference between the situation in western Europe and in the Byzantine empire lay in the fact that the Byzantine guilds developed in the shadow of a great centralised state which, following tradition dating from antiquity, controlled production and distribution for its own political purposes, and would only tolerate the existence and activity of craft guilds if they did not frustrate its political purpose.

Whether there were such guilds outside Constantinople at this time we do not know. They certainly did exist later, and it is probable that they date back to the ninth century if not earlier. They may have developed more freely and represented more closely the interests of their own members, since they did not directly affect the politically sensitive capital city. They are likely to have been much more limited in number than at Constantinople and confined to a few major cities

such as Thessalonika. Where we have no evidence, however, speculation is unwise.

The third pattern of production and sale is that of the private
producer working on his own with no more aid than that of his family
or possibly one or two wage labourers or slaves, subject neither to
regulation nor to protection by others. This was probably the commonest pattern in the production of articles for everyday consumption. Such producers usually sold directly to the ultimate consumer.
Middlemen were not prominent. And such enterprises were always
small, catering for a limited local clientele. There were no economic
advantages to be gained by concentration of production in these
cases.

It should however be borne in mind that far more was produced
by the user for himself than in the modern world. Thus spinning,
weaving, tailoring or dressmaking were regular domestic activities,
and much agricultural equipment was made by peasants themselves,
supplemented by the occasional work of the travelling smith—
kōmodromos—and the wheelwright. In addition monasteries often
produced almost all their own requirements, not only for the monks
but also for the numerous laymen employed by a rich monastery.
The trades represented in the great monastery of St John of Studios
at Constantinople are mentioned elsewhere in this book. The signa-
tories of an Athonite document of 1154, monks of the relatively
small monastery of St Philotheos, include a carpenter, a shoemaker,
a cooper, a tailor, a weaver, as well as a fisherman and a boatman.[5]
A list of monks at Lavra of approximately the same date includes
shoemakers, carpenters, a cook, a boatman, a builder, a shipwright
and a rope-maker. The situation was broadly similar two or three
centuries earlier. In the same way owners of large estates tended to
produce what they needed from their own resources and with their
own labour.

This tendency towards autarky, together with the low standard
of life and the high cost of transport were factors limiting the development of commodity production for an extensive market in the
Byzantine empire. In fact the whole economy was organised for
consumption by a limited group—the court, the church, the state
dignitaries, the wealthy landowners—not for mass consumption. The
Byzantine city drew food, raw materials and semi-manufactured
goods from the surrounding countryside, but it did not in return
supply the countryside with the products of its industry on any scale.

The peasants were paid in money, most of which they used to pay their taxes.

Byzantine international trade was in a somewhat different position. The technical superiority of Byzantine methods of production enabled the empire to export luxury goods such as gold and jewellery, enamels, textiles, carved ivory etc. for consumption by the wealthier classes of the western and northern world. Much of this export was non-commercial in character, taking the form of gifts to foreign potentates. Indeed many luxury goods were not allowed to be exported by private individuals at all. Travellers' luggage was examined by customs officers—*kommerkiarioi*—at frontier-posts and forbidden goods were confiscated, as Liutprand of Cremona discovered to his cost in 968. Another export was technical skill. Byzantine architectural expertise contributed to the building and decoration of churches all over northern and western Europe, from St Sophia in Kiev to Charlemagne's basilica in Aachen. No doubt Byzantine skill made its contribution to the production of less durable artefacts of all kinds. We know little about the way in which this export of know-how was organised. In many cases craftsmen would be sent directly from Constantinople to a foreign capital by the emperor to carry out a particular task. In other cases the export may have taken place from a Byzantine provincial town and had a more commercial character.

Foodstuffs and bulk goods of Byzantine origin were not normally exported in the middle Byzantine period. On the contrary food was imported to the capital from foreign territory and in particular from Bulgaria. A considerable part of Byzantine trade consisted in the re-export of goods imported from southern and eastern Asia—spices, silk, incense and other luxury goods of small bulk. The rate of commercial profit on these re-exports was probably high, as the Byzantines still had a virtual monopoly of the supply of these essential commodities to western and northern Europe.

Byzantine imports from the west and north fall into two main categories—raw materials and labour. To the former belong the hides, furs, dried and salted fish, amber and honey imported from Russia; the furs, linen, honey and metals from the northern Balkans, etc. The latter comprise the numerous slaves imported from central and northern Europe through Venice, Thessalonika and the capital itself, to work as domestic servants, industrial labourers—often mere sources of energy—and land workers.

Foreign trade was fairly rigidly controlled, particularly as regards exports. There was no attempt at an export drive, no desire to conquer new markets, for there were probably none to conquer. Byzantine merchants did not themselves travel far afield to sell their goods. They waited in Constantinople and Thessalonika for foreigners to come to them, driven by the economic forces generated by a sharp difference in productivity. Much foreign trade was governmental in character, and not necessarily commercially profitable. The merchant occupied a humble and undistinguished station in Byzantine society, though he could raise capital fairly easily. Legislation of Leo VI permitted loans of money at 4 per cent per annum (*Novel* 83).

Nevertheless, the empire's balance of trade was a positive one, such was the demand in the developing countries of northern and western Europe for Byzantine luxury manufactured goods. The disparity was made good by the import of gold, which flowed from all over Europe to the treasuries of Constantinople.

In spite of apparent restrictions upon commercial enterprise, it is clear that in the period under discussion Byzantine industry and trade was immensely more developed than in other parts of Europe, and comparable to those of the Moslem world. Commodity production for an extensive market obviously played a large role, its importance being indicated by the amount of money in circulation. This kind of evidence is extremely difficult to use, and expert opinions vary on the interpretation of numismatic evidence. For what it is worth, however, the number of coin finds, both in hoards and in single coins, outside the confines of the empire and within its bounds, begins to rise again sharply early in the ninth century after a sudden general drop about the middle of the seventh. It has been argued that this is evidence of the growing prevalence of a natural economy during the Dark Age of the seventh and eighth centuries, and the resurgence of a market economy based on money from the beginning of the ninth century. The argument is put most forcibly by A. P. Kazhdan, *Derevnja u gorod v Vizantii ix-x vv.*, (1960), 260-72 and 'Vizantijskie goroda u vii-xi vv.', *Sovetskaja Arkheologija* 21 (1954). More cautious, perhaps sometimes too cautious, attitudes are expressed by P. Grierson, 'Coinage and Money in the Byzantine Empire 498-c. 1090'. *Settimane di Studio del Centro Italiano di Studi sull'Alto Medioevo* 8 (1961), 411-53; R. S. Lopez, 'La crise du besant au Xe siècle', *Mélanges H. Gregoire* II, (1950), 412; P. Charanis, 'The significance of coins as evidence for the history of Athens and Corinth in the seventh and eighth centuries, *Historia* 4 (1955), 169ff; D. M. Metcalf, *Coinage in the Balkans 820-1355,*

(1965) 1-47. The general conclusion, supported by narrative texts and by other archaeological evidence, that a resurgence of the Byzantine market economy and a movement away from natural economy began in the early ninth century, is generally accepted.

If Byzantium was at this time a land of money economy, Bulgaria was one of natural economy. The Bulgarian state issued no coinage of its own. Byzantine coins are certainly found in Bulgarian sites, but hardly in any numbers until the middle of the tenth century, and then only in urban sites. There is nothing to suggest that they were used to a significant extent in internal trade. They were rather used by the rich as a means of hoarding wealth in a portable form or for purchasing foreign luxury goods. The almost total absence of money in Bulgarian society is strikingly brought out by contemporary evidence. Land taxation was entirely in kind, and the Byzantines were forced to maintain such a taxation in kind after the conquest. When in 1040 they tried to convert the land tax to a money payment, which had long been the practice in other regions of the empire, they found themselves faced with a revolt on a national scale headed by Peter Deljan. The treaty signed by Michael II and Omurtag in 815 allowed the ransoming of Byzantine prisoners held by the Bulgarians at the rate of two buffaloes for each man.[6] The Arab geographer al-Masudi, writing in the tenth century but reflecting conditions somewhat earlier, says that the Bulgarians paid for goods in oxen and sheep.

These facts indicate an economy very different in its total structure from that of the Byzantine empire, in spite of the many detailed similarities between them. With this in mind we can begin to examine the scanty data furnished by written sources and by archaeology. Bulgarian society started from a position of relative technological backwardness. The cities, centres of industry in the late Roman period, had been largely destroyed and the craftsmen in them killed or dispersed. The Slav communes were practically self-sufficient, producing food, clothing, houses and such tools as they needed themselves. The two possible exceptions were probably pottery and iron goods. A common type of wheel-turned pottery with incised designs and out-turned lip is found in Slav sites all over central and eastern Europe. They were probably produced by village potters who served the needs of several surrounding villages. Similarly the iron tools which the Slavs certainly used were the product of village smiths or travelling smiths.

Bulgar society was technologically sophisticated in the sense that its ruling class used, either by purchase or by forced labour, the products of numerous artisans, who may have been largely non-Bulgar. The silver-ware found in a probable Proto-Bulgar site at Nagy Szent-Miklós in Hungary is more indicative of Bulgar taste than of Bulgar technology. Nevertheless there must have been many craftsmen working around the courts of the Khan and his principal boyars.

We read in the works of John the Exarch and others of numerous craftsmen—shipwrights, coppersmiths, goldsmiths, weavers, tanners, blacksmiths etc. Excavation at Pliska, Preslav and elsewhere reveals much sophisticated metal-work—including a dentist's probe—besides well-turned pottery, including much polychrome-ware resembling, but not copying, contemporary Constantinopolitan ware, jewellery and other luxury articles.[7] This was probably largely produced for the court and the upper classes of the capital. Surviving buildings or those clearly defined by existing ruins testify to the skill of the architects and builders but also to their unfamiliarity with contemporary Byzantine building practice. Sculptors decorated these buildings with reliefs in which Byzantine and oriental motifs are fused. The latter may be due to the tastes and traditions of the Proto-Bulgars.

Side by side with this industrial production within the cities for a limited urban market, the economic life of the countryside went on with scarcely any change—autarkic, without money, and largely without a market. This last point needs some qualification. Cosmas the Presbyter in the mid tenth century speaks of peasants coming to the city for trade. But in the absence of money this was probably a matter of exchanging occasional surpluses for such products of city industry as might be readily available. The cities of Bulgaria were essentially fed from two sources, the cultivation of the land immediately surrounding their walls, and the product of the tax in kind redistributed by officials and magnates to their dependents. Trade was a secondary source. It is noteworthy that there is no word for 'price' in early Slavonic texts: *cěna*, which later has this meaning, means 'compensation' or 'fine' in the Bulgarian legal code.

It is this relative absence of internal trade which explains the dependent situation in which many of the craftsmen found themselves. Cosmas the Presbyter writes of craftsmen working for their lord during the day and praying by night. The craftsman had only a few customers, or possibly only one, for whom he worked to order, probably with materials provided by the customer. He was dependent on his customer or customers for the necessities of life, and indeed was, *mutatis mutandis*, in the same position as those soldiers who are described in early Bulgarian inscriptions as 'kept men' of the Khan. He was essentially unfree. There were, however, also free workers negotiating contracts with their customers.

At the same time Bulgarian industry did not remain static. There was some overspill of technique from the royal capital to smaller cities, where it was adapted to local needs. At Oescus (Gigen) in the tenth century much domestic pottery of a traditional type was produced. But a curious closed vessel was also found, with three vent pipes uniting at the top, which has been variously interpreted as a perfumery still or a ritual object (the last resort of the archaeologist who does not know!).[8] And one industry which processed Bulgarian raw materials seems to have made the crucial step from domestic to craft industry in the period under study. The *Book of the Prefect* speaks of Bulgarians bringing linen to Constantinople, which they cannot sell directly in exchange for such Constantinopolitan goods as they need.[9] This passage has been variously interpreted. It may be that these Bulgarians are peasants from Bulgarian Thrace, part-time weavers rather than merchants. Earlier in the same chapter of the *Book of the Prefect* (9.1) we hear of linen 'from beyond the Struma' which is paid for in money by the drapers. This linen is presumably brought to Constantinople by merchants operating under the terms of the commercial treaty between the two countries. At any rate these passages point to the existence of an exportable surplus of textiles. There are indications elsewhere that dressed skins, sheepskin rugs and the like were imported from Bulgaria to Constantinople. So here again we may have a case of the change from subsistence production to market production.

Why did this development of productivity not lead to a more generalised market economy and the use of coined money in Bulgaria? The answer, apart from the general economic backwardness of the country, may lie in the fact that the Bulgarian proprietors, who controlled not only the agricultural surplus, but also such industrial production as existed, found it easier to dispose of their surplus in the nearby Byzantine empire in exchange for Byzantine luxury goods than to encourage the development of home markets, as sometimes happened in western Europe. Church property would be particularly important in this respect. It is perhaps significant that Cosmas the Presbyter condemns monks who 'engage in buying and selling, sending letters and instructions everywhere, and seeking to become known even in other lands.' Thus the proximity of the empire with its—in medieval terms—developed market economy enabled the Bulgarian feudal magnates to avoid the dilemma created by their own growing wealth and the poverty of the agricultural world in which they lived; it prevented the Bulgarian economy developing in the directions taken in the contemporary Frankish Kingdom, for example.

Another factor limiting the free development of the Bulgarian economy lay in the needs of the army. Krum put in the field an army of 30,000 men in defensive armour—*holosidéroi*—with 5,000 wagons with iron tyres, and a variety of siege engines.[10] We have no comparable information regarding Symeon's armies, but there is no reason to regard them as smaller or less well-armed. Rather the contrary. The equipment and maintenance of such an army must have involved virtually all the metal workers, wheelwrights, harness-makers, carpenters etc. of the country. How this was organised we do not know. There is no sign of long-established government arms factories or arsenals. Presumably it was done by direct personal mobilisation of such craftsmen as were not already working under the direction of the ruler or of one of his boyars. Armaments production, especially under Krum or Symeon, clearly represented a much larger part of the total industrial production of the country in Bulgaria than it did in Byzantium. To that extent industry was isolated from the market and encouraged to specialise in certain limited types of product for which there was little or no outlet on the market.

Bulgaria of course lay on important international trade routes. Some of the trade between the Byzantine empire and the west—some of which was, in its turn, an extension of Byzantine trade with the Moslem world and regions further east—must have passed through Bulgaria. The Byzantines succeeded in profiting by this long-distance trade but the Bulgarians seem not to have done so, or at any rate not to a significant extent. In Byzantium this was done by an elaborate system of customs barriers, both at the frontiers with foreign states and at points within the empire itself, at each of which a *kommerkia-rios* levied tolls on goods in transit in accordance with a complex and sophisticated scheme.[11] No such system seems to have existed in Bulgaria. The frontiers were constantly guarded in the time of Boris, and no doubt later, but the prime purpose was military security rather than fiscal advantage. The picture which John Cameniates paints of Byzantine-Bulgarian relations in the neighbourhood of Thessalonika—

incidentally at a time when the two countries were at war! —does not suggest the existence of any serious customs barrier on the Bulgarian side. No doubt the Bulgarian rulers levied duty on foreign goods in transit. But they had not the reserve of literate minor functionaries needed to make such a control effective.

Thus in a variety of ways the Bulgarian economy, which was at the start relatively underdeveloped, was distorted by the closeness of the Byzantine empire, by its domination of international trade, and by the demands provoked by the frequent military conflicts between the two countries. Regions with an economy equally well developed, such as the Arab world, derived advantage from the proximity of the empire. Those which were significantly weaker saw their subsequent economic development hindered rather than helped by this proximity.

7 Political Structure

The Byzantine empire in the ninth and tenth centuries was, in its political ordering as in so many other things, the heir of the later Roman Empire. The changes which had taken place since the age of Diocletian and Constantine were great, but they had in general been made by way of adjustment to the challenge of successive crises rather than as part of a well thought-out plan of reform. The only significant exception to this may be the introduction of the *theme* system. But there is still no agreement on the date, purpose and method of this radical change. What is certain is that it took place slowly, over a period of as much as two centuries, so it is in no way comparable to the restructuring of the Roman administrative system by Diocletian, a reform carried out in a few years and under the rule of one man.

By the early ninth century stability had been reached after a long period of slow change. By the later tenth century that stability began to be upset by innovations in the pattern of land-tenure and consequently in the provision of soldiers and the collection of taxes, and a new period of change was inaugurated which was only stabilised once again in the reign of Alexios I Comnenus (1081-1118). What is here described is the political structure during the long period of relative stability, with only occasional references to the periods of change preceding and following.

All power was vested in the emperor, who was not merely a head of state but a divinely appointed ruler whose authority was potentially ecumenical. His office was not hereditary, but had to be conferred. On the death of an emperor his successor was theoretically appointed by the army, the senate and the people, and consecrated by the patriarch. As the army and the people had no deliberative or executive organs, and the senate by this time virtually none, the real forces involved might be very different. Sometimes a mere conspiracy among the palace guards sufficed; more usually it was a consensus among the leading civil and military officers of state. Often an emperor appointed a junior colleague during his lifetime, usually a son, and such a junior emperor might expect to succeed his predecessor without formal appointment. Coronation by the patriarch was not essential for the exercise of imperial power, and was sometimes long delayed for various reasons. Where there were several co-emperors, only the senior actually exercised imperial functions.

The traditional and official view of the functions and duties of a Byzantine emperor in the ninth century is summarised in Title 2 of the *Epanagoge,* a brief codification of the law promulgated by Basil I about 880, probably as part of the preparation for the restoration and revision of Justinian's legislation. The passage is as follows:

1   The Emperor is a legal authority, a blessing common to all his subjects, who neither punishes through hostility nor rewards through partiality, but behaves like an umpire making awards in a game.

2   The object of the Emperor is to protect and secure by his ability the powers which he already possesses; to recover by vigilant attention those that are lost; and to acquire by wisdom and by just habits and practices those he does not possess.

3   The goal set before the Emperor is the conferment of benefits; this is why he is called 'benefactor'; and when he wearies of conferring benefits he manifestly falsifies the royal stamp and emblem, as the ancients put it.

4   The Emperor is supposed to enforce and maintain first of all everything that is set out in the Holy Scriptures; then the doctrines established by the seven sacred councils; and furthermore the current Roman laws.

5   The Emperor ought to be distinguished in orthodoxy and piety, both as regards the doctrines established about the Trinity, and as regards the views clearly and unerringly defined concerning the nature of being of our Lord Jesus Christ according to the flesh. This he will do by maintaining the identity of essence in the three substances of the Deity, indivisible and uncircumscribable, and the union of the two natures in the substance of the one Christ, unconfounded yet indivisible, perfect God and perfect man in one person, consequently without passion yet subject to passion, incorruptible yet corruptible, impalpable yet palpable, beyond circumscription yet circumscribed, possessed of dual will and operation without contradiction, impossible to depict yet depicted.

6   The Emperor must interpret the laws established by the ancients, and must on the analogy of these decide questions on which there is no law.

7   In interpreting the laws he must observe the custom of the state, but must not admit as a model anything contrary to the canons.

8   The Emperor must interpret the laws benevolently, and in cases of doubt adopt a generous interpretation.

9   The Emperor must not alter laws which have a clear interpretation.

10   Regarding issues on which there is no written law, the Emperor must pay heed to habit and custom, and if these fail he must follow precedents analogous to the issue in question.

11   As the statement of law is either written or unwritten so its repeal is either the result of a written enactment or of unwritten disuse.

12   We follow the custom of the state or of a province when it has been confirmed after discussion in court. Rules approved by long custom and maintained in force for many years are no less valid than written laws.

13   We do not permit wrong decisions to be confirmed even by long custom.

The compilatory nature of this hodge-podge is evident on first reading. Yet it is interesting as a contemporary formulation of the role of an emperor. And it is typically Byzantine in its accumulation of material from varied sources, brought together through the needs of practice without any attempt at systematisation.

In spite of the aura of sanctity surrounding an emperor, if he were deposed or killed by a rival, that rival, once formally proclaimed, was usually accepted by the whole of Byzantine society. Failure was an indication that divine favour had been lost. Success by a usurper marked him as the man chosen by God. This meant in effect that the absolutism of imperial power was tempered by a right of revolution—provided it was successful. In fact several such acts of usurpation took place between the mid ninth century and the mid tenth century. On 23 September 867 Michael III was murdered on the orders of his co-emperor Basil I, who succeeded to power without further incident. In the years 918-919 the *drungarios* (admiral) Romanus Lecapenus succeeded in setting aside the council of regency appointed during the minority of Constantine VII, and in marrying his daughter Helena to the young emperor. By December 920 he had himself proclaimed co-emperor, which in this case implied the exercise of effective power, since his colleague was a minor. In the following four years his sons were proclaimed co-emperors along with him. Twenty years later in December 944 Romanus Lecapenus was arrested on the order of his two surviving sons, deposed and deported to an island in the Sea of Marmara. A month later the sons themselves were arrested and deposed by Constantine VII, and sent into exile, where both soon died a violent death. Constantine VII himself was poisoned in 959 by his son and co-emperor Romanus II who succeeded him, only to die three years later, probably poisoned by his wife. In all these cases the transfer of power was effected relatively smoothly without the intervention of the army and without civil commotion.

The emperor's functions were representative, legislative, executive, and on occasion judicial. Representative functions occupied a great deal of his time, as can be seen from the manual of court ceremonies compiled by Constantine VII. Many of these were performed inside the palace, and involved the reception of foreign envoys, presiding at banquets, and attending a variety of religious ceremonies in the palace churches. Those which took the emperor outside the palace were mainly religious. On a great many days in the year he made his way in procession to the Church of the Holy Wisdom. Other occasions took him to different churches in the capital and to those outside the walls, both in Europe and in Asia. No Byzantine public occasion was wholly non-religious. But such imperial occasions as the vintage-festival at Hieria—on the Asiatic side of the Bosphorus—or the so-called Gothic Games, celebrated within the palace *enceinte,* had a minimal religious content. And finally under the emperor's representative functions must be included attendance at the chariot races in the Hippodrome, the protocol for which is recorded by Constantine VII in *De Caerimoniis* I, 78-80.

The emperor was the source of all law, but was bound by existing law unless he expressly repealed it. Many emperors seem to have issued no laws of their own. The Macedonian emperors, on the contrary, were active both in the codification of existing law—which always involves some modification of it—and in the promulgation of new laws, the so-called *Novels.* Basil I produced two summaries of the law, the *Prochiron* and the *Epanagoge,* issued *Novels* of his own, and set in motion a kind of revised edition, in Greek translation and with the removal of matter which had become obsolete, of Justinian's Corpus of Civil Law. This new codification, the *Basilica,* was probably completed by his son Leo VI, who also issued 113 *Novels* emending and tidying up the law of the Justinianic Corpus, and, in the *Book of the Prefect* promulgated new regulations for the industrial and trade guilds of Constantinople. Several collections of excerpts having legal validity were also issued by the Macedonian emperors, though they cannot always be unequivocally attributed to a particular author.

In the performance of his representative and legislative functions an emperor was surrounded and supported by a hierarchy of courtiers and officials, in whose hands he might be a virtual puppet. His executive functions could only be carried out through the intermediacy of a series of departments of state and of provincial and regional officers. This is no place to enter into a detailed description of the administrative structure of the empire in the ninth and tenth centuries. Certain preliminary points must be made clear, however, before entering upon a more detailed examination of regional administration and military command, two aspects of the emperor's executive function which lend themselves to comparison with those of Bulgaria. First, the division of responsibilities between different departments of state was not the result of any well-thought-out scheme based upon principles. It was the end product of a long series of makeshift adjustments and of individual acts of initiative in small matters. It occurred to no one to undertake a radical reform or to seek logical justification for the *status quo.* Different types of revenue were raised by different departments, and there was no single central treasury. Expenditure was similarly sub-divided, hence anything corresponding to a budget was impossible. Most items of revenue and expenditure were fixed by custom if by nothing else, but there was enough variability to rule out any but the most rudimentary financial planning.

Next, there were departments of state and there were provincial governors, but there was no government. Each department and each provincial governor was responsible to the emperor alone. The main qualification which has to be made to this general statement is that representatives of certain central departments were attached to the staffs of provincial governors, whose activities were to this extent brought under the control of other officers of state. An energetic emperor, interested in the exercise of power, might make a great many decisions of policy himself. Most of them probably only made decisions when they were asked to do so by their senior officers, or not even then. Such interventions as they did make tended to be arbitrary and capricious. There being no constitutionally established machinery for making day-to-day decisions of policy, decisions were often made by individuals or groups enjoying no constitutional authority. A series of imperial 'favourites', sometimes holding high office, sometimes related by blood or marriage to a reigning emperor, concentrate the levers of power in their hands, and only surrender them after a bloody palace revolution. At other times there is a vaguely defined group of high officials who sort out most problems themselves. The Senate still exists, of course, as a venerable survival of the Roman Republic. However it is no longer a body which meets to transact business, but is an order, membership of which goes with certain ranks and/or offices. In fact an emperor normally consults a group of officers of state before making important executive or legislative decisions, but the membership of this group is neither constant nor constitutionally determined. It depends in part on the emperor's personal whim, in part on the balance of power among the great officers of state.

Apart from decisions of policy, which were certainly far rarer than in a modern state, the administration of the empire went on almost automatically, thanks to a numerous corps of professional civil servants, who were the direct continuation of those of the later Roman Empire. They were arranged in a hierarchy of ranks, with increasing money salaries as well as allowances in kind. The holder of any particular office was given the rank appropriate to it, normally for life or until further promotion. During the period under study the correspondence between rank and office is regular. By the later tenth century the correspondence breaks down and ranks begin to be devalued. These civil servants are recruited from students at the University founded — or refounded — by Caesar Bardas in 863, or from the pupils of schools in which a classical education in grammar and rhetoric is given. The correspondence of the head — who was the only permanent teacher — of one such school in the first half of the tenth century shows the process of enquiry and testimonial-writing (a veritable 'old-boy system') which led pupils to lucrative posts in the civil service.[1] These civil servants seem in the main to be recruited from the class of small and medium landowners of the regions near the capital, who were beginning to form a kind of civil or bureaucratic nobility. It was the same class which supplied the church with its numerous functionaries — often deacons of the Church of the Holy Wisdom — and consequently most of its prelates. They were not of course a closed group. The Byzantine bureaucracy was permeable to the 'lad o'parts' if he found some patron to help him along. But they formed a self-conscious intellectual élite, with a very strong sense of tradition and a respect for culture sometimes amounting to fetishism. In a sense they might be described as the ruling class of the empire at this period. But the exercise of their power was strictly limited. They did not necessarily supply the highest officers of state, who might be chosen from among the emperor's kinsmen or favourites, and hence the highest decisions of policy were often taken out of their hands, even if they could influence them considerably by preparing the papers. And they did not hold military commands. As a result provincial governorships were usually beyond their grasp, though they did provide the staff for the office of provincial governors, and were able in this way to exercise some control over them.

The principal sub-division of the territory of the empire was into themes — *themata*. These were both units of civil government and of military recruiting, and were governed by a military officer, the *stratēgos*. Some of the themes, particularly those of western Asia Minor, were formed in the seventh century, as part of the process of adaptation to the Arab conquest of Syria, Palestine and Egypt, and the continuing Arab pressure on Asia Minor. Others, particularly those in Europe, were formed in the eighth or the early ninth centuries. The newer themes were generally smaller in extent than the older ones. There is also a significant difference in nomenclature. The old Asiatic themes are called after the army units, which withdrew to them before the Arab thrust — Armeniakon, Opsikion, Anatolikon etc. The newer themes have geographical names — Hellas, Peloponnese, Strymon, Macedonia etc. The theme was further sub-divided into *tourmai* and *banda* or *topoteresiai*, which are both administrative circumscriptions and military recruiting areas. The *stratēgos* is both governor of the theme and commander of the theme army — of which more later — and is appointed by and responsible to the emperor. He generally had the rank of *patrikios*, sometimes that slightly higher of *patrikios kai anthypatos*. He was generally appointed for a term of three to four years, and was not appointed to his native province. He was forbidden to acquire real property in the theme which he governed. He had delegated to him all of the imperial functions in so far as they applied to a single province. To enable him to carry these out he had a staff of both military officers and civil servants, as well as an entourage or court of dignitaries. Functionaries from different departments of state in Constantinople were attached to his staff for fiscal and other purposes, and were theoretically under his authority. His second-in-command, the *ekprosōpou*, often functioned as a kind of lieutenant-governor of a section of the theme. The *stratēgos* had power to intervene in any kind of dispute between citizens or legal personalities such as monasteries, including the power to arrest persons and to seize property. In maintaining public order he had the assistance of a kind of military police under his direct command known as *taxeōtoi*. The *stratēgos* himself acted as judge in dealing with military crimes. Jurisdiction in ordinary civil and criminal cases was exercised by the *praitōr* or *kritēs,* who also appears to have had charge of the fiscal officers of the theme. In the course of time, with the breakdown of the theme armies, the *kritēs* became independent of the *stratēgos* and eventually became the effective governor of the theme. But there are few traces of this growing independence of the *kritēs* before the second half of the tenth century. In the major cities of each theme there were officers appointed by the *stratēgos*, with full executive powers in civil matters. They seem generally to have had the neutral title of *archontes*.

Not all the territory of the empire belonged to themes. Apart from the capital, which constituted a separate administrative unit under a prefect appointed by the emperor, there were many small regions near the frontiers or controlling an important mountain pass or other strategic point, which formed independent military and civil circumscriptions. Known as *kleisourai,* they were governed by a military officer of lower rank than a *stratēgos*, but appointed directly by the emperor. Their civil administrative structure seems to have been similar to that of themes, though no doubt on a smaller scale. The only *kleisoura* which we hear of in Europe during the period under study was that of Strymon, which became a theme in the tenth century. In the period of Byzantine expansion in Europe and Asia in the second half of the tenth century and the early eleventh century many new *kleisourai* were established in newly-conquered territory, and some of these were subsequently raised to the status of themes.

The Proto-Bulgars when they settled south of the Danube towards the end of the seventh century were no mere fortuitous grouping of nomad tribes. They had a strong political organisation, a developed system of officers of state, and a tradition of government. Some of their political structure and ideology they brought with them from their Turkic homeland in central Asia. There are valid points of comparison with the society revealed by the Orkhon-Yenisei Turkic inscriptions.[2] Other features may be due to Iranian influences, either from Sassanian Persia or from the Sarmatians and Alans who shared with the Proto-Bulgars and their ancestors the life of the steppe north of the Caucasus.

At the head of the Proto-Bulgar state stood the Khan. In surviving

inscriptions written in Greek he is called κανα συβιγι.[3] The Bulgar
state was not a confederation, and the Byzantine ethnographic
commonplace of the *polyarchia* (plurality of rulers) of the pastoral
peoples is never applied to Bulgaria. The position of Khan was hereditary, normally passing from father to eldest son. When the Bulgar
state first appears, the royal dynasty belongs to the clan or family
of Dulo. When this became extinct or was overthrown in 739—the
meagre sources are discussed by Zlatarski, *Istorija* I. 193ff.—the
monarchy passed to the clan of Vokil. Otherwise we hear nothing
about tribal or clan organisation among the Bulgars. It is unlikely
to have played an important role in the period under discussion.

The Khan was legislator, executive, judge, military leader, and probably priest. The earliest record of Bulgarian legislation is the entry in
the Suda, s.v. *Boulgaroi* concerning the laws promulgated by Krum
(802-814). Its immediate source is probably the *Excerpta historica*
of Constantine VII. Its ultimate source is Greek, not Bulgarian, but
cannot be identified. The account of the legislation is embodied in
a moralising story of the reasons for the downfall of the Avar empire,
but there is no reason to doubt its general reliability. The new laws
were promulgated at an assembly of all the Bulgars—a topic which we
shall examine further—and dealt with procedure for prosecutions,
punishment of thieves and those who gave them shelter, prohibition
of viticulture, and maintenance of the poor. These are presumably
only a selection of the topics covered by Krum's legislation, and they
are probably not reported as accurately as the historian would desire.
But they reveal the mechanism for legislation—the formal proclamation by the sovereign before an assembly, which presumably accepts
or ratifies the laws. There is no question of a written text. And the
initiative rests entirely with the Khan, the assembly's role being
quite passive. In so far as we can validly discuss the content of Krum's
legislation, it appears to replace archaic procedures such as oath and
ordeal by formal prosecution before a court, it lays great emphasis on
offences against property—a thief is to have both his legs broken—and
it takes account of a new class of paupers, for whom the traditional
social security of family or commune can do nothing. After the conversion of Bulgaria Slavonic translations were made of the *Ecloga*
and other Byzantine manuals of law, but it is not clear to what extent
they had legal force. Towards the end of Boris' reign or early in that
of Symeon a new Bulgarian legal code—this time a written text in
Slavonic—was promulgated, no doubt before an assembly of the people.

This code, the *Zakon Sudnyj Ljudim*, drew both on the *Ecloga* and on Bulgarian customs, and at the same time asserted feudal property rights and the new privileged position of the church.

Of the Khan's executive, military, and judicial functions less need be said. All three were carried on largely through the inter-mediacy of a series of officers of state, with Proto-Bulgarian titles whose meaning is not always clear, and most of whom seem on occasion to have combined civil and military functions. Of these the most important were the *tarkhan*, essentially a military officer, the *kavkhan*, whose principal duties were civil, the *ičirgu boila*, who may have been a kind of mayor of the palace, and others. This administrative structure was brought by the Bulgars from the steppes, and the function of many of these officers was no doubt modified with the change from pastoralism to settled life. It was also certainly changed as the Bulgars first established authority over and then gradually merged with the more numerous Slav population of Bulgaria. It is this rapid adaptation which largely explains the vagueness of the functions of Bulgarian officials. The administrative structure was continually modified to cope with new tasks.

The most important officers of state formed a council which advised the Khan. Under Symeon this council allegedly comprised twelve members, but the number was probably not fixed. A slightly later text mentions 'the six great boyars'. A weak Khan could be dominated by a united council; a strong Khan would find his authority reinforced by it. These boyars forming the royal council and living at court are often called *boule* or *synklētos* (senate) by Byzantine authors. They are possibly to be identified with the 'inner boyars' mentioned by Constantine Porphyrogenitus, *De caerimoniis* p. 681, and in Proto-Bulgarian inscriptions, though these are probably a wider group of officers of the central government.[4]

As well as his boyars, who probably belonged to powerful Bulgar families, at any rate until the ninth century, the Bulgar Khan also had an entourage of fighting men whom he maintained and whose loyalty to him was a personal one. These *threptoi anthropoi*, as they are called on the memorial inscriptions which the Khan set up for them, are probably to be identified with the *oikeioi anthropoi* men-tioned in Byzantine sources. Whether they are a specifically Bulgar institution, for which analogies are to be sought in the Orkhon-Yenisei inscription, and in the Mongol *nokod*, or whether they are merely an example of a phenomenon universal in a military society

in which tribal organisation is breaking up, has been much discussed
without any clear conclusion being reached.[5] Eight *threptoi anthropoi*
are commemorated in inscriptions set up by Omurtag and one in an
inscription of Malamir. All have Bulgar names, and most hold some
office or rank. The institution was probably a short-lived one, a
stage in the process of development of feudal society, but while it
lasted it may have given the Khan some freedom of manoeuvre in
the tribal politics of the Bulgar. The unfeoffed knights of early
Norman society, permanently maintained in royal or baronial
households, offer some parallel to these *threptoi anthropoi.*

Thus far we have scarcely mentioned the Slavs. When they crossed
the Danube and moved into the former Roman provinces they had
the simplest of political organisations. They were divided into tribes,
based on real or fictitious common ancestry. The same tribal names
recur again and again throughout the Slavonic world, and may have
been brought by the Slavs from their central European homeland.
But many of them are geographical in origin—Men of the North,
Men of the Lake, and so on—so too much should not be made of this
common nomenclature. There was probably no tribal nobility,
merely individuals chosen by the assembly of heads of families to
perform particular tasks. Beneath the tribe the only unit was the
village or commune of twenty to thirty families, perhaps forming one
or more extended families. As the Slavs settled in the Balkans and
came directly or indirectly under the influence of Mediterranean
society, a process of social differentiation and political unification
began, which led to the growth of larger units with a permanent
leading or ruling group. Such larger communities and their leaders
appear again and again in the Byzantine sources for the seventh and
eighth centuries. They were often called Sclaviniae. In so far as the
Byzantine authorities had any dealings with Slav communities in the
Balkans it was through the rulers of these Sclaviniae, men who often
had some superficial acquaintance with Byzantine ways of life. Such
must have been the situation in the northern Balkans when the
Bulgars crossed the Danube. The pastoral societies of the steppes
easily moved from herding animals to herding men. The principles
are the same. One must shear one's sheep, not flay them, and one
must encourage natural increase. The Bulgars imposed the payment
of tribute—mainly in the form of agricultural produce—on the Slav
communities between the Balkan chain and the Danube, and sometimes moved them to new areas. Thus Asparuch transferred the

Slavonic Severi from the area of the Veregava pass to the more sensitive zone to the east, as a defence against Byzantine forces based on the Black Sea cities, and left the Seven Tribes, another nascent political unit, as tributaries in their former area of settlement. Like the Byzantines, the Bulgars dealt with the Slavonic communities through their rulers. And as in Byzantine-dominated regions these rulers became to some degree Byzantinised, so where the Bulgars were the ruling power they became Bulgarised.

There must have grown up a kind of dual administrative structure, on the one hand the Khan and his Bulgar boyars, concerned with tribute and security, on the other hand the Slavonic princelings and village headmen dealing with the day to day life of their compatriots. Thus in 764 Byzantine agents in Bulgaria kidnapped Slavon, the ruler of the Severi, who had caused much damage in Thrace. Slavon seems to have carried out his raids independently of Khan Pagan. This dualism was only slowly liquidated as feudal relations developed and as the two peoples merged. And it left in Bulgarian society a certain independence and even resentment of the central power, which helped the progress of Bogomilism, but which also conferred an immense toughness and durability on the lowest units of Bulgarian society. In this respect it was rather different from Byzantine Society. When Krum's conquests brought vast new areas of Slavonic settlement under Bulgarian control this dualism was extended and strained. The tribalism of the Sclaviniae with their *archontes* co-existed uneasily with the centralised Bulgar state. Krum seems to have begun to resolve the conflict between them by transferring to palace officials some of the powers of the Slav *archontes.* This process was continued by Omurtag, who replaced the *duces* of three Slavonic tribes by *Bulgarici rectores*,[6] by Malamir and Persian, and above all by Boris. The result was to replace the half-autonomous Sclaviniae by provinces (*comitatus*) headed by royal officials appointed and controlled by the Khan. Some of these officials might of course be members of the Slav tribal nobility who had fused together with the Bulgar leadership to form the ruling class of the developing feudal society. Thus the ninth century was a period of very rapid political and social change in Bulgaria.

The adoption of Christianity as the state religion provided a sanction for the power of the ruler equally valid for Bulgars and Slavs, and discouraged local or separatist loyalties. When it was followed by the adoption of Slavonic as the language of state and church it led to the growth of a common ethnic feeling and tradition.

The Bulgar state had no body of literate civil servants at its disposal. The Khan and his officers no doubt had subordinates and menials, but nothing approaching departments of state. The use of Greek in Proto-Bulgarian inscriptions is evidence that such records as were needed were kept in Greek, presumably by Greek slaves, captives or defectors. The earliest such inscription surviving is that carved on the rock-face at Madara (Beševliev No. 1) commemorating the cooperation of Khan Tervel in the restoration of Justinian II. Beševliev dates it between 705 and 707.[7] It is evident that persons able to speak and write Greek — of a kind — were available in the service of Bulgarian rulers in the first generation after their crossing of the Danube and settlement in the Balkans. Most of the other surviving Proto-Bulgarian inscriptions belong to the ninth century, in particular to the reigns of Krum and Omurtag. The most interesting from the point of view of government administration are the lists of arms and weapons held by various officers (Beševliev Nos. 48-53), which are presumably copies on stone of documents prepared in government offices. Some were found at Preslav, others nearby; they probably all originate in Preslav. It is noteworthy that two out of the six inscriptions are in Proto-Bulgarian written in Greek characters (Beševliev Nos. 52, 53). This is more likely to be the work of a Greek who had learned Bulgarian than of a Bulgar who had learned to write Greek. What is striking about these inscriptions when compared with similar texts from the same period in the Byzantine world, like the lists of troops and equipment for expeditions against Crete preserved by Constantine VII in his *De caerimoniis*, is their extreme simplicity. They deal with few different articles, and merely list the numbers of each, usually without any overt syntactical structure, like a shopping list or inventory. They suggest that Bulgarian administrative methods were fairly simple and unsophisticated. It should be borne in mind that much of the complex financial administration performed by Byzantine departments of state had no counterpart in Bulgaria, where a natural economy prevailed and where most, if not all, taxes were levied in kind, and no doubt weighed and checked on the spot without much in the way of book-keeping.

The administrative sub-divisions of the Bulgarian state before the ninth century cannot even be guessed at. As has been suggested emergent Slav political communities co-existed with the centralised Bulgar state. From the early ninth century the picture becomes a little clearer. An inscription of Krum (Beševliev No. 47) appears to divide the newly conquered territory in northern and eastern Thrace into three sub-divisions governed respectively by the Khan's brother, by the *ičirgu-boila* Tuk, and by the *kavkhan* Iratais, each with *stratēgoi* under him. But this is more probably a temporary arrangement for military purposes during the period of conquest than a lasting administrative pattern. The process of replacing Slavonic tribal administration by Bulgarian state administration was probably a slow one, begun by Krum but only completed by his successors. At any rate we find Omurtag replacing Slavonic princes by Bulgarian governors in the central Danube area.[8]

The distribution of early episcopal sees may correspond to the administrative sub-divisions of the country in the later ninth century. During Boris' reign bishops are attested at Belgrade, Bregalnitsa, Cherven, Devol, Dristra, Moravsk (=Margus), Ochrid, Philippopolis, Probaton (= modern Provadia, half way between Varna and Shumen) and Serdica. Other early bishoprics are found at Develtos, Drembitsa-Velitsa (of uncertain location, and perhaps identical with some other episcopal see), Preslav and Strumitsa. But it is likely that the boundaries of Bulgarian administrative districts were frequently changed and new districts created for various purposes, often quite temporary. Thus when Clement was sent by Boris to Macedonia to form clergy and set up the church organisation, we are told that the monarch separated Kutmichevitsa from Kotokios and appointed as its governor Dometas, after relieving Kurt of his office. The precise location of these districts is uncertain, but it is clear that some rearrangement of administrative sub-divisions took place.[9]

What the title and powers of such a provincial governor were is not entirely certain. The title probably varied from case to case, and the powers always seem to have included both command of military forces in the area and authority over the civil population. It is unlikely that they were defined with any precision. The Bulgarian commander at Belgrade who received the pupils of Cyril and Methodius in 886 apparently had the title of *Boritarkan* 'deputy or lesser *tarkan*', *hypostratēgos*. Other provincial governors' titles probably included the element '*tarkan*'.[10] In Greek texts the governors of districts in Bulgaria are often called *komēs* (for example Cedren. II. 347, 434). The same title appears in Proto-Bulgarian inscriptions in Greek. An interesting example is Beševliev No. 46, set up in 904 at Nea Philadelpheia, 22 kilometres north of Thessalonika, to mark the frontier between Bulgaria and the Byzantine empire. Mention is made there of Symeon ἐκ θεοῦ ἄρχοντος Βουλγάρων Theodore ολγου τρακανος and Dristros (or Dristres) Κόμης. The title ολγου τρακανος occurs only here, and probably designates some high officer of the central government. Dristros the *komēs* is likely to be the local governor. In fact he is probably to be identified with Dristros the *komēs*, who appears in *The Life of the Fifteen Martyrs of Tiberiopolis* as a Bulgarian local official in the area of Tiberiopolis-Bregalnitsa (eastern Macedonia) in the reign of Symeon (MPG 126.213).

The Bulgarians were taking over elements of the Byzantine administrative system even before the conquest of Bulgaria by the Byzantines. But there was not, under the first Bulgarian Kingdom the wholesale imitation of Byzantine political organisation which we find under the second Bulgarian Empire, after nearly two centuries of Byzantine rule.

The Byzantine theme was a military as well as a civil administrative unit. Each theme had permanently stationed in it an army unit, also known as a theme, and commanded by the *stratēgos*. The army unit was sub-divided into *tourmai*, *droungoi* or *moirai*, and *banda* or *tagmata*, corresponding more or less to the administrative subdivisions already mentioned. The soldiers of the themes were not permanently mobilised, but were called up as required, and normally at least once a year for training. The call-up or mobilisation was known as *adnoumion*, from Latin *ad nomen*. The soldiers were maintained by heritable grants of land, to each of which was attached the duty of providing one soldier with his horse and equipment. These military holdings were also exempted from certain taxes and *corvées*. The system dated from the origin of the themes in the seventh century. Ideally the soldier who served was the tenant or his son. This was often still the case, but the matter had become more complicated with the passage of time, and by the ninth century the tenant or tenants of the military holding sometimes fulfilled their duty by paying a man to serve. The soldier himself received pay—*roga*—and in some cases rations when called up for service. The minimum value of a military holding furnishing a cavalry soldier was four pounds of gold. We do not know the figure for an infantry holding; it may well have been two pounds of gold. At any rate the tenants of military holdings were very substantial peasants, almost small gentry, to use a term from a later period and another region. They sometimes held estates much exceeding the minimum value appropriate to their military duties.

In such a case only part of their estate enjoyed the fiscal immunities of a military holding. Nicephorus Phocas (963-969) instituted a new type of military holding, with a value of twelve pounds of gold and the duty of providing a heavily-armoured cavalryman. This was probably done by extending to the remainder of the estate of the richer military tenants the fiscal immunities of a military holding, in order to meet the demands of new developments in military technology. Some military holdings had become divided between a number of tenants. In such cases these were jointly responsible for providing a soldier, either one of their own number or more often a mercenary.

The strength of these theme forces is difficult to estimate. Constantine VII appears to speak of a paper strength of some 3,000 men. Leo VI in his *Tactica* speaks of 9,000 to 10,000 as normal, and 24,000 as a maximum never to be exceeded. Perhaps the difference is due to counting or not counting the infantry, or to discrepancies between paper strength and real strength. And there must have been differences between one theme and another, even before the proliferation of small themes which began in the later tenth century. A judicious estimate for the period under study would be an average real strength of 3,000 men per theme.[11]

The theme armies had a primarily defensive role. But they could of course form part of an expeditionary force, and on several occasions in the ninth and tenth centuries did so. There were elaborate contingency plans for the mobilisation of the Asiatic themes to participate in an invasion of Moslem territory. *Kleisourai* were similarly garrisoned by soldiers with land holdings. Presumably *kleisoura* soldiers were mobilised for longer periods than those of themes, especially in the frontier region. We do not know whether this greater liability was compensated by greater fiscal immunities.

The system of theme armies remained in full operation throughout the period under review. Soon after the middle of the tenth century, however, it began to break down, through a combination of impoverishment of the poorer military tenants and acquisition of military holdings by local magnates. From the later eleventh century we hear no more of the theme forces. This change, which we are not here called upon to discuss in detail, involved not only a reduction of the defensive power of the empire but the destruction of a whole class of substantial peasants standing outside of the peasant communes described in the *Farmer's Law* and yet independent of the great landowners.

The theme soldiers were not the whole of the Byzantine army. There were also units of full-time professional soldiers, the *tagmata*. Certain of these go back to late antiquity, for example the *Scholae*, the *Hikanatoi*, the *Excubiti* etc. Some of these ancient élite corps had become by the ninth century more ornamental than militarily effective. But new units of the professional army were constantly being created. Many of these were composed of Byzantines, presumably largely younger sons of peasant families. Others drew their recruits from ethnic minorities within the empire, particularly from the inhabitants of those mountainous regions which had always served as reservoirs of tough manpower. Still others were composed of mercenaries from outside the empire. This last category increased in importance throughout the tenth and eleventh centuries. Each unit of the *tagmata* was independent of all others, under the command of an officer appointed by the emperor, though they might be put under the operational command of a single officer, sometimes the *Domesticus*, who was in his own right commander of one such unit, the *Scholae*. The commanders of *tagmata* units are called by various titles in our sources, and which of these titles are official is uncertain. The units were generally stationed in the capital, but detachments or whole units were often attached to themes. The commander of such a detachment had the title of *doux*. The relation between a *doux* and the *stratēgos* in whose theme he was stationed is not always clear. Sometimes he was subordinate to the *stratēgos*, but on other occasions he seems to have been under the direct command of the emperor or of a senior officer in Constantinople. Whether in such cases he also commanded some of the theme troops is not easy to determine. It is probably wrong to expect uniformity in such matters.

The soldiers of the *tagmata* received pay and rations from the central authorities, and had no land holdings. Nothing is known of their terms of service. They seem in general to have been volunteers engaged for life. There is no trace of any system of land-grants or money pensions on retirement, so presumably they were supposed to provide for their old age out of their pay. But there is room for research here. The old soldier is not a feature of Byzantine society as he is of certain others.

There is very little precise information available concerning the Bulgarian army. Much of what follows must therefore have a conjectural character. The Proto-Bulgars were originally a pastoral people of the steppes. When they fought, it was as cavalry. And the army presumably consisted of all the men of military age. But by the time they settled in the Balkan peninsula they had been in contact with the Roman empire for nearly two centuries. Bulgarian corps had fought as *foederati* or as mercenaries in Roman armies in various parts of Europe and probably also in Africa. As a result military service had become a career rather than an obligation falling upon all members of the community. No doubt a levy of the people could be made in an emergency. But there was also something resembling a standing army of professional soldiers, maintained by the Khan and loyal to him. The 'kept men', *threptoi anthrōpoi* of the Proto-Bulgar inscriptions are probably commanders of units of this standing force. Of its detailed organisation we know nothing. It was probably better armed and equipped than the mass of Bulgar horsemen, who were unlikely to possess defensive armour of their own.

The Slavs, when they appeared in the Balkans had no large-scale military organisation. In the words of a Byzantine writer, they were *ataktoi kai anarchoi* (Mauricius, *Strategicon* 9.3). Each tribe or ephemeral confederacy made war and peace on its own, and its army consisted of its able-bodied men. Renowned for their 'toughness', at their best in difficult country, skilled at laying ambushes for their enemies, expert boatmen and swimmers, armed only with short javelins and bows with poisoned arrows, careful to avoid pitched battles, these Slav peasant soldiers inspired a healthy respect in the Byzantine commanders who had to face them.

Such were the materials out of which the Bulgarian rulers fashioned an army which for a time dominated the Balkans. Throughout most of the eighth century the army must have consisted in principle of armoured Bulgar cavalry supported by Slav light infantry called up as and when required. The army which Khan Tervel brought to the aid of Justinian II in 705 is described as 'the whole host of Bulgars and Slavs' (Theoph. p. 374). It could not be kept in the field at full strength for long. Its strength lay in ambushing defiles and in sudden cavalry charges. It was not equipped or trained to face a force of professional soldiers in a regular battle on open ground. The hard core of Bulgar cavalrymen of the Khan's retinue were full-time soldiers, given board and lodging by the ruler. The remainder, cavalry and infantry alike, received no pay, but got a share of any booty taken.

A radical change in the early ninth century is associated with the name of Krum, though its first stages may date from before his reign. The army began to be equipped with defensive armour and with a variety of artillery and siege engines. Krum is said by a Byzantine

134 *Byzantium and Bulgaria*

source to have put 30,000 men in armour into the field. The figure is likely to be exaggerated. But the ability to equip and train such a force implies a degree of central organisation previously lacking. Armour has to be distributed to selected individuals, who have to be trained in its maintenance and use, it has to be regularly inspected, and so on. And smiths have to be available in the right numbers and at the right places, with the necessary raw materials, to manufacture and repair so many suits of armour. What is happening is that a semi-professional military body is separating out from the mass levy of peasants, and is being brought under centralised state control. This accords with what we know of Krum's efforts to strengthen the power of the central government and to weaken that of tribal and local leaders.

Similarly his considerable artillery park is something which the old system of tribal levies could not provide. It required engineers and craftsmen of many kinds to create and maintain it. Many of these were doubtless Byzantine deserters or *émigrés,* like the commanders with Christian Greek names whom we find fighting under Krum. We know a little of several of them, including a certain Euthymius, a military engineer belonging to the garrison at Serdica. After the capture of that city by Krum he tried to rejoin the Byzantine forces under Nicephorus I, but was rejected by them and then took service under Krum. An Arab engineer who had served in the Byzantine forces under Nicephorus I, went over to the Bulgarians and took charge of the successful siege operations against Mesembria in 812 (Theoph. p. 498). The men who operated these sophisticated engines cannot have been peasants called up for a campaign, but professional soldiers in constant training.

In the early ninth century then, the Bulgarian army was organised under stricter central control, and equipped with armour and artillery provided by the central government. This better trained force must have been smaller than the body of peasant levies who could be put into the field. Krum, we hear, had a force of 30,000 men in armour. Subsequent Bulgarian armies were probably in general smaller, say 10,000 to 15,000. Doubtless they could be supported in an emergency by a general levy. But the main weight of defence and attack was borne by a relatively small but well-equipped force. Apart from the retinues of the Khan and some of the magnates, the technicians required for the artillery, and the forces employed on frontier guard duties, it was not a full-time army. We learn from the *Responsa* of

Nicholas I that when the army was called up, its equipment was inspected and those who were found negligent were severely punished. And we find inventories of weapons and armour held by various officers. So, a part-time peasant force, with arms and equipment supplied by the state. What was the difference between a peasant who became a soldier and one who remained a peasant? Unfortunately we do not know. There may have been a system of military land holdings on the Byzantine model, but we hear nothing of such an institution. Perhaps the soldier peasant was given some tax-exemption. Most probably his principal advantage was the right to share in any booty.

The Bulgarian army had as its standard before the conversion a horse's tail. This was probably later replaced by a cross or other Christian symbol. Before going into battle it sought to learn the outcome by divination or to influence it by incantations. These no doubt received a Christian colouring after the conversion. Its discipline was ferociously strict — cowardice or disobedience in the field were punished by death. The supreme command lay with the Khan, who usually took the field at the head of his army. Subordinate commands were held by a variety of high officers of state. There seems to have been no clearcut distinction between civil and military office.

Of the arrangements for supply we are almost totally ignorant. Weapons were held in reserve by various officers for distribution.[12] Presumably they were manufactured at the capital. As regards food, a Bulgarian army lived off the land. There seems to have been no kind of quartermaster's department. It is precisely this absence of an infrastructure which distinguishes the Bulgarian army from its Byzantine counterpart. Hence the need for booty which sometimes diverted the army from its main objective.

We know nothing of the organisation of the Bulgarian army during Symeon's years of war with the empire. But there is no reason to believe that there were any radical changes. Formidable as it was, the Bulgarian army had always a short-term, provisional character. It was not organised for long wars. It was Symeon's error that he insisted on fighting a long war. And concentrated as he was on the prospect of taking Constantinople and ruling the Byzantine empire, he never seems to have had time or inclination to modify the structure of his own army for the new role which he required it to play.

The Byzantine empire, even after the loss to the Arabs of Syria, Palestine, Egypt, Cyrenaica and the remaining North African provinces, was essentially a maritime power. It had a very long coastline, and its provinces were so grouped around the Black Sea and Propontis, the Aegean and the Adriatic that the shortest distance between them was most often by sea. The Arabs under Mu'awiya had begun to challenge Byzantine command of the sea, which was not firmly reasserted until the middle of the eighth century. The seizure of Crete in 827 by a force of western Arabs from Andalusia, operating from Egypt, put the Aegean once more at risk. A generation later the attack on Constantinople by the Russians showed that even in the Black Sea Byzantine naval strength could not be allowed to weaken without disastrous results.

The war fleet was therefore an important part of the Byzantine defence force. As so often in the Byzantine empire new arrangements were superimposed upon old without definitely replacing them. As a result the organisation of the fleet in the later ninth and early tenth centuries was complex and arbitrary. As with the land forces, there was a basic distinction between local fleets, manned by local sailors, who were paid for by grants of land with immunity from certain taxation, and the central fleet under imperial control, which was a force of professionals, recruited from all over the empire and beyond its frontiers. There were in fact at this time three 'naval themes', whose defence force was not an army but a fleet; the Cibyrrheot theme on the southern coast of Asia Minor, the theme of Samos, and the theme of the Aegean Sea. The latter two were instituted to meet the new situation created by the Arab occupation of Crete. The forces of each of these were commanded by a *stratēgos,* who was also civil governor of the region from which the sailors were drawn. The central fleet, commanded from Constantinople, was partly held in reserve in the capital, partly detached to various ports in the Aegean, the Propontis and the Black Sea. Its commander was the *droungarios tou ploimou,* a post probably created after the Arabs took Crete. Its detachments, which were very numerous, were commanded by *hyparchoi, eparchoi, archontes,* and *praefecti.* This force was the descendant of the old Roman navy of the age of Justinian. In addition there were various fleet units scattered about the Aegean and elsewhere, whose status is not clear to the historian, under the command of *archontes.* They may be akin to the detachments of the *tagmata* stationed in the territory of a theme under the command of a *doux.* But one must not seek in Byzantine organisation and administration a uniformity which was alien to it.

This diverse but powerful fleet was supported by a series of naval bases, at which facilities for victualling and repair were available, and by a developed ship-building service. Each unit of the fleet had its own naval carpenter — *naupēgos* — under the command of the captain. Naval carpenters and other specialists at naval bases were probably under the same command as the fleet which they served, though there is some uncertainty about the arrangements. Ship-building, as distinct from repair and maintenance, was a centrally organised service, dependent upon the *vestiarios,* a high financial official, and headed by the *exartistes,* who had subordinate officers in various centres throughout the empire where ship timber was readily available. This ship-building service — known as the *exartysis* — involved the training and direction of a great variety of specialists, the maintenance of workshops, operation of bulk purchase arrangements, whether compulsory or not, and so on. It also required large sums of ready money. A special branch of the naval supply service was concerned with the manufacture and distribution of Greek fire — and presumably with the training of specialised personnel to operate the *siphones* through which it was discharged. Manufacture was confined to the arsenal at Constantinople, but vessels equipped to use Greek fire were stationed at various bases throughout the empire and supplies of the fluid held in stock at the bases from which they operated.

The Bulgarians had nothing to correspond to the Byzantine fleet. At no time do we hear of any Bulgarian warships taking part in operations against the Byzantines. The port of Odessos (Varna) with its large land-locked harbour seems to have fallen to the Bulgars soon after they established themselves south of the Danube, say about 700. A little more than a century later the Byzantine naval bases of Mesembria, Anchialos and Sozopolis were captured by Krum, and Mesembria at least remained in Bulgarian hands for some time. But there is no sign that the Bulgarians ever thought of using these cities as bases on which to build a fleet which could challenge Byzantine command of the Black Sea. It is important to remember that the Black Sea coast of Bulgaria was regularly patrolled by Byzantine warships. There was probably for a time a special naval command of the coast between Mesembria and the northernmost arm of the Danube delta, under an *archōn Boulgarias.*[13] This fleet detachment was not directed primarily against the Bulgarians, who were powerless at sea, but against the Russians who came down the west coast of the Black Sea in their *monoxyla* from the mouth of the Dnieper. The most likely date for its establishment would therefore be in 860, the year when the Russians made a lightning raid on the capital itself.

The reasons for the failure of the Bulgarians to develop a war fleet to counter Byzantine thalassocracy, as the Arabs had done in the seventh century, are worth examining.

One consideration is the poverty of good harbours on the west coast of the Black Sea. The Byzantines themselves had no major naval bases or shipyards on that coast. Yet the poverty was only relative. Mesembria and Sozopolis offered good shelter for small fleets; Odessos and the Gulf of Burgas could contain large fleets in their estuarine waters provided they were not allowed to silt up; and the Danube delta could shelter a large fleet (the Byzantine naval base there seems to have been at Lykostomion, to the admiral of which Photius dedicated his *Lexicon*). Another factor might be shortage of good ship timber. But even today the Balkan range is much more densely forested than the mountain systems surrounding the Aegean, and has plenty of lofty firs on its higher slopes. And timber from the thickly wooded Rila mountains would have been available to the Bulgarians after Krum's conquests in western Thrace; it could have been floated down the Iskăr to the Danube. Sailors to man ships must have been available either among the inhabitants of the coastal towns incorporated into the Bulgarian state or among the numerous Byzantine prisoners, deserters or defectors whom we find in Bulgaria in the ninth century.

The problem was probably rather the technical backwardness of Bulgarian society compared to that of the empire and the weak development of internal trade. The building and maintenance of a fleet requires the concentration and coordination of the work of a great number of specialists—shipwrights, blacksmiths, coppersmiths, sailmakers, rope-makers, architects etc. And naval weapons were more sophisticated and involved a greater concentration of resources than did land weapons. It is significant that when Krum captured 36 bronze 'siphons' and a considerable quantity of Greek fire at Mesembria in 812 he was unable to do anything with it, in spite of Byzantine consternation at the secret weapon falling into enemy hands. Yet by 835 Muslim warships from North-West Africa operating in the Tyrrhennian sea were equipped with Greek fire, and by 844 the Spanish Umayyads were using it. Krum, we are told, had an army of 30,000 *holosidēroi.* The figure may be exaggerated, but clearly the Bulgarians could put in the field a large armoured force. This called for the co-ordinated work of a large number of smiths, many of whom probably belonged to the entourage of the monarch or his magnates. It did not call for the services of a variety of specialists who would otherwise be producing for private customers or for the market. Commodity production was not sufficiently advanced in Bulgaria to support such a variety of specialist craftsmen. And in so far as craft production did develop, the craftsman tended to fall into dependence on an individual magnate and so did not produce for the market.[14]

Therefore the Bulgarian state, although it could put into the field an army that was a match for the Byzantines in point of armour, siege equipment etc., was quite unable to challenge Byzantine naval superiority even off its own shores, and at a time when Byzantine naval power was passing through a serious crisis. In the end this weakness proved fatal for Bulgaria. Under John Tzimiskes Byzantine forces were freely transported by sea past the Bulgarian coast and up the Danube, and landed in the rear of the main Bulgarian army. This more than anything else contributed to the collapse of Bulgarian power and the re-establishment of Byzantine rule in Moesia and Thrace after a gap of three centuries. It was no sudden strategical innovation. Constantine V in the eighth century had regularly sent his flotilla up the Danube, cutting off Balkan Bulgaria from its Transdanubian provinces and making raids in force. It is impossible that either Boris or Symeon can have been unaware of this basic strategic weakness of his country in face of the Byzantine empire. Boris was probably not thinking in terms of military confrontation, but Symeon was. If therefore he made no serious attempt to develop Bulgarian sea power it can only have been because he had not at his disposal the requisite technical resources. It is noteworthy that the Slavs of Bulgaria, living in a mountainous land with few navigable rivers, seem to have lost that familiarity with boats which struck the writer of the *Strategikon* attributed to Maurice, and which in the ninth century enabled the eastern Slavs of Russia to launch their formidable fleet of dug-out canoes on to the waters of the Black Sea, and in 860 to make a lightning raid on Constantinople itself. Yet this point must not be overstressed. The Bulgarians—doubtless descendants of those who came to Macedonia with Kuber—who took part in a revolt against Leo III in 718 advanced from Thessalonika to Herakleia by land and sea, using dug-out boats, presumably built by their Slav allies or subjects (Niceph. *Brev.*55-56). However to build boats is one thing, to keep a war fleet at sea is another. This latter was beyond the capacity of Bulgaria.

8   Religion

Little is known about the religious beliefs and practices which the Proto-Bulgars brought with them from north of the Danube. Exposed as they had been for centuries to the influence of the Iranian Sarmatians and Alans and to the prestige of Christianity, Islam and Zoroastrianism, their religion is likely to have been highly syncretistic. Yet they preserved certain traits of the religion of their Turkic forefathers in Central Asia. An inscription of Omurtag from Madara records a sacrifice to Tangra, who is clearly the Turkic sky-god Tängri.[1] Byzantine sources describe sacrifices of human beings and animals offered by Krum outside the walls of Constantinople before the horrified eyes of the Christian defenders of the city.[2] There was probably a Proto-Bulgar cult site at Madara, where a late Roman church seems to have been demolished to make way for a large rectangular building with six wide doors, in front of which stood a monolith of rock. Nearby is another enclosure surrounding an immense hewn stone in the shape of a throne. In the outer city at Preslav is a square building with a stone pylon, later converted by the addition of an apse into a church. The *Responsa* of Pope Nicholas I to Boris make it clear that sacred stones or rocks played a prominent part in Bulgarian religion. We hear of oaths taken by Bulgarian envoys according to vaguely described pagan rites. But Proto-Bulgar religion remains nebulous and uncertain. Was there a national religion? How far did it involve participation by the mass of Bulgars? Had separate tribes, clans or families their own observances? Was participation in Bulgar religious observances open to non-Bulgars, and in particular to the numerous Slav subjects of the Bulgars? Are scholars justified in assuming that the *Responsa* of Pope Nicholas refer specifically to the religion of the Proto-Bulgars? To these and related questions no clear answer can be given. It seems likely, however, that the progressive Slavisation of the Bulgars in the course of the ninth century weakened the hold of their traditional religion.

On the beliefs and practices of the Slavs we are better informed. Most of the evidence, it is true, refers to the Slavs of north-western Europe. But there is no reason to suppose that it does not give a fair picture of the whole Slav world at a time when linguistic and cultural differentiation had only begun. It corresponds quite closely with the evidence from pre-Christian Kiev, in the far east of the Slav world.

There was a large pantheon of gods, whose exact relations with one another cannot now be determined. The supreme god, in so far as there was one, was Perun, god of the thunder, who wields an axe which returns to his hand after he throws it. Perun is also connected with oak trees and forests. Etymologically and probably cult-wise he is identical with Perkunas, the thunder-god of the Baltic Lithuanians. A wooden figure of Perun with a silver and gold head was set up on a hill outside Kiev by Vladimir, together with statues of other gods— Khors, Dažbog, Stribog, Simargl and Mokosh. These latter are mere names, tempting to the etymologist, for instance Simergl has been connected with a legendary animal of Persian mythology. Vladimir's uncle Dobrynja set up a similar statue of Perun above the river Volkhov at Novgorod. It is likely that the pre-Christian building at Peryn—the name preserves the memory of the pagan deity—is the cult site established by Dobrynja. German sources describe the temple of pagan Wends at Arkona on the island of Rügen with its huge statue of the god Svantevit in an inner room supported by columns, bearing a drinking horn in his right hand. A similar statue, though no doubt smaller than that described by Saxo Grammaticus, was recently found at Zbrucz in Galicia.[3]

Other temples on Rügen were sacred to Rugievit, Porevit and Poremit. Christian missionaries are not always the most reliable authorities on the earlier beliefs and practices of their converts, and there may be some confusion here. Otto of Bamberg describes a temple dedicated to Triglav, the three-headed principal deity of the Polabi. The Wendish god Rugievit had seven heads, and other polycephalous gods are known from the western Slavonic area. A three-headed statue, now in the Museum of Slavic Antiquities at Split, is probable evidence for the cult of such a god among the Slavs of the Balkans, and stone statues of three and four-headed gods have been found in the upper Dniester area, the original home of the Slavs, in a context attributable to the fourth century A.D. Another god whose name is mentioned in connection with the early Slavs in several regions is Veles/Volos, god of flocks. His name is probably to be associated with *Velaeda* or *Veleda*.[4] Old Irish *Felmac*, Latvian *Vels*, god of the underworld and guardian of cattle, Lithuanian *Velinas* (=devil), and ultimately with *Varuna* in the Rig-Veda. The western and southern Slavs share a belief in *Vile*, semi-divine maidens to whom offerings are left in the open air, and who are often connected with water. In modern folk-tales they appear as naked girls carrying arrows or other weapons, but they may change into swans, falcons, snakes and other animals. They doubtless represent a debased fragment of early Slavonic religion, though their relation to the great gods who were worshipped in the temples is not clear to us and may not have been clear to the early Slavs. A number of hilltop sites in the western Ukraine have been identified as early Slav cult sites. Offerings of grain, acorns etc., as well as dogs and horses, have been found at these sites, together with a type of pottery found all over the early Slav area. Human burials, associated with horses, weapons, furniture etc. indicate belief in an after-life, at any rate for some. But the Slavs during their period of migration seem to have generally disposed of their dead by cremation rather than burial.[5]

How much of this body of beliefs and practices the Slavonic settlers in the Balkans brought with them is an open question. No such great cult sites have been discovered there as in more northerly regions. They called for a degree of economic concentration and political centralisation not attained by the Slavs of the Balkans when they came under either Bulgar or Byzantine control. It is likely, however, that the Balkan Slavs shared in a system of rituals and in a complex mythology which we can only dimly discern behind the ill-formed observations of hostile witnesses. This body of beliefs and actions did not vanish on the official adoption of Christianity. Symeon himself, though brought up as a Byzantine Christian and for some time a monk, seems to have participated in pagan religious ceremonies, either from conviction or as a matter of policy. In the countryside pagan beliefs and practices lingered on, in some cases until the present day. Some were taken over and 'Christianised', others degenerated into peasant mummery. But the mass of common motifs, beliefs and rituals in the folk poetry of the southern Slavs and the Ukrainians—and to a lesser degree the Russians—testifies to the survival through centuries of Christianity of much of the common Slavonic religious tradition.[6] This circumstance must certainly have coloured the pattern of Bulgarian rural life, and made it in many ways different from that of Greece or Asia Minor, where Christianity had become the sole publicly-professed religion much earlier. This seldom emerges in our sources but was certainly a factor distinguishing Bulgaria from the neighbouring Byzantine territories.

The traditional religions of Slavs and Bulgars were a disadvantage to them in a world in which the only powerful and durable states were either Christian or Moslem, in that they isolated their adherents. Both at individual and at state level they presented all kinds of problems.

How was an oath to be administered? How could a marriage be celebrated between a pagan and a Christian? How were treaties to be guaranteed? And so on. Unlike the great monotheistic religions they could not provide universally valid sanctions for the conduct of individual or community, or endow their adherents with the conviction that their lives formed part of a process of cosmic importance. Closely linked with family and clan, with particular persons and places, traditional religion was of no help to a man once he was removed from his familiar environment.

There were Christians in Bulgaria from the first—citizens of the Black Sea coast cities taken by Asparuch, such as Dionysopolis (Balchik) and Odessos (Varna); and of the few Danube forts which were still inhabited; Romanised Moesian and Thracian peasants still living north of the Balkan mountains; Byzantine prisoners, both military and civilian; defectors, merchants and others. But the ecclesiastical organisation of the northern Balkans, based as it had been on the cities, virtually disappeared under the tide of Slav settlers.

From the first the prestige and power of the Byzantine empire exerted an attraction upon the upper class of Bulgarian society, be they Bulgar or Slav. Khan Tervel, to whom Justinian II appealed in 705 to help restore him to his throne, was given the rank of Caesar. It is inconceivable that he can have remained overtly a pagan, and presumably the leading members of his entourage accepted baptism too, however formally. Yet Christians must have remained an insignificant and occasionally persecuted minority in Bulgarian society until early in the ninth century. The use of ὁ θεός in inscriptions of Khan Krum is not an acknowledgement of Christian belief, but an imitation of Byzantine forms of expression, perhaps due rather to the Greek redactor of the text than to the Bulgarian ruler. With the victorious campaigns of Krum large numbers of Christians became subjects of the Bulgarian state. They included not only the inhabitants of the Black Sea and Thracian cities—Serdica, Philippopolis and Adrianople were the most noteworthy—captured by Krum and transported to Transdanubian Bulgaria and elsewhere, and the numerous Byzantine soldiers captured in battle, but Christian, Slav and Greek inhabitants of the Macedonian and Thracian countryside, among whom missionary activity had been going on for some two centuries.

Byzantine military defeats led many senior officers to desert to the Bulgarians, and take service under Krum. Several of these are mentioned in a contemporary Bulgarian inscription (Beševliev No. 47), and Theophanes mentions others in his account of events from 809 to 811 (485.9 the *spatharios* Euthymios, a military engineer; 490.14 Byzantios, a high official of the emperor Nicephorus), as does the Scriptor incertus (347.7ff. Constantine *ho tou Patzikou*, who married a sister of Krum). Krum's victories and the resulting territorial expansion meant that Bulgaria was now challenging the empire for control of the Balkans. Christians by then formed a substantial minority of the Bulgarian population, but they were potentially suspect as owing allegiance to emperor and patriarch. So the next few decades were marked both by the expansion of Christian influence among the Bulgarian ruling class and by intermittent persecutions. Thus Voin or Bajan, the eldest son of Khan Omurtag and brother of Khan Malamir, was converted, according to tradition by a Byzantine prisoner, but put to death in 833 during the repression of Christians by Malamir.

In these years the problem of the attitude of the Bulgarian state towards the Christian religion became an acute one, whose solution could not be indefinitely put off. In the first place the number of Christians among the Khan's subjects was probably growing, and included not only members of the ruling class of boyars and Slav tribal leaders, but almost all the men with high technical skill who were indispensable to a state which was on the way to becoming a European power. More important, perhaps, normal international relations with neighbouring and more distant states were impossible so long as the archaic—and probably decaying—religion was that of the state. Thirdly, the traditional religious beliefs and practices were divisive, in so far as they distinguished between Bulgar and Slav, while the fusion of the two ethnic groups—or the absorption of the Bulgars by the more numerous Slavs—was going on apace in the ninth century. They were divisive too, because of their links with tribal and clan organisation, while Bulgarian rulers in the ninth century were striving to establish centralised government in place of tribal polycentrism, and indeed had to succeed in doing so if they were to build a viable state which could survive on territory which the Byzantines regarded as rightly theirs. Fourth, and connected with the preceding, was the need of the ruler to establish a universally valid sanction for his rule, such as the Byzantine emperor had *par excellence*, and other Christian rulers had in lesser degree. These considerations meant that the situation could not be allowed to drift, on the assumption that in due course Christianity would either spread through the population, or die out. This urgency was quite independent of the views of this or that ruler.

It is clear that Khan Malamir, for instance, was personally hostile to Christian influences, and that Boris became a sincere and devoted Christian. Even had he not been such he would probably have to take the course of action which he did in 864, the mass conversion to Christianity of rulers and people, by decision from the top.

The problem that faced Boris was that the adoption of Christianity as the religion of state and ruler meant becoming part of the divine plan for the salvation of mankind, of which the Byzantine emperor was the earthly guarantee. In other words, was it possible to enjoy the advantages of Christianity without falling under the political sway of the empire, without seeing in every village of the country a priest whose allegiance was to the patriarch of Constantinople, without allowing an ideology centred upon Byzantium to determine the attitudes and values of Bulgarian society? The dilemma was less pressing in Moravia or Russia because they were far from Constantinople. For Bulgaria, on the doorstep of the empire and always potentially in conflict with it, there was no avoiding the issue.

By the early sixties of the ninth century Boris was actively grappling with the intricate tangle of religious and political issues involved. The Byzantines had probably been making semi-official overtures. The empire, after two centuries of retrenchment, was once again pressing forwards its frontiers, especially in the east where the dualist Paulicians had established a state between the empire and the Caliphate. This was a situation in which military power and spiritual influence clearly went hand in hand. In Greece the evangelisation of the Slavonic communities was being actively pursued. The new patriarch, Photius, a distinguished civil servant and scholar, regarded the conversion of peoples outside the frontiers as one of his prime duties. Missions were sent to Kiev and to the Khazars during his patriarchate. He saw clearly the link between religious and political alignment. When King Rastislav of Moravia, feeling that the evangelisation of his country by Latin clergy was but the forerunner of subjection to Germany, turned to Byzantium for help, Photius sent an ecclesiastical mission headed by Cyril and Methodius to establish a Slavonic-speaking church. Cyril and Methodius, natives of the bilingual area around Thessalonika. and scholars of distinction, already had Slavonic versions of some of the principal liturgical texts prepared when they left for Moravia in 862. It is unlikely that these had been prepared in advance against the eventuality of an appeal from distant Moravia. And there is no evidence that the Byzantines ever attempted to introduce a Slavonic liturgy into the Slavonic-speaking regions of peninsular Greece. It is most likely that these versions were prepared, under Photius' direction, for use in the conversion of one of the Slav peoples near the frontiers of the empire. The most likely candidate was Bulgaria. It thus seems likely, though it is nowhere directly attested, that shortly after Photius' accession unofficial feelers were put out to the Bulgarian court at Pliska to sound out the possibility of conversion of the country.

Boris was alarmed by the eagerness of the Byzantines. And he had to beware of certain groups among his own ruling class, perhaps the descendants of the Bulgar clan leaders, who were unsympathetic to his project of bringing Bulgaria into the concert of civilised states. In 862 he sought to counter-balance Byzantine pressure by establishing friendly relations with another Christian state, far enough away to pose no threat to Bulgarian interests. Louis the German, King of the Franks, had asked for Bulgarian aid against his son Carloman, who was supported by Moravia; and Moravia had a common frontier with Bulgaria. In summer 862 Boris and Louis met at Tulln on the Danube, near modern Vienna. The main subject of their discussions was doubtless military collaboration. But religious policy was probably also on the agenda, and Boris may have asked Louis to send Frankish clergy to Bulgaria. At any rate rumours were soon circulating that Louis expected Boris and his people to embrace Christianity.

The Byzantines recognised that their own plans were threatened. Fresh from victories against the Moslems on the eastern frontier, they switched their field army to the west and invaded Bulgaria. Boris, realising that no help could come from the Franks and that his own forces were no match for the experienced Byzantine soldiers, agreed to accept Byzantine terms without a battle. He was by temperament a diplomat rather than a soldier. These terms included the break-up of the Bulgarian-Frankish alliance and the baptism of Boris and his people into the Byzantine church, which would supply clergy and liturgical books for the establishment of churches throughout the country. Boris' ambassadors were baptised in Constantinople, where they had been sent to sign the peace treaty, while the patriarch Photius sent an ecclesiastical mission to Bulgaria to baptise Boris himself and his family and entourage. His godfather—by proxy—was the emperor Michael III, whose name Boris took. Neither the date nor the place of this event is certain but it is thought to have been either 864 or 865 (the complex arguments involved are irrelevant to the present discussion) and probably at Pliska. Thus the acceptance of Christianity by Boris occurred as part of a new assertion of Byzantine power and influence on the northern frontiers of the empire. It must have rankled with Boris, however sincere his religious convictions, and it clearly fulfilled the worst fears of the reactionaries in Bulgaria who mistrusted Boris' new policy.

Soon Byzantine clergy began to arrive in Bulgaria and set up their organisation. A bishop was appointed, subordinate to the Patriarch of Constantinople. Emissaries shuttled back and forth between the new head of the Bulgarian church—almost certainly a monoglot Greek, though we do not know his name—and his superior on the Bosphorus. The bewildered Slav peasants were rounded up by the Bulgarian army and marched to the nearest river or lake, in which they were immersed *en masse* while a priest from Constantinople intoned the formula of baptism in a tongue incomprehensible to his hearers. Churches were set up in which a Greek liturgy was followed on Sundays by a homily in Greek, which can have done little to edify its audience. Though the Byzantines had now finally recognised Bulgarian control of the area south of the Balkan chain first occupied by Tervel a century and a half earlier, there was little in the new situation to reassure the more conservative boyars who distrusted the Greeks *et dona ferentes.* There was a revolt by these elements which Boris only just succeeded in crushing. Many of the rebel leaders were put to death, along with their families.

Boris' worst fears were realised. The Bulgarian church, wholly under the control of Constantinople, acted as the agent of the Byzantine government. The Slav peasants and townsmen of Bulgaria saw their inherited customs and values treated with tactless contempt by the new Christian clergy. Their ruler seemed to have abandoned them and gone over to the enemy. A letter sent by Photius to Boris in 865 demonstrates the situation clearly.[7] The Patriarch reads his convert a slightly patronising lesson on the duties of a Christian monarch, who owes obedience to the church and to the emperor. There is to be no suggestion of ecclesiastical autonomy, as there was for more distant Moravia. Bulgaria was to become in effect a Byzantine vassal state. What the Byzantines had been unable to obtain by force of arms they looked like getting through their church and the demoralising effect of a rapid and forced acculturation.

In the meantime tension had been growing between Photius and Pope Nicholas I. Nicholas, a fervent believer in the authority of the church even in civil matters, had been horrified at the sudden elevation of a layman to the patriarchate, and was eager to assert the authority of Rome over Constantinople. He turned first to the old quarrel about the ecclesiastical province of Illyricum. A series of muddles and misunderstandings, in which the astute Photius manoeuvred the Papal legates into an untenable position, led ultimately to a break between Nicholas and Photius, whom the Pope refused to recognise. It therefore seemed to Boris that the best way to counter growing Byzantine influence in Bulgaria would be to appeal to Rome to set up an ecclesiastical organisation in his country. Nicholas could scarcely refuse without surrendering his claim to Illyricum, and in any case he would welcome an opportunity to humiliate Photius. The whole of Boris' diplomacy from 866 to 870 was directed to this end, in which as usual it is difficult to separate religious from political motives. In summer 866 he sent a mission headed by the Kavkhan Peter, his kinsman, and the boyars John and Martin—members of the Bulgarian ruling class who supported his policy of Christianisation—to Rome to ask the Pope to set up an independent church, and to pose a number of questions on ecclesiastical and civil organisation, Christian conduct, etc. The envoys reached the Lateran on 29 August 866. Boris at the same time sent a mission to his old ally Louis the German at Regensburg, asking him to send Frankish bishops and clergy to Bulgaria. The envoys no doubt also raised the question of military support.

The Pope, who had certainly known in advance of the approach of the Bulgarian mission, was delighted at this opportunity to extend the authority of the Roman see and to snub the Byzantines. He received the Kavkhan and his companions with every mark of respect and prepared for them about a hundred brief answers to questions raised by Boris. These are based in part on the instructions given by Pope Gregory the Great to Augustine of Canterbury when he sent him on his mission to evangelise the English. But they also contain much interesting material dealing with specific Bulgarian problems. There is little theological profundity in them, and no attempt to dazzle Boris with intellectual subtleties, as Photius had done in his letter of the previous year. They give simple practical advice on Christian life and church organisation and practice, and make allowances for some of the difficulties of the Bulgarian situation. Boris is reassured that Bulgarian dress—trousers and a turban—may continue to be worn without offence. The Roman marriage rite it described, but the King is assured that where the participants are too poor, consent is enough to validate a Christian marriage. But polygamy, which had been practised by some Bulgarians, is unconditionally forbidden.

To Boris' request for an independent church, that is one in the same relation to himself as that of the Byzantine church to the emperor, Nicholas refused to accede, though he was careful not to offend the new convert. If Bulgaria was to come under Rome rather than Constantinople, appointment of prelates would have to rest with the Pope. It was too early yet to consider the appointment of a patriarch. Bishops must first be appointed, then in due course an archbishop. In the meantime Boris is enjoined to do nothing until he receives a bishop from Rome. These replies were sent by the hands of two bishops, Formosus of Porto and Paul of Populonia, who headed a mission which accompanied the Kavkhan Peter and his companions on their return journey to Pliska. They arrived there in November 866. Boris at once began to expel the Byzantine clergy from his dominion, as the Romans prepared to undertake their evangelical work. It would be interesting to know where they found the necessary interpreters. There were many who knew Greek in Bulgaria, but Latin speakers must have been few indeed.

At the beginning of 867 Boris' negotiations with Louis the German bore fruit. A large delegation of German clergy arrived headed by Hermanrich, bishop of Passau. They brought with them church vessels, liturgical books and other requirements for Christian worship. When the Pope heard of the presence of the German mission in Bulgaria he was displeased. It was no part of his intention to increase the power and prestige of the Frankish church, and he soon persuaded Boris to expel the newcomers from his dominions. The astute Bulgarian monarch, though possibly puzzled by this development, did not find it unwelcome. It gave him a means of exercising pressure on Pope Nicholas, should the need ever arise.

Towards the end of 867 a series of changes took place in the situation of south-eastern Europe. The emperor Michael III was murdered by his protégé and co-emperor, Basil the Macedonian, who donned the imperial purple in his stead. Photius was at once deposed by the new emperor, who regarded him as a creature of Michael's, and Ignatius reinstalled in the patriarchate. Nicholas I died and was succeeded as Pope by Hadrian II. The ostensible ground for the schism between Rome and Constantinople had now been removed, but relations remained cool at first. Hadrian made no move to appoint an archbishop of Bulgaria as promised by his predecessor. But in the meantime Formosus and his companions began a campaign of church-building in Bulgaria. Sometimes they built on the ruins of earlier Christian churches surviving from late antiquity, sometimes on new sites, and probably sometimes on former pagan cult sites which had been exorcised and consecrated. Roman ritual replaced Byzantine throughout the land, and the slow work of Christian education of the masses of newly-converted Bulgarians went on. Boris seemed to have succeeded in getting Christianity without submission to Constantinople. But his goal of an independent church was still not realised. He had grown attached to Formosus of Porto, who impressed him by the sincerity of his beliefs, the simplicity of his life, and his organising ability. In the autumn of 867 he had sent Peter the Kavkhan and three other high officers of state to Rome to request Nicholas to appoint Formosus archbishop of Bulgaria. Nicholas realised that this would be a step towards a Bulgarian church less directly under Papal control. He feared the alliance of Boris and Formosus. So the request was refused. It was not difficult to find good canonical grounds for the refusal. The news of the refusal was to be conveyed to Pliska by Dominic bishop of Triva and Grimoald bishop of Polymartia. By the time they left Rome Nicholas was already dead.

Coolness began to develop between Pliska and Rome, a coolness which the new Pope Hadrian did nothing to alleviate. Preoccupied with the Arab threat in southern Italy, against which the Byzantine army offered the only effective defence, Hadrian was unwilling to do anything which might aggravate his already bad relations with Constantinople. Indeed in February 868 he recalled Formosus and Paul of Populonia to Rome. They were accompanied on their journey once again by the trusty Kavkhan Peter. Peter delivered to Pope Hadrian a letter from Boris pressing him to appoint an archbishop of Bulgaria, and probably suggesting the names of suitable candidates among the Roman prelates whom the Bulgarians knew.

It was while this mission was in Rome that Pope Hadrian received Cyril and Methodius on their return from Moravia and blessed their Slavonic translations of the Gospels and other liturgical texts. We know that Formosus met them, and presumably told them of the situation in Bulgaria. It is virtually certain that they also met the Kavkhan Peter in Rome, and that their work of evangelisation in the Slavonic tongue was in this way brought to Boris' notice.

In due course the Pope appointed his archbishop, one Sylvester, apparently still a sub-deacon. His qualifications for the post are unknown. At any rate he was not one of the candidates suggested by Boris. This was a direct snub to the Bulgarian monarch, and it can hardly have been unintentional. There was developing a clear conflict of intention between Boris and the Pope. Rome wanted Bulgaria as an advance post in a struggle with the Church of Constantinople for ecclesiastical control of the Balkans. Boris wanted an independent Bulgarian church under his own control, as the only means of maintaining a viable Bulgarian state on the northern frontier of the aggressive and expanding Byzantine empire of the late ninth century. Boris soon saw that his aim could not be realised by the Roman connection, and decided to change course.

His motives can only partly be discerned. Dissatisfaction at the high-handed action of the Pope no doubt was a factor. More important probably was the realisation that now that Photius was deposed and Ignatius restored, Rome was likely to patch up an understanding with Constantinople over his head, and leave Bulgaria in a vulnerable position. Of still greater moment was the change of régime in Constantinople itself. Basil I and his ministers were anxious for an understanding with Rome in the matter of spheres of jurisdiction. And they saw their principal military task in the final suppression of the Paulicians on the eastern frontier. It is likely that this new direction in policy was explained to Boris by Byzantine envoys, or by his own agents in Constantinople, and secret negotiations begun. Boris had come to realise that a compromise with Constantinople was preferable to a complete victory which depended on Papal approval, and in the last resort on the very uncertain hope of Frankish military support. He made one more attempt to put pressure on Pope Hadrian. The hapless Sylvester was sent packing back to Rome with a letter from Boris insisting that either Formosus or the deacon Marinus—who was well known in Pliska as a Papal legate—be appointed archbishop of Bulgaria. The Pope, as unwilling as his predecessor to countenance the establishment of a quasi-independent church in Bulgaria, tried to temporise. But Boris was not prepared to wait. His negotiations with Basil I and his patriarch were bearing fruit. On 5 October 869 a council opened at Constantinople which is regarded by the Roman church as the Eighth Oecumenical Council. Its main task was to heal the rift caused by the Photian schism. It completed its work on 28 February 870. Towards the end of its proceedings there arrived a Bulgarian delegation, headed by the indispensable Kavkhan Peter, which invited the Council to decide to which obedience the Bulgarian church ought to belong. There was a long and heated discussion at an extraordinary session. But most of the members of the Council were eastern churchmen, and the outcome was never really in doubt. The Council decided that the Bulgarian Church fell within the jurisdiction of Constantinople. There seems also to have been a tacit understanding that it would enjoy internal autonomy. Doubtless these points had been settled in private negotiation before the debate in the Council. The Papal representatives had no choice but to accept the decision of the Council concerning Bulgaria, particularly as it formed part of a 'package-deal' containing much of which they approved.

The Roman clergy were sent back to Italy, and the Patriarch Ignatius consecrated an archbishop of Bulgaria, who arrived at Pliska later in 870 accompanied by numerous clergy. The name and identity of the first archbishop is unfortunately not known for certain. He may have been called Nicholas, George, Joseph or Stephen, and he was probably a Greek, but perhaps a Greek from Bulgarian territory. At any rate he was a candidate acceptable to Boris. And he was probably appointed not directly by the Patriarch of Constantinople, but by an oecumenical council at which all five patriarchates were represented. So he could not be interfered with unceremoniously by the Byzantine ecclesiastical authorities. The semi-independent status of his archbishopric is indicated by a tenth-century list of bishops in which the archbishop of Bulgaria appears side by side with the archbishop of Cyprus. Everyone knew that the Cypriot church had been autocephalous since the fifth century. Boris had thus won a partial victory in his struggle to bring his country into the Christian world without becoming a puppet of the emperor in Constantinople.

There were occasional attempts by the Roman church to reassert its supremacy in Bulgaria, but they had more the character of diplomatic manoeuvres than of serious endeavours to upset the settlement of 869-70. Pope John VIII, who succeeded Hadrian II, pressed his claim to authority over the Bulgarian church in a series of letters addressed to Boris and to Basil I. When a Papal mission came to Constantinople in the spring of 878, Ignatius was already dead, and Photius, who was again patriarch, was quite disinclined to make concessions to Rome. Negotiations continued between Pope and patriarch until the Pope virtually had to admit his defeat at a council held in Constantinople in 879-80. In spite of efforts made by the Papal legate Cardinal Peter to put Roman claims to Bulgaria, the Byzantine clergy skilfully evaded the issue. In the meantime a representative of the autocephalous Bulgarian church took part in the deliberations of the Council. This amounted to *de facto* if not *de jure* recognition of the situation in Bulgaria by Rome. Further Papal protests were ignored in Constantinople and in Pliska alike.

Throughout these years the church was gradually built up in Bulgaria. An ecclesiastical organisation corresponding more or less to that of the civil government was set up. Churches were built throughout the country, some of them by Boris himself, who is credited with constructing seven cathedrals. Monastic communities were established, largely in north-eastern Bulgaria. The western provinces seem to have been relatively neglected, except for a few key fortress-towns. All this activity, however, went on in Greek. Inevitably the leading clergy, even if Bulgarian by origin, were men who had spent the formative years of their lives in study in Constantinople. We hear of a school for young Bulgarian set up there on the initiative of the patriarch Photius. One of its pupils was Boris' second son Symeon, whom his father had destined for an ecclesiastical career. It is likely that he may have thought of him as a future archbishop, perhaps the first patriarch of a fully independent Bulgarian church. Such men, when they returned to Bulgaria, must often have felt disorientated and disappointed. They had exchanged the subtle sophistication of the Constantinople of Leo VI the Wise for a bucolic life in a land where most men were illiterate, and where hands sprang to sword hilts with terrifying readiness. The intellectual leaders of Bulgarian society were becoming alienated not only from the mass of the people, of whom few spoke Greek and fewer had a literary education, but also from the political and military leaders, including those descendants of the Bulgar aristocracy who clung most tenaciously to the ancient traditions of their people. In the Byzantine empire too, of course, there was a gulf between the tiny educated minority who manned the civil service and the Senior ecclesiastical posts and the great majority of the people. But at least they generally spoke the same language, or different varieties of it. And the educated did not feel allegiance to another state and its culture. In Bulgaria their situation must have been almost schizophrenic. Whether Boris saw things in these terms may well be doubted. But he was certainly keenly aware of the growing influence of Greek culture and Byzantine ways on those very people to whom he looked to raise their countrymen out of semi-barbarism, and of the danger of a Byzantine fifth column in Bulgaria.

As for the mass of the people, there is little evidence for what they did, said or thought. An alien clergy preached to them in a foreign tongue. No doubt interpreters were available, but it is likely that during the years of Byzantine ecclesiastical supremacy the veneer of Christianity remained pretty thin in the Bulgarian countryside, and that pagan cult practices and beliefs were far from extinct.

Boris, who was conspicuously well-informed on what was going on outside Bulgaria, was aware of the progress of evangelisation in Moravia under Cyril and Methodius and their pupils, and of the advantages of a Church using the Slav language. If the same principle could be applied to his own Bulgaria, the precarious independence of the Bulgarian church might become a reality, as it would have to train its own native clergy, and the stranglehold of Greek culture and Greek ways on Bulgaria would be broken. The expulsion of the pupils of Cyril and Methodius from Moravia by the pro-Latin King Svjatopolk would not pass unnoticed in Bulgaria. Boris may even have been in touch with the exiled clergy and have invited them to seek refuge in Bulgaria. Be that as it may, when a group of these, headed by Clement, Naum, Laurence and Angelarius, reached the Bulgarian frontier-post at Belgrade in 885-6, they were enthusiastically welcomed by the local governor, the Boritarkan Radislav, who sent them on to his master with every mark of respect. It may be significant that no mention is made of the bishop of Belgrade in the accounts of their arrival, yet Belgrade was the seat of one of the bishoprics established by the settlement of 870. This may be evidence of a certain coolness on the part of the Greek hierarchy in Bulgaria towards advocates of the Slavonic liturgy. Yet Methodius appears to have left Slav teachers and Slavonic liturgical books in Constantinople after his visit there in 882. It is likely that in Byzantine eyes what was permissible in distant Moravia could not be tolerated in Bulgaria. In any case Basil I and his advisers were under no illusions that Boris would take every step open to him to increase the independence of the Bulgarian church.

Boris at once seized on the opportunity offered by the arrival of the Moravian missionaries with their liturgical books. Naum was kept at court, at Pliska or more probably at the new royal residence at Preslav. Clement was sent to Macedonia, where he was given property and other privileges. A modification was made in the local provincial boundaries, the precise significance of which escapes us, and a new governor sent out to ensure that Clement met with no hindrance. Clement was probably of Macedonian origin and may have preferred to work in his native land. But another reason for his being sent there was certainly that Macedonia, and the western provinces of Bulgaria in general, had been much less affected by Greek missionary activity than the north-east. Clement could begin with what was virtually a *tabula rasa*, free from interference by Byzantine clergy.

Laurence and Angelarius died soon after their arrival in Bulgaria. The tradition of Slavonic Christianity depended entirely on Clement and Naum, men already middle-aged. The first task was the rapid training of Slavonic-speaking clergy and the multiplication of Slavonic liturgical books, both by copying existing texts and by new translations from Greek. With every encouragement, material and moral, from Boris, Clement and Naum began this task. The accounts of their lives and the subsequent history of the Bulgarian church make it clear that the task was given a high priority by Boris, who had by now decided to aim at replacing Greek clergy by native Bulgarian Slavs in the shortest possible time. It was a task which called for the kind of material resources that only the ruler could provide. Suitable young men had to be found, lodged and fed during their studies, and taught to read and write their mother tongue before the most elementary theological training could begin. Clement and Naum must each have been supported by an army of copyists, parchment-makers, bookbinders, secretaries, cooks, servants, messengers, and so on. Naum at the capital had access to Boris either directly or through the King's brother Doks, who was a monk; Clement was looked after by Dometa, the provincial governor sent to Macedonia with him. Clement, according to our sources, taught 3,500 pupils in seven years. The figure may well be near the mark. He no doubt followed the practice of Byzantine schools of his time, by which the more advanced pupils taught the less advanced, and the teacher confined himself to taking the highest class and regularly testing the work of the lower classes. But by any standards it represented an educational undertaking almost without parallel in the Middle Ages, when we consider that there was no pre-existing tradition of Slavonic letters.

The alphabet invented by Cyril and Methodius, the Glagolitic, was cumbersome to write and totally unlike the Greek alphabet. Clement continued to teach it all his life. In north-eastern Bulgaria it was replaced, we do not know exactly when, by a new alphabet, the so-called Cyrillic, whose letter forms were where possible based upon those used in contemporary Greek liturgical manuscripts. Whether this change took place while Boris was still on the throne or early in the reign of his son Symeon is uncertain. Boris may have been aware of the problem, which was particularly acute in the capital, where many Bulgarians could read Greek. But speculation on the part he may have played in the change is futile. After all, we do not know whether Boris could read himself or not. The probability is that he could not. In the event it was the Cyrillic alphabet which became the vehicle for Slavonic literature in Bulgaria and later in Serbia and Russia.

For a number of years after 885-6 there were both Greek and Slavonic missionaries at work in Bulgaria, and Greek and Slavonic liturgies in use in the churches. In the nature of things those who preached in the language of the people must have had much more success than those who could be understood, if at all, only through an interpreter. If there was no outside interference, the Bulgarian church would soon be almost entirely Slavonic-speaking and hence largely beyond the day-to-day administrative control of Constantinople. But there might well be outside interference, especially after Basil I died in 886 and was succeeded by his son Leo VI, who showed signs of intransigence in his relations with Bulgaria. Boris no doubt attended the outcome of his new policy with some disquiet. But in fact there seems to have been no serious attempt by the Byzantine church to interfere with the process of Slavisation of the church in Bulgaria. A curious work by a Bulgarian monk, Hrabr, which probably belongs to the closing years of Boris' reign or the opening years of that of Symeon, is evidence of polemical discussion in Bulgaria of the question whether God could be worshipped in other tongues than Hebrew, Greek and Latin. But the date and context of Hrabr's work are uncertain, and it would be unwise to base precise hypotheses upon it. It may be concerned rather with a dispute between adherents of the Glagolitic and Cyrillic alphabets than with the introduction of the Slavonic liturgy.

For seven years the training of Slavonic clergy went on in the monastery of St Panteleimon at Ohrid in Macedonia and in the Bulgarian capitals of Pliska and Preslav. It was long thought that Naum centred his activities in the large monastery of St Panteleimon near Preslav, but recent archaeological work suggests that his school was more probably in a small monastery near the great basilica which

Boris caused to be built in Preslav as the counterpart to the Hagia Sophia in Constantinople. He later joined Clement in Macedonia. In 889 Boris, after a reign of 36 years, was sure enough of the success of his policy to abdicate and enter a monastery which he had himself established at Preslav. His withdrawal may have been the result of a vow taken in a serious illness. His successor on the throne was his eldest son Vladimir or Rasate.

Boris had misjudged the situation. Though nominally a Christian Vladimir was under the influence of the pro-pagan and anti-Byzantine conservative wing of the Bulgarian aristocracy, who saw not only the ideals of their youth rejected, but their own political position weakened as Boris pursued the policy of centralisation of power and liquidation of the Bulgar and Slav tribal survivals begun by Krum. There was possibly an element of anti-Slav Bulgar ethnic feeling underlying the action Vladimir took. He began to persecute the Greek hierarchy, imprisoned archbishop Stephen and other clergy (and possibly closed churches and restored Bulgar pagan cults), and at the same time entered into negotiations with King Arnulf of Bavaria with a view to forming an anti-Byzantine military alliance. What was in essence a political struggle between different sections of the ruling class took the form of a religious dispute in late ninth-century Bulgaria, where religious belief and religious organisation were not inherited unchanged from an immemorial past but imposed as part of the rapid adaptation of Bulgarian society to the challenge of being a great power. The effect was to undo much of what had been done in the previous generation, to bring to the forefront again old racial and tribal differences, and to risk war with Byzantium, which Boris had carefully avoided throughout his reign. At first the old man stayed in his monastery and prayed. But finally in 893 the growing chaos and division in the country and the appeals of his old friends and collaborators prevailed on him to return to the world which he had forsaken. Supported by his old guard and by his younger son Symeon, who after his return from his years of study in Constantinople was now a monk, probably in the same monastery as his father, he arrested Vladimir and his principal followers and took control of the state himself. His authority enabled him to carry through the deposition of his son without too much bloodshed. Some of Vladimir's friends were executed. Vladimir himself was blinded—a Byzantine punishment which rendered its victim incapable of exercising supreme power. A little later Vladimir apparently died, perhaps a natural death.

Order was soon restored. Boris found in his son Symeon a decisive and energetic collaborator and outwardly a convinced Christian. By autumn 893 he was able to summon a council of boyars and other magnates to whom he presented Symeon as their new ruler. He also announced the final transfer of the capital from Pliska, where two centuries earlier Asparuch had established his fortified camp, to Preslav. Pliska was probably too closely connected with pre-Christian religion. And most important of all, he proclaimed Slavonic to be henceforth the official language of the Bulgarian state and church. Since the days of Asparuch the Bulgarian rulers had communicated with the outside world in Greek, and also used Greek for such internal written communications as were necessary. They were probably dependent on Greek-speaking inhabitants of their territory for the redaction of these texts. But these men often had no Greek literary education, and so the Greek inscriptions of the early Bulgarian state were written in something approaching the spoken Greek of their time. A few military inventories were written in the Proto-Bulgarian tongue in Greek letters. There may well have been occasional Slavonic texts similarly written in Greek letters, though none survives. Many Greek inscriptions probably belonging to Boris' reign have survived — for example the record of his adoption of Christianity, in Balshi in present-day Albania,[8] the epitaph of a Bulgarian monk dating from 871, found near Červen,[9] the seal of the Kan-bagatur Ioan Irtkhituin from Pliska,[10] the sepulchral inscription of Anna, recently found at Preslav, and possibly belonging to the tomb of Boris' own daughter,[11] etc. From the beginning of the tenth century these Greek inscriptions virtually disappear, and sepulchral and other texts in Slavonic begin. No doubt Greek was still used for the diplomatic correspondence of the Bulgarian state. But for internal use it was replaced by Slavonic, the language of the overwhelming mass of the people. In the ecclesiastical sphere the effect was even more striking. Slav-speaking clerics were available in sufficient numbers to man the posts required. Greek clergy who could not or would not perform the liturgy in Slavonic were sent back to Constantinople, though no doubt an exception was made for places with a substantial Greek-speaking population, such as some of the coastal towns.

The development of Old Slavonic literature in ninth- and tenth-century Bulgaria forms the subject of another chapter of this book. The spread of the Slavonic liturgy to Russia and its wide-ranging effects are outside its scope.

Together with the Christian religion in its Byzantine form the Bulgarians had adopted the institution of monasticism, again in its Byzantine form. We hear of a number of monastic communities from the time of Boris, such as that of St. Panteleimon at Ohrid, several at Preslav, and so on. These were rich monasteries founded by the king or a member of his family, and endowed with extensive landed estates on the produce of which the monks lived. These estates must have come from royal land, or from the confiscated lands of defeated opponents of Boris, or from tribal or communal land which was treated as individual property. Later on, in the first half of the tenth century, the hermit St John founded his great monastery in the mountains of Rila. If these large monasteries were anything like their Byzantine exemplars they not only engaged in agricultural production but in industrial production too. Thus the great monastery of Studios in Constantinople not only had estates comprising agricultural land, meadows, hay-fields, vineyards, orchards, vegetable gardens, water-mills and cattle-powered mills, wine and olive presses, but it also employed specialist craftsmen, both monks and laymen, as tanners, shoemakers, tailors, goldsmiths, blacksmiths, chain-makers, net-makers, masons, carpenters, icon-painters, scribes, bookbinders etc. The economic activity of Bulgarian monasteries was probably less developed than was the case in Constantinople, since the latter were operating in a market economy, the former in an economy in which most units were virtually autarkic. But they did bring the church directly into the economic life of the country, above all as landowners, and inevitably developed a community of interest with other landowners which spread from the rich monasteries to the church as a whole. Side by side with these large and wealthy monasteries there were no doubt many smaller monasteries in the countryside, established by a minor landowner, a group of peasants, or a single peasant. The farm that had through division become too poor to maintain a family might very well maintain one or two monk-farmers. But of these we hear very little.

Every city of the Byzantine empire, almost every village, had its own saint or martyr, whose tomb or other relics were venerated by the inhabitants. Local peculiarities of cult, local legends, all contributed to link each community to the transcendent world of God's elect, and to give it a sense of special protection. Bulgaria was poor in saints. The cult of those connected with places in the northern Balkans had largely ceased during the Slav and Avar invasions;

their churches were destroyed, their relics removed or lost and their clergy dispersed. And in so far as they were known, they were known through Greek texts and assimilated to the Byzantine world. For Bulgaria to be a fully developed Christian country it had to have its own saints, and by preference native Bulgarian saints. The earliest recorded one is Voin or Bojan, eldest son of Khan Omurtag and brother of Khan Malamir, who had been converted by a Byzantine prisoner and died a martyr during the persecution of Christians by Malamir in 833. It is interesting to compare this royal saint with Boris and Gleb, the first Russian saints, whose position in society was very similar. Voin, like Boris and Gleb, contributed a kind of supernatural validation to the political power of his collateral descendants. Cyril and Methodius, Clement and Naum were recognised as saints by the Slavonic church first, and only later by the Byzantines. Similarly St John of Rila seems to have found late and grudging acceptance by the Church of Constantinople, as did also St Gabriel of Lesnovo, founder of a monastery in Macedonia. Boris himself was canonised by the Bulgarian church shortly after his death in 907, and seventeen years later appears, if we may believe a letter of the patriarch Nicolaus Mysticus, to have been recognised as a saint by the church of Constantinople.

In the reign of Boris' son Symeon (893-924) Bulgarian relations with the Byzantine empire were mostly hostile. For many years on end Symeon's armies invaded northern Greece or Thrace, and on several occasions besieged Constantinople. Symeon hoped to exploit a crisis of power in the empire to become emperor himself, no doubt of a new empire as much Bulgarian as Byzantine. He saw himself as the successor of Constantine and Justinian. In spite of the victories of his forces and the concessions he forced from a dismayed and divided clique in Constantinople, his great ambition was not realised. And in fact his military victories cost Bulgaria dear in men and resources and confidence, and prepared the long period of decline under his son Peter, when Bulgaria sank from being a great power to the state of a Byzantine protectorate.

The relative isolation from Byzantium resulting from the wars, the heady enthusiasm of victory, and the fruition of the plans long laid by Boris, led to a flowering of Slavonic culture under Symeon. Symeon had been educated in Constantinople and had then become a monk in a monastery at Pliska or Preslav. Few men were temperamentally less fitted for the monastic life, but his love of letters and scholarship seems to have been genuine enough. He may well in his monastic days have taken part in the great work of translation and writing inspired and organised by Clement, Naum, Tudor Doksov, Constantine the Presbyter and others. As monarch he encouraged by his patronage their work and that of their successors. He continued the building activity of his father. To Boris' great basilica and palace church at Pliska, church of the Virgin on the acropolis at Ohrid, church of St. Germanus at Bregalnitsa and other monuments, he added a series of churches, monasteries and palaces in Preslav, the new capital, which had been sacked by the Magyars in 895. The impression which his buildings made on the eyes and minds of contemporaries is vividly conveyed by John the Exarch in his description of the Palace. Symeon's reign saw a continued flowering of the new Slavonic Christian culture. We must not forget, however, that the great figures of the previous reign survived long after Symeon's accession. In particular Boris lived on until May 907, and all the indications are that he was far from inactive. His brother Doks survived him, we do not know for how long. Naum died in 906, Clement not until 916; Constantine the Presbyter probably survived even later. So it would be unwise to attribute the whole inspiration of this golden age of Bulgarian literature and art to Symeon, a monarch who spent much of his life at the head of his army, and who was interested above all in power.

The firm establishment of a church organisation, the training of sufficient clergy, the provision of liturgical and other books in the language of the people, the adoption, at any rate superficially, of Christian patterns of life and Christian ethical standpoints were the achievements of the sixty years from the conversion of Boris to the death of Symeon. They represent a rapid transformation of Bulgarian society and a radical process of acculturation corresponding to the new role of Bulgaria in European politics. But they are only one side of the picture. There were others. The church hierarchy, whether Greek or later Bulgarian, lived in close contact with the ruler and his boyars and shared their style of life. Indeed the Bulgarisation of the hierarchy probably meant that it was recruited more and more from the same class as the boyars. The church at the same time became a great landowner, extracting rents and services from its tenants exactly as did the boyars and other magnates. The church's tenants shared in the growing dependence in which the tenants of lay landlords found themselves in the later ninth and tenth centuries. The teaching of the church became the principal ideological support of the established order, an order in which the protection of tribe, clan, or village commune was crumbling away and more and more of the peasantry were being exploited with increasing efficiency and harshness by the rising territorial magnates. It was thus inevitable that in the eyes of many the church, or at least its hierarchy, should be identified with the apparatus of exploitation which kept them in grinding poverty, and took away their sons to die in war in distant lands. Even at village level the church was seen exacting payments for baptism, for marriage, for burial etc., as well as collecting rents.

At the same time the very novelty of Christianity meant that unorthodox interpretations of it flourished. Clergy were thin on the ground during the first decades after the conversion and in some regions long after that. Strange fusions of pagan and Christian thought took place in the minds of simple men. Rites and practices of pagan origin, some of them perhaps taken over from the Romanised or Hellenised Thracians, were given a Christian colouring. Among these were spring and midsummer festivals, sacrifices on beginning buildings, rituals involving transvestism, etc.[12] There were many heretical or doubtfully orthodox teachers about. As early as 865 Boris had to deal with a layman representing himself as a priest and giving baptism to large numbers.

Constantine V (741-775) had transferred several groups of dualist Paulicians from the eastern marches to Thrace to guard the frontier against the Bulgarians. The Paulician communities had flourished and spread, and much of the territory in which they were settled had since early in the ninth century formed part of Bulgaria. These militant, well-organised neo-Manichaeans with their puritan rejection of the church and its sacraments, their dualist solution of the problem of evil — the material world was the creation of the Devil and could not be sanctified — and their claim to represent an earlier, truer form of Christianity found ready hearers among the downtrodden Bulgarian peasantry, and contributed to their dream of a better world to which they and not the official church held the key. About 872 Peter of Sicily sent the newly-appointed Archbishop of Bulgaria a treatise on the errors of the Paulicians, and John the Exarch in his Shestodnev (*c.* 915) argues at length against the view that the created world is evil. There is evidence of the arrival in Bulgaria in the ninth century of Paulician teachers from Cappadocia, the heartland of Paulicianism. There were other heretical groups at work in Bulgaria, contributing to this ferment of underground Christianity. Messalians, who believed that in each man there is concealed a demon who can only be expelled through continuous prayer, and who rejected as worthless the sacraments and other ministrations of the church, were certainly engaged in missionary activity, particularly in the monasteries of Bulgaria. Syrian Monophysites had been settled in Thrace by Leo IV in 778, and had doubtless maintained their religious separatism. There were also many monophysite Armenians in the Black Sea cities, in Thessalonika, and engaged in long-distance trade through Bulgaria. The followers of the shadowy Leucius, author of apocryphal additions to the New Testament with a strong Manichaean and Eucratite undertone, sought refuge in Bulgaria shortly after the conversion, when they were banished from Rome. Jewish colonies were found all round the Sea of Azov and on the northern shore of the Black Sea, where they actively sought proselytes, and there were similar Jewish communities in most of the cities of the Balkans. Boris asked the advice of the Pope in 865 regarding baptisms performed by a Jew in Bulgaria.

Out of this confusion of religious teaching and practice, in a situation of great religious instability, in a society in which the exploitation of the primary producers was increasing in intensity and assuming new forms, social discontent took religious form, and religious heterodoxy had social implications. The early stages of this ground-swell of protest are impossible to trace, as they are almost completely neglected by our scanty sources. John the Exarch as early as *c.* 915 attacks 'heterodox and filthy Manichaeans and all pagan Slavs . . . who are not ashamed to call the Devil the eldest son (sc. of God)'. This passage is interesting both because it shows the link between heterodoxy and paganism in Bulgaria and also because the doctrine that the Devil is the eldest son of God is never attributed to the Paulicians but is a feature of later Bulgarian dualist theology. It suggests that the peculiar Bulgarian amalgam had already taken shape as early as 915. No particular social views are attributed to the heretics thus attacked. But no arguments can be drawn from this, as John the Exarch is speaking in a theological context.

Some time later, probably in the thirties of the tenth century, this current of religious thought which was at the same time a movement of social protest was given a clear conceptual form and possibly also some kind of institutional embodiment by a parish priest called Bogomil. We know nothing of his life or of the region of Bulgaria in which he worked. There is some likelihood that it was in Macedonia.

At any rate Macedonia was the centre of the Bogomil movement in the first Bulgarian Empire.[13] There are only two contemporary sources on the origin and doctrines of the movement associated with Pop Bogomil: a letter of the Byzantine patriarch Theophylact to King Peter of Bulgaria, and the sermon of the Presbyter Cosmas against the heretics. Neither can be dated with precision, and they do not always agree in the details of what they recount. Cosmas gives the more detailed and concrete account, based on personal observations, while the Patriarch was concerned with fitting what he had been told into a preconceived scheme of heresies. What emerges from the two documents is that a new heretical movement was sweeping through Bulgaria. Its adherents tried to pass as orthodox Christians. The material world, they said, is the creation of the Devil, Satanael, who is the brother of Christ. It is therefore unsanctifiable, and the eucharist is an absurdity. Christ was not born in the flesh, but was an immaterial apparition. Only the Gospels and Acts of the Apostles were divinely inspired. Marriage, and the use of meat and wine, were to be avoided, not from Christian asceticism, but because they were evil. They rejected all the sacraments and in particular baptism: John the Baptist was the forerunner not of Christ but of Antichrist. All material vehicles of grace they rejected, such as icons and the cross. Churches as built by men in the material world were abodes of the devil. The Gospel accounts of miracles operated in respect of material objects were to be interpreted allegorically. The order of priesthood and the hierarchy of the church were inventions of Satanael. The Bogomils seem in fact to have made no very clear distinction between priesthood and laity, though certain of their members were recognised as teachers. Probably these were the 'perfect', who practised in full the asceticism enjoined by Bogomil doctrines, while the mass of their followers merely did what they could. Their organisation, so far as we can discern it, was extremely democratic. Their church was built from the bottom up, not from the top down. Its basic unit was the local conventicle, of necessity clandestine. They rejected the liturgy of the orthodox church, with the exception of the Lord's Prayer. They confessed to and gave absolution to one another. 'They teach their own people,' says Cosmas, 'not to obey their masters, they revile the wealthy, hate the king, ridicule the elders, condemn the boyars, regard as vile in the sight of God those who serve the king, and forbid every serf to work for his lord' (Cosmas, *Treatise* ch. 19).

To the patriarch Theophylact the doctrine of Bogomil and his
followers was a mixture of Paulicianism and Messalianism. And it
is no doubt true that most of what Bogomil preached was borrowed
from these two sources. From the Paulicians he took their dualism,
and their rejection of the material world and hence of the church. But
Bogomil's dualism was not absolute. The Devil for him was not, as
for the Paulicians and the Manichaeans before them, an independent
principle of evil equipollent with God, but a subordinate figure, a mere
emanation of God, whose ultimate victory is assured. From the Messalians he took their puritanism and in particular their rejection of
marriage and procreation, but brought this puritanism out from the
monastery into the world. His radical anarchism was a contribution
of his own, reflecting the social and economic reality of the world in
which he preached. The Paulicians had opposed the Roman empire,
but they did so on the field of battle, as disciplined soldiers. The systematic civil disobedience of Bogomil and his followers—who soon came
to be called Bogomils—was something different.

Such was the doctrine which emerged from the ferment of religious
teaching and thinking in early tenth-century Bulgaria, and which was
associated with the name of Pop Bogomil. It spread rapidly among
the dissatisfied and alienated Bulgarian peasantry, and soon had
considerable following in the Byzantine empire. In due course its missionaries—for the Bogomils were fervent evangelists—laid the foundation of a great movement of religious and social protest in Bosnia and,
in central and western Europe, inspired that of the Cathari or
Albigenses, which was suppressed with the utmost severity but with
very varying success. To follow the later fortunes of Bogomilism in
Bulgaria—where it survived until after the Turkish conquest—in
Byzantium, where it flared up in the twelfth century, or in the west,
is no part of our present design. This glance into the future merely
serves to show the unerring skill with which its mysterious founder
expressed the doubts and aspirations of oppressed medieval peasants.

In Bulgaria in the tenth century Bogomilism had in addition a certain ethnic tone. It was popular and Slavonic rather than aristocratic
and Greek. The period of its origin and early spread was the reign of
Peter, when Bulgaria, weakened by Symeon's wars and by the increasing enserfment of its population, became a Byzantine satellite, and
Greek influence spread among the ruling class. The Bogomils preached
in the language of the people, and their message was understood by

the people. In particular, they composed a number of apocryphal evangelical and hagiographic texts in Slavonic, in which they not only illustrated their doctrines, but embodied material from Slavonic folklore. This apocryphal literature is the earliest free narrative literature in Slavonic.[14] The Bogomils were persecuted in Bulgaria. But their loose organisation, their attractive solution of the problem of evil, and their commitment to social protest made their movement virtually indestructible. And eventually, in the western Bulgarian Kingdom of King Samuel at the beginning of the eleventh century they may even have enjoyed some covert support from the civil authorities because of their anti-Byzantine attitude.[15]

The religious history of Bulgaria from the mid-ninth to mid-tenth centuries has been treated in some detail. It was a period of rapid change, when questions of religious affiliation and doctrine were of the utmost importance to the ordinary man, if only because social and economic relations were so often and so clearly given religious expression. When we turn to the Byzantine empire we find a very different picture. There are plenty of religious disputes, but they are essentially of interest to theologians and clergymen. The lay masses seem to have been scarcely involved.

Byzantine society had been Christian for centuries. The Christian religion was closely interwoven with the everyday life of individuals and of the community in a variety of ways. The Church penetrated throughout society, as a teacher, as an organiser of social welfare, as a landlord, as a judicial body, and in many other ways. This stable relation remained unchanged and indeed unquestioned throughout a period of fairly intense theological and ecclesiastical argument.

Serious non-Christian belief was confined to the Jews, a tolerated minority whose function in the Byzantine scheme of things was exemplificatory, and to the Neo-Manichaean Paulicians, largely in Cappadocia and on the eastern frontier. Non-Christian practice was found both in these groups and in the degenerate form of peasant mummery here and there in the countryside. (On the latter cf. Canon 62 of the Council in Trullo of 692 and the comments thereon of John Zonaras in the twelfth century.) Neither these beliefs nor these practices offered the slightest threat to the position of the Church in Byzantine society.

That society had just passed through a century of acute religious division, the iconoclast crisis, which was 'a period as decisive for the spiritual development of the Byzantine empire as the struggle against the Persian and Arab invasions had been for its political existence'.[16]

During the iconoclast crisis there is no doubt that religious beliefs had been closely interwoven with social, political and ethnical demands, though scholars differ on the precise relations between them. After the final victory of the Iconodules, symbolised by the proclamation of the Synod of March 843 restoring the veneration of icons, this link was broken, and all parties avoided doing anything likely to rehabilitate it. The settlement was essentially a compromise, in that only the leadership of the iconoclast clergy was liquidated, while the rank and file were allowed to change sides with no questions asked. That this should be so was the wish of the empress Theodora, widow of Theophilus, and the logothete Theoctistus, the power behind the throne, and also of the new patriarch Methodius, an enlightened man who favoured the interest in profane, classical education shown by Theoctistus. Those who saw less far, or felt more bitter, saw this compromise as a betrayal. Their centre was the monastery of St John of Studios in Constantinople, and their strength lay among monks rather than laymen. These Zealots, as they called themselves, fought the new iconodule régime with as much fervour as they had fought the once victorious iconoclasts. What was essential was to keep the Zealots from winning support among discontented elements in the mass of the people. Only thus could a potentially dangerous situation be defused.

On this ecclesiastical level the dispute was pursued with fervour, and Patriarch Methodius before his death in 847 excommunicated the Studite monks and their leaders. His successor Ignatius was a strict monk, and his elevation to the patriarchate implied a certain concession to the point of view of the Zealots. But any effect which this might have had in unifying the church was more than offset by the conflict between Ignatius and Photius, which dragged on for nineteen years, and in which the Church of Rome became involved. The resulting schism was healed, but it was a foretaste of the situation in the eleventh century, when the schism between the two churches became permanent. Yet its effect upon the ordinary laymen in the period under discussion must have been extremely slight. No parallel church was set up, no one but church dignitaries was called upon to stand up and be counted.

The dispute on the canonicity of the fourth marriage of Leo VI aroused more passions among the lower clergy and the mass of laymen. Subjects with sexual overtones are particularly liable to stimulate strong, if not always rational, feelings. Two parties were in fact formed among the Byzantine clergy, and the patriarch Nicolaus Mysticus was deposed and exiled. After a long struggle, in which provinces as well as the capital were involved, he was restored and his rival Euthymius deposed. As the event which had provoked the dispute receded into the past and the participants themselves began to vanish from the scene, the Nicolaites and the Euthymians were reconciled by the Tome of Union promulgated by the council held at Constantinople in 920. After Nicolaus' death in 925 the energetic emperor Romanus Lecapenus brought the Byzantine church firmly under imperial control, and so it remained for the rest of the period. Of the three disputes which had arisen only the last spread beyond the hothouse atmosphere of the Holy Synod. And none of them appears to have been in any way linked with the burning social question of the time, the growing power of the magnates, who were ousting free peasants and military tenants from their land in the rapidly accelerating process of feudalisation, and against whom a series of laws was directed by successive emperors.

The Church had its problems and its successes. They were those connected with the expanding, aggressive nature of Byzantine power. The Paulicians on the eastern frontier, many of whom fought on the side of the Arabs, had to be eliminated. But this was on the whole done by military rather than by missionary means, as the Paulicians were not as a rule open to conviction by theological arguments. The settlement was a bloody one. And the deportation of Paulicians to Thrace and elsewhere contributed, as has been seen, to the development of the Bogomil movement in Bulgaria. There must have been many crypto-Paulicians left in the Byzantine world, particularly in the east. But the Paulicians had little aptitude for underground conversion, and the Byzantine church was far too firmly rooted in Byzantine society to be permeable by neo-Manichaeism.

The other side of Byzantine expansionism is the readiness with which the Church planned and undertook large-scale missionary enterprises. The patriarchate of Photius was marked by several, directed to the Khazars, the Russians and the Moravians. And the sudden conversion of the Bulgarians was in part the result of Byzantine pressure. None of these enterprises, as it turned out, had much lasting effect except the conversion of Bulgaria, and that took a turn which would have horrified Photius. They were all based upon assumptions regarding the relations of the church—any church—and the Byzantine government which did not correspond to the realities of ninth-century international relations. To this extent the energy, devotion and professional skill which went into these missionary enterprises was largely wasted.

Religion played a different role in Byzantine and Bulgarian society in the ninth and tenth centuries. In the former church, state and society were so inter-connected and in such stable equilibrium that a kind of homoeostasis reigned. Religious disputes were either quickly settled or confined to a restricted group in society. The balance was rapidly restored after any deviation. Religious organisations provided an indispensable aid to the political enterprises of the Byzantine state. In Bulgaria, on the other hand, the Christian religion was new, and had not become intimately linked with traditional patterns of life. Boundaries were unclear, and equilibrium uncertain. What began as an act of state policy with the conversion under Boris became within a generation or two an essential element in the new national consciousness of the Bulgarians, and in turn gave birth to a movement which was not merely a 'vote of no confidence in the universe', but the vehicle of the very concrete and particular social discontents of tenth-century Bulgaria.

9   Culture

The image which the Byzantines formed of themselves and of the world was based upon the synthesis of classical and Christian traditions made in the fourth and early fifth centuries and given institutional form largely in the age of Justinian. Constantinople and its empire were both the New Rome and the New Israel. The empire was a state *sui generis,* a crucial part of the divine plan of salvation for mankind, and in essence if not in concrete reality co-extensive with the inhabited world—the *oikoumenē.* Christian myths, legends and images provided an elaborate code of symbols through which men communicated with one another, at all levels, from the most sophisticated speculation concerning the nature of the universe to the most trivial popular magic. Emperor and patriarch were both God's agents on earth—and hence to be treated with submission—and the people's representatives before God—and hence recallable if their mission was a manifest failure. Disasters, natural or military, were *prima facie* evidence of such failure. Side by side and intertwined with this specifically Christian picture of the world was another, drawing its values and its imagery largely from the rhetorical literary culture of late antiquity. Men still read the pagan classics and appreciated them. Photius the future patriarch in his *Bibliotheca* discusses a large number of pagan classical works which he had read and evaluates them as literature quite independently of their content. Citations from Homer figure side by side with those from the Psalms in literature. In fact classical mythology and certain concepts of classical philosophy provide for the educated a code of symbols available to complement or replace those of Christianity.

This complex, double picture of the world was maintained through the generations by a system of education which is the direct descendant of that prevailing in the Roman empire, with little but the most superficial concessions to Christianity. Elementary schools, where boys learned to read and write, were common enough in towns and there seem quite often to have been village schools.[1] The schoolmaster was often the local letter-writer and lawyer, drawing up petitions, deeds of sale etc., for those unfamiliar with such matters; these are the men whom Theodore Balsamon calls *notarioi paidodidaskoloi.*[2]

What corresponds to secondary education, involving the systematic study of grammer, some acquaintance with selected works of classical literature, and training in self-expression according to the rules established by the rhetoricians of the Roman empire (in particular Hermogenes and Aphthonius), was available only in the larger cities, and at some periods probably only in Constantinople; St Nicephorus of Latmos, early in the tenth century, was sent by his parents at the age of eight from his native town of Basileion in Galatia to Constantinople to attend school. The pupils of such a school usually went directly on completion of their studies to junior posts in the civil service. There was however at certain periods in the ninth and tenth century a still higher form of education available, comprising the study of philosophy, mathematics, astronomy and literature. A school or university providing such a higher education under imperial patronage was founded by the Caesar Bardas in the reign of Michael III. There may have been an earlier foundation by Theoktistos the Logothete, chief minister of Theophilus. Whether Bardas' 'university' continued in unbroken existence till the middle of the tenth century or whether, as is more probable, there was a succession of refoundations, there are traces of such an institution of higher education at various dates throughout the period which concerns us. The details are obscure, and of limited relevance to our subject.[3]

Photius' wide knowledge of profane literature has already been mentioned. His younger contemporary Arethas, Metropolitan of Caesarea, was a scholar and bibliophile who sought out rare classical texts — including such un-Christian works as the *Meditations* of Marcus Aurelius — and had them copied by the best calligraphers. He then furnished them with marginal commentaries to facilitate their reading, commentaries drawn in part from the surviving débris of ancient exegetical literature, partly from his own wide reading.[4]

The early and middle tenth century saw the compilation of a number of encyclopedic works intended to make the classical tradition more readily accessible to non-specialists. These include not only the monumental Excerpts from classical, Hellenistic and early Byzantine historians made on the order of Constantine VII, of which only fragments survive, and the *Suda,* a vast dictionary of literature designed to explain the allusions to be found in classical texts, but also works on court ceremonial, on agriculture, on medicine, on veterinary science, and so on.[5] These works imply the existence of a reading public. And although literacy was certainly not widespread in the Byzantine empire in the ninth and tenth centuries, and real acquaintance with classical literary tradition was confined to a small upper crust, nevertheless far more men could and did read in Byzantium than in any other European state, and probably as many as, if not more than, in the contemporary Moslem world. And literacy, whether we mean mere ability to read or some degree of acquaintance with the classical tradition, was not the monopoly of the clergy, as in the West. There was in the cities and in particular in the capital a class of literate and educated laymen, from which the state drew its higher functionaries.

As well as this general, literary education, specialised professional education was available, through which something of the tradition of ancient science and technology was transmitted. Doctors and architects, to name only two groups, studied the ancient authorities. At a later period we find institutional arrangements, under the patronage of the emperor or the patriarch, for instruction in medicine. There is no evidence for such arrangements in our period, and it is probable that there were none. But somehow the science and tradition of antiquity did filter through.

The literature of the ninth and tenth century reflects the conscious re-establishment of contact with the classical, non-Christian past, both in its form and in its content.[6] The visual arts of the period show a similar imitation or re-creation of classical models, a flexible and sophisticated humanism contrasting with the rather rigid and symbolic art of the Dark Ages.[7]

There was always another strand in Byzantine culture, that of those who opposed the Christian-classical synthesis and based their view of life solely on Christian tradition. For them the adoption of Christianity meant the rejection of the pagan, classical part. The biographies of saints often record that their subjects knew nothing of classical literature and thought, and studied only the Bible and the fathers of the Church. This radical rejection of one half of Byzantine culture could imply a critique of the established order. It was probably commonest among monks, whose prestige in Byzantine society was always high. At times of stress it had a strong appeal for many in Byzantine society. But it never became the ideology of an effective opposition. And it was itself riddled with contradictions, both in theory and practice. For instance the fourth-century fathers themselves were men who were brought up in and respected the classical educational tradition. And the monks of the great monastery of St. John of Studios in Constantinople, who in the early ninth century led the radicals and sometimes came near to claiming complete independence of the Church from the Byzantine state, were often themselves men of learning, engaged in copying not only texts of liturgical and theological content, but profane literature also.

The Byzantines, then, saw in themselves not only God's chosen people, whose order of being transcended that of other nations, but also the heirs of the pagan Hellenistic and Roman world. The two traditions had long been fused together, and for most men presented no problems. In the period which we are studying the growth of Byzantine political power and economic wealth was accompanied by a growing emphasis on the Hellenic side of their tradition, one at first no doubt confined to limited circles of men of learning in the capital, but which in the course of the tenth century spread to wider elements of the literate population. It led to a highly sophisticated literature and art, with subtle and varied means of expression at its command, and a vast and complex universe of reference and allusion, and it was sustained and developed by a tenacious educational system, involving text books, methods of instruction, institutions and so on.

We know very little about the Bulgarians' view of the world and of themselves before their conversion to Christianity. But certain features stand in clear contrast to the situation in Byzantium. The Bulgars no doubt brought with them a complex culture. There has been much talk in the past of strong Iranian influences which may well have existed, but there is little indisputable trace of them. The Bulgars had, however, a fairly sophisticated political system. They formed a centralised monarchical state, unlike many of the nomadic peoples of the steppes who invaded eastern Europe in the Middle Ages. The monarchy was hereditary, passing normally to the eldest son, though he may have had to be confirmed in his office by a council of tribal leaders. The monarch was served by a hierarchy of officials bearing Proto-Bulgarian titles and with clearly defined duties, though we cannot always be sure what these were. The people were divided into clans or tribes, and it was probably from the leaders of these that the high officers of state were selected, in order to ensure the loyalty of the clans to the Khan. The Khan had in addition an entourage of men at arms maintained by himself and living at his headquarters, which provided a counterbalance to the potential power of the clan leaders. The Khan probably claimed some kind of religious sanction for his rule, though what it was we do not know. At any rate we find him performing sacrifices on behalf of his army. He strengthened his prestige by recording his exploits in grandiose inscriptions set up in his capital and elsewhere. This is not a Byzantine custom and may have Iranian origins. But such inscriptions recording the *res gestae* of rulers were set up in central Asia and southern Siberia by the Orkhon-Yenisei Turks in the eighth century. And the predominant cultural influence upon these came not from Iran, but from China. So we may have to seek there the primary influence which led to the recording of their exploits on stone by the pagan Bulgar Khans.

Most of the Khan's subjects, however, were not Bulgars, but Slavs. The process of fusion of the two ethnic groups—or of absorption of the Bulgars by the more numerous Slavs—had begun already in the eighth century and was rapidly advancing in the ninth. Already in its earliest decades we find a Slav, Dragomir, acting as Krum's ambassador to Constantinople. Three of Khan Malamir's sons bore names which appear to be Slavonic. Unfortunately we know virtually nothing of the way in which the fusion came about, though it has many parallels in history. The Slavs brought with them a body of religious beliefs and practices, which have already been described, an organisation by families—probably usually extended families—and clans, with a clan nobility gradually differentiating out of the mass of the peasant clansmen and loose unions of clans beginning to form; they would doubtless also have brought songs, stories, music and visual art which we can only reconstruct by extrapolation backward from later periods and by comparison with what we know of other Slavonic peoples, particularly the western Slavs. As well as Bulgars and Slavs there were also the descendants of Romanised and Hellenised Thracians, the ancestors of the later Vlachs and Saracatsans, who had probably already taken up their pastoral way of life.

Bulgaria, then, was not ethnically homogeneous—but neither was the Byzantine empire. Its culture was not uniform, as was that of the Byzantines, and above all it was not a literate culture. Its only vehicle was oral tradition, which is particularly liable to weaken in a period of rapid social change, like that of the absorption of the Slavonic clans by the centralised Bulgar state. There was therefore little sense of the past, few ready-made and universally-recognised symbols through which ideas could be projected. There was not even, in the middle of the ninth century, a national language. Slavonic was not written. Some of the inscriptions set up by the Khan or his officers are in Proto-Bulgarian written in the Greek alphabet (Beševliev Nos. 50, 52, 53). But most are in Greek, a language certainly not in familiar use by either Bulgars or Slavs. They were probably carved by Greek captives, deserters or emigrants in the service of the Khan and his officers, men who could read and write—another testimony to the relative frequency of literacy in the Byzantine empire—but who had not had a literary education. They are a valuable testimony to the popular Greek of the time. It is significant of the state of Bulgarian culture that the Khans generally sought to project their power in Byzantine terms. Thus they often prefixed their inscriptions with a cross, not as evidence of Christian belief, but because they saw in it a powerful magical symbol, as indeed did most Byzantines. Omurtag, Malamir and Persian called themselves *ek theou archōn* not, as has been suggested, because they were translating a traditional Turkic title, but in imitation of the titulature of Byzantine sovereigns of the time.[8] And in their acclamations and other court ceremonial there is evident imitation of Byzantine models, which carried far more prestige than anything in their own traditions.[9]

Christianity was not unknown in Bulgaria in the mid-ninth century. Krum's conquests had brought under Bulgarian control areas in Thrace and on the Black Sea coast where the church was well established. Many inhabitants of former Roman territories had been deported as prisoners to other parts of Bulgaria. They included Manuel, Bishop of Adrianople; and among Omurtag's senior officers appear three called Bardanes, Ioannes and Gregoras, doubtless Christians and probably Greek.[10] Ioannes and another Christian officer named Leo were beheaded by Omurtag a little later during his persecution of Christians.[11] Two of Omurtag's own sons adopted Christianity, and one of them was put to death by his brother Malamir on his accession.[12] Boris' own sister, Maria, was a Christian, educated in Constantinople. So we have two strands in early Bulgarian Christianity, that of the common people and that of the court.

Nevertheless, the cultural heritage of Byzantine Christianity was scarcely familiar to Boris' subjects, high or low, at the time of the conversion in 864 or 865. (The details of the conversion are recounted elsewhere.) Potentially it provided moral and theological justification for the power of the ruler, gave him, through the church, a means of exercising influence on all his subjects, and brought Bulgaria into the comity of civilised nations. But much had to be done before this potentiality could be realised. And the difficulties were great. There was no common language. The Greek-speaking clergy who came to Bulgaria could not communicate with the mass of the people, who had been marched to the nearest river or lake by

Boris' soldiers to be baptised. And many of the boyars, perhaps the majority, were in sullen opposition to the new state of affairs. We have very little information on the progress of Christianity in Bulgaria for thirty years, and that little does not suggest that Byzantine Christian ways of thought and life made much progress. Boris sent his son Symeon to Constantinople to be educated, probably intending that in due course he should become head of the Church in Bulgaria, either as patriarch or as archbishop. But his eldest son and heir apparent, Vladimir, was kept at Preslav.

The arrival of the exiled pupils of Cyril and Methodios in 885-6 was evidently welcomed by Boris as providing him with clergy who spoke Slavonic and had the necessary liturgical texts in Slavonic. Such clergy were available in Constantinople among the pupils of Methodios who had remained there. But the Byzantine authorities showed no inclination to send them to Bulgaria or to train Bulgarians to use the Slavonic liturgy. Their expectation was that Greek would become the language of church and state in Bulgaria. At best it could only have become the language used by the upper classes on formal occasions, and could never have become the second language of the people and the vehicle of their national culture. The four pupils of Cyril and Methodios who came to Bulgaria were welcomed at Preslav and given facilities to continue their work of teaching and translating. The tradition of Slavonic letters was preserved by two men, Clement and Naum. In 893, only seven years after the arrival of the Moravians, four years after Boris' abdication and immediately after the deposition of his eldest son Vladimir, Boris, returning from his retirement in a monastery, was able to proclaim Slavonic as the language of the Church in Bulgaria, which is a testimony to the success of Clement and Naum's work. It was a momentous step, and the reasons for which it was taken were not necessarily wholly political.

Boris had vision enough to see that the adoption of Greek culture, however superficial, by the upper classes could only have a divisive effect on Bulgarian society. There were difficulties enough in the new policy. First, the exiles from Moravia had brought with them the cumbersome Glagolitic alphabet, arbitrary in its letter forms and slow to write. It would be particularly unacceptable to those who could already read Greek. It long continued to be used in Macedonia, but in Preslav and eastern Bulgaria it was replaced soon after 893 by the new Cyrillic alphabet, based on the uncial letter forms still used for liturgical books in the Byzantine empire. There are a few Glagolitic graffiti in Preslav, but Cyrillic was the writing used by court and church, and in due course it supplemented or replaced Glagolitic in the far west of the kingdom. How the training of copyists, bookbinders and others was set on foot we do not know. Symeon's powerful patronage doubtless smoothed over many difficulties. Be that as it may, the last decade of the ninth century and the early decades of the tenth saw an upsurge of writing in Slavonic, both in translation from the Greek, and as original composition, which has no parallel in early medieval Europe. The details, so far as we can reconstruct them, will be discussed later. Here it must suffice to point out that the adoption of Slavonic as the language of church and literature, and indeed as the national language of Bulgaria—it had always been the language of the mass of the people— ended any remaining antagonism between Bulgar and Slav and quickly led to the development of a native literate class, the setting up of schools in Preslav, Ohrid etc., and finally to a sense of dignity and pride. This feeling of pride emerges strongly in many of the early Slavonic writings, for instance in the polemical piece on Slavonic writing by the monk Hrabr—probably a pseudonym, but guesses at his true identity have no foundation to build upon.[13]

The main centres of translation and original writing were Preslav and Ohrid and their neighbourhoods. It is not always possible to determine where particular texts were written. The Bible or most of it had already been translated by Cyril and Methodius and their disciples. The same is true of the most essential liturgical texts, the three liturgies of John Chrysostom, Basil, and Gregory the Great. The rarer liturgies of SS. James and Peter were probably also translated early. The remaining liturgical books, some of them of great length—the *Euchologion, Gospel Readings, Praxapostolos, Psalter, Horologion, Triodion, Pentekostarion, Oktoechos, Menologies* etc.—were all translated in Bulgaria, probably before the end of the tenth century. These were in principle close word-for-word translations. But local Slavonic saints were added to the *Menologies*. And hymns which had to be sung to a fixed melody could not be literally translated.[14]

Among patristic texts the great fourth- and fifth-century fathers were extensively translated. No complete survey has ever been made of the many unpublished versions. The *Apostolic Canons* exist in an early Slavonic version, as do a number of apocryphal works, including apocryphal Gospels. But it is not always clear whether these are Bulgarian or later translations. Other rarities, which testify to the thoroughness with which Christian literature was rendered into Slavonic and the erudition of some of the translators, include Severian of Gabala, Diadochos of Photike, Ephraim Syrus and Isaac of Antioch. Ascetic works were also among those early translated, which was natural since many monasteries were centres of translation. John Climacus, Dorotheus, Maximus Confessor, John Damascene and Theodore of Studios belong to this category. More than these liturgical, dogmatic, pastoral and ascetic texts was needed, however, to render Byzantine Christian tradition accessible to Slavonic readers. The *Christian Cosmography* of Cosmas Indicopleustes, itself originally a polemical work directed against the Christian Aristotelians of Alexandria, was translated, probably in Bulgaria in the tenth century, as an introduction to the Christian view of the physical world. It is noteworthy that Photius in his *Bibliotheca* comments upon the *Christian Cosmography* favourably. It was probably a text recently 'rediscovered'. The Christianised version of Epictetus' *Encheiridion*, a favourite Byzantine introduction to ethics, exists in an early Slavonic translation.

One essential body of information which neither the liturgical texts nor the church fathers could furnish concerned the history of the world, and in particular of the Roman empire. There is no sign of Slavonic translation of any of the Greek historians of antiquity and the Middle Ages, in spite of the great interest shown in them at the court of Constantine VII. What was translated were Byzantine Chronicles, presenting the history of the world in a naïvely theological framework, without the investigation of causes and the interest in human character which Byzantine historians in the tenth century were relearning from classical models. Malalas was translated at the beginning of the tenth century, from a fuller version of the Greek original than that now surviving. The *Breviarium* of Nicephorus was translated about the same time, as was also the *Chronicle* of George Syncellus. Whether the Slavonic translation of George the Monk, of whom there are two versions, was made at this period is uncertain. It may be the work of a translator of the second Bulgarian empire.[15]

A Christian state whose ruler derived his authority from God needed a body of law. Boris asked Pope Nicholas I to send him a code of laws in 867. There is evidence of early translations of the *Nomocanons* of John Scholasticus and John Nesteutes. These are compilations of ecclesiastical and civil law, which would be used primarily by churchmen. The *Ecloga* and the *Farmer's Law* were also translated and adapted, presumably very early, before the publication of the *Procheiron* and the *Epanagoge* by Basil I or Leo VI. But the Bulgarians did not go on trying to adapt Byzantine law to their own rather different society. They compiled their own legal code, as we shall see.

Of belles-lettres remarkably little was translated until a very much later period. Yet this was an age of literary renaissance in Byzantium. But the historical works of men like Genesios and Theodore Daphnopates, the tortuous rhetoric of Photius or Arethas—or indeed of Symeon himself when he wrote in Greek—and the elegant if often tasteless Byzantine epigrams of the *Greek Anthology* alike aroused no echo in Symeon's Bulgaria. The kind of sophisticated reading public with a literary education hardly existed there. Indeed, it is unlikely that many laymen could read at all.[16]

Bulgaria's programme of acculturation is astonishing both in its range and in the gaps it shows. The intensive practice of translation rapidly made of Old Slavonic a literary tongue, suitable for original writing. Original texts are in fact found from before the adoption of Slavonic as the church language in 893, but the main period of this 'first wave' of original Bulgarian literature belongs to the last decade of the ninth century and the first half of the tenth, the reigns of Symeon and Peter. It was in this period that the Byzantine twelve-syllable line was adopted for Slavonic poetry which followed Greek models, such as the *Introduction to the Gospel* of Bishop Constantine, or the anonymous panegyric of King Symeon. Many works are anonymous, and there are problems both of authorship and of dating, which need not be gone into here. However certain literary personalities do emerge, and it is primarily with these and their works that we shall deal.

Little is known of the life of John the Exarch, who evidently lived in the late ninth or early tenth century. He translated John Damascene, and composed the *Shestodnev,* an account of the creation largely based on the *Hexaemeron* of St Basil. Both works have long adulatory prefaces addressed to King Symeon, which are informative on contemporary life and thought as well as on his theory and practice of translation. He seems to have worked at Preslav, the magnificence of which is described in the preface to his *Shestodnev.* It is not clear what his title of Exarch implies, though the most probable suggestion is that he was a kind of ecclesiastical visitor, responsible for teaching and discipline throughout a diocese.[17] Constantine the Presbyter became Bishop of Preslav in the reign of Symeon. His literary work belongs to the nineties of the ninth century. His principal work was a compilatory Gospel commentary based on patristic sources, which seems to have been written in the first years of Symeon's reign. It is prefaced by an acrostic prayer in verse modelled on that which Cyril had prefixed to his translation of the Gospels. There is also a treatise on the organisation and services of the church, drawing on but not slavishly following Byzantine models. To a quite different category belongs Constantine's *Outline of History*, a free adaptation of the *Breviary* of Nicephorus. A translation of Athanasius' *Tracts against the Arians* has a preface in which Constantine declares that it was made at the command of Symeon in 906-7.

The monk Hrabr (probably a pseudonym) was the author of a short treatise on the Slav alphabet, probably written as a defence of the Glagolitic alphabet against those who wished to introduce a writing system more closely based on Greek models. The author shows acquaintance with Greek grammatical theory, but great disdain for chauvinistic Greek attitudes in cultural matters. The work must date from about 893 when the question of alphabets was a living issue.[18] Cosmas the Presbyter, author of a *Treatise against the Bogomils,* belongs to a later generation. His work is probably to be dated *c.* 969-72.[19] Symeon not only sponsored and patronised literature, but seems to have taken part himself in the translation of a collection of homilies of John Chrysostom known as the *Zlatostruj.*[20] He also caused to be translated a collection of sayings of the Greek fathers, together with grammatical notes by George Choeroboskos, citations from the ninth century Patriarch of Constantinople Michael Syncellus, a short chronicle from Augustus to the reign of Constantine VII and Zoe, and other matter. This *Sbornik,* formerly falsely associated with the Russian prince Svyatoslav, is of course not an independent compilation but the translation of a popular Byzantine encyclopedia.[21] Gregory the Presbyter, the translator of the Chronicle of Malalas, and of a compilation of Old Testament texts, was thought by some to have translated for Symeon a romantic version of the Fall of Troy, based on Hellenistic pseudepigrapha which were also used directly or indirectly by many Byzantine writers. If this were true it would be most interesting, as it would be the unique example of an early Slavonic translation of a wholly non-

Christian text made at this time. But the argument depended entirely on the appearance of the Tale of Troy in the same manuscript as undoubted works of Gregory the Presbyter. It has now been shown to belong linguistically to a later period.

In spite of Symeon's Byzantine education, there is no evidence that the programme of translation which he encouraged comprised any work of pagan classical literature. Not only could this literature 'fulfil no spiritual need in a country of such young civilisation'[22] but it would have been largely incomprehensible and unappreciated. It is not just a matter of factual knowledge; it would have been possible to translate Byzantine encyclopedias. The problem was that the whole classical aesthetic tradition would have to be re-created on Slavonic soil. For this the necessary social structures and educational institutions were missing. So we have the strange circumstance that a period of classical renaissance in Byzantine culture had virtually no effect on an emergent Bulgarian culture which was closely and even slavishly modelled upon Byzantine exemplars. The Bulgarians took over to themselves one half of the Byzantine past but totally rejected the other.

It is interesting to compare the selective way in which they adopted and adapted Byzantine culture with that pursued at the same period by the Moslem world. For the ninth century was the golden age of translation from Greek into Arabic at the court of the Caliphs in Baghdad, though some translation had certainly taken place earlier. In the Moslem world there was no place for the basic texts of Christianity or the commentaries upon them by the church fathers, nor for the homiletic and ascetic literature necessary for the practice of an officially Christian community. On the other hand Moslem society had a cultural level and an institutional framework, including libraries and schools, which enabled it to absorb much of the philosophy and the scientific thought of Hellenic antiquity and even to develop it creatively. The problem of providing a rational account of the world which was at the same time in accordance with revealed religion was one which Moslem thinkers of the ninth and tenth centuries tackled with the aid of what they could discover of Hellenic philosophy. Their translations were often made not directly from the Greek but through Syriac or occasionally Pehlevi versions. This circumstance reminds us that, when the Arabs in the seventh century swept over Egypt, Syria, Palestine, Mesopotamia and Iran, they found not a desolation of ruined cities and abandoned settlements but a flourishing society with a delicate balance between urban and rural areas, with extensive literacy in several tongues, and established techniques of communication between different ethnic communities. The Slavs and Bulgars, on the other hand, found something approaching a *tabula rasa*, from which they had to build, painfully and largely by their own efforts, the rudiments of civilisation. Only then did the adoption and adaptation of the cultural traditions of Greco-Roman antiquity become a possibility. But that adoption was made on terms that were unique.

The Byzantines, as has been observed, had two pasts, Greek and Judaeo-Christian, two frames of reference into which they could fit their impressions of the world around them, whether expressed in language or in one of the visual arts. In becoming a completely Christian community they had not rejected the traditions of their own pre-Christian past, though some of them had to be modified or pushed into the background. Sometimes the adoption of Christianity had led to the reinstatement of older traditions with a new emphasis.[2] In the same way, though to a much lesser degree, the Latin-speaking Christian world of the West had not turned its back upon its earlier, non-Christian ways of thought and scales of value. Its schoolbooks were still Virgil, Cicero, and *'Livio che non erra'.* The same was not true of other communities who adopted Christianity from Byzantium or Rome after the synthesis of the fourth/fifth century. The Armenians and the Georgians preserved little interest in their own pre-Christian past. The situation in Egypt was even stranger, since in late antiquity the Coptic-speaking mass of the population totally rejected the pagan Egyptian past, while the Hellenic or Hellenised upper classes, who in an earlier age would have despised most things Egyptian, developed a kind of *Schwarmerei* for such ill-understood fragments of Egyptian tradition as were accessible, even going so far as to revive hieroglyphic writing. This movement did not last long, and from the late fifth century until its Islamisation Egypt was a solidly Christian country, which had forgotten its pagan past. The local characteristics of Egyptian art in late antiquity, marked though they are, owe very little to earlier Egyptian traditions.

The adoption of Islam generally meant total effacement of a people's past. The Arabs themselves, though they had a literature of sorts and thus the technical means of conserving memories of the distant past, were not merely uninterested in the Jáhiliya. They washed it from their minds—all except a few poems—in a conscious act of purification and rebirth. Even the Iranians under Islam only succeeded in maintaining a pale shadow of their own distinguished past. There was no such creative fusion as took place in Byzantium between Christianity and Hellenism.

The Bulgarians' sense of their own past was probably too confused and ill-remembered, and above all too tied up with pagan religious practices and beliefs to form the basis for a Byzantine-type synthesis. And their past was not embodied in a literature, apart from a few inscriptions in Greek. Other than the mysterious *List of Princes* nothing seems to have survived of the Proto-Bulgars' picture of their own past. The traditions embodied in the *List* have certainly been tampered with in ways difficult to determine, but they have not been Christianised, not even by the kind of banal chronological linking which would have been so easy. And the Slavs, though they must have had a mythology if not a history, forgot it speedily. Or rather they isolated it in a kind of sub-literary world of folk-belief and folk-song. Professor Ivan Dujčev has recently drawn attention to the few pieces of evidence for oral narrative poetry in early Bulgaria. For all his thoroughness, the harvest is meagre.[24] The Bulgarians in fact took over the Byzantine picture of the past ready-made and in close detail. In doing so the Christian elements were adopted with no change. But the Hellenic elements, always the preserve of a minority in Byzantine society, were much less successfully incorporated. They were too strange and too dependent on the existence of a class of literate laymen and a sophisticated educational system to be re-created in Preslav, even by Symeon who himself moved with ease in the world of the Byzantine intellectuals. What the Bulgarians did from the first was to stake out their own little plot within the larger Byzantine-Christian territory by the recognition of Slavonic saints— just as the Russians did later. By the time Slavonic was adopted as the language of the Church—and one must not imagine the change taking place instantaneously and simultaneously throughout the vast lands of Bulgaria, like a currency reform in a modern state—the process of rejection of their own past and the adoption of that of the Byzantines had gone too far to be arrested, even if anyone had seriously wished to arrest it.

A legend related by a Byzantine historian tells that Boris, still a pagan, sent for a painter from Constantinople to adorn his new palace at Preslav with hunting scenes. The painter, a monk named Methodios, seized the opportunity to paint the Last Judgement. Boris was so

terrified by the picture that he at once begged to be received into the
Christian church (Theoph. Cont. pp. 162-3). The story is probably
apocryphal, though Symeon the Logothete does mention a Byzantine
painter named Methodios who worked in Bulgaria after the conversion.
But it symbolises the fact that in adopting Christianity the Bulgarians
perforce took over an iconographic tradition developed over many
centuries, and a style imposed by the metropolitan masters who
enjoyed prestige. Boris was a great builder of churches and monasteries, which were all no doubt fittingly decorated. We hear of seven
metropolitan churches built by him, of a 'White Church' on the river
Bregalnitsa in Macedonia, of the Church of the Archangels at Ohrid,
a church at Vodocha near Strumitsa, of a church dedicated to the
Martyrs of Tiberiopolis, and so on. None of these buildings survives.
The great basilica at Pliska must have been the second largest church
in the Balkans. But it is not completely certain that it was the work
of Boris. His son Symeon followed his father's example: several
churches at Preslav were built at his instigation, as well as others
throughout Bulgaria. The oldest part of the great Church of the Holy
Wisdom at Ohrid may belong to his reign, but it is probably later.
His son Peter, politically a protégé of Constantinople, continued to
build churches and public buildings. So little of this architecture and
its accompanying decoration survives that it is worth quoting the
words of John the Exarch, a contemporary eye witness:

> If some poor peasant from far away comes to the door of the royal
> court, he is seized by wonder. But his amazement grows as he
> enters and sees on either hand buildings decorated with timber
> and stone. And if he enters the King's dwelling place and observes
> the lofty palaces and churches embellished on the outside with
> stone and timber and paint, and on the inside with marble and
> bronze, silver and gold, he knows not what to compare it with,
> since in his own homeland he has seen nothing but huts. He is filled
> with such wonder and astonishment as if he had lost his wits.

Just as the Bulgarians took over, in part at least, Byzantine literature and thought as they were in the ninth century, so too they took
over the architecture, the iconography and the style of contemporary
Byzantium. This has never been in doubt. The question is whether
they also had other sources of artistic inspiration, and if so what they
were and whence they came. Much has been written on this topic,

some of it more marked by patriotism than by scientific judgement. What does seem to be true is that Bulgarian art of the ninth and tenth centuries shares certain features with the art of Asia Minor, Syria and Egypt. Such are the type of church with four corner towers, the 'Syrian' façade with twin towers, a type of frieze or moulding running round the walls and framing doors and windows, development of a narrative in an uninterrupted frieze, and many iconographic details for which parallels must be sought at Bawīt, in Syria, or in the cave churches of Cappadocia.[25] The explanation appears to be that local artists did not always follow the latest metropolitan exemplars, with which they might not be personally familiar, but drew their inspiration from monuments nearer at hand, particularly in the Black Sea cities, which were relatively undamaged. There they would find not only buildings and decorations from late antiquity, but also works of pre-iconoclast Byzantine art, which embodied many oriental features. But one cannot rule out direct influences from eastern Asia Minor, perhaps via the Paulicians settled in Thrace by Basil I.

Another possible influence is that of pre-Christian Bulgar art. The magnificent silver vessels found at Nagy-Szentmiklós in Hungary give us some idea of the art of the steppe peoples, in which Sassanian influences are clearly visible. Some of the capitals and decorative relief plaques recently found in ninth- or tenth-century contexts at Bulgarian sites have a striking stylistic resemblance to the Nagy-Szentmiklós treasures. Such are the lions and griffons from Stara Zagora,[26] a capital from Novi Pazar with a griffon attacking a lion,[27] an altar plaque with peacocks from Stara Zagora, the bronze handle with a lion in relief from Pliska,[29] the sculptured animal head from Preslav,[30] the bone plaque from Preslav,[31] etc. Before making up our minds on this question it would be well to await the results of the further excavations going on at Preslav and elsewhere. But there is certainly a *prima facie* case for influences of this kind. A more remote possibility is that of Slavonic influence, remote because we know so little of the art of the Slavs before their conversion. Yet here too there are suggestive resemblances. The small metal crosses with a rather primitive figure of Christ found at Pliska and elsewhere, and often referred to as 'Palestinian', find close parallels at Zlaté Moravce, Trnovec and Sady,[32] and in belt buckles from Mikulčice with a primitive effigy of a saint in the attitude of an Orans.[33] The round churches of Bulgaria—of which the one at Preslav is the most noteworthy—are without parallel in contemporary Byzantine architecture. But round churches were built in the mid-ninth century at Mikulčice and Staré Město.[34] Are these correspondences between Bulgaria and Moravia the result of western (? Frankish) influence, of parallel development, or of common Slavonic tradition? The question must at present remain open.

Christian Bulgaria then became an artistic province of the Byzantine world in the course of adopting and adapting Byzantine Christian traditions. But it did retain and develop some traits in the visual arts which do not stem from the Constantinople of the Macedonian dynasty, though neither their extent nor their origin can at present be precisely defined. Visual artistic traditions are not dependent for their survival upon a literary tradition; they may endure when all that depends upon the use of words is destroyed in the process of acculturation.

10 Everyday Life

Thus far we have looked at the large-scale features of human societies in our comparison of Bulgaria and Byzantium. Each of these is reflected in the situation of the individual and in his life-style. There are however other features which may be very important in the life of individuals or small groups but which scarcely emerge in a large-scale study. Some of these form the subject matter of the present section.

First would come the question of language, which has already been discussed. Apart from the bilingualism common in frontier areas, in urban society, in coastal towns and ports and so on, a Bulgarian was likely to be a monoglot Slavonic speaker, a Byzantine rather less likely to be a monoglot Greek speaker. The Bulgarian would call his native tongue *slověnĭskij ęzyk* or *bŭlgarskij ęzyk*—Slavonic or Bulgarian. The former term was also applied to Slav speech spoken outside of Bulgaria. To this extent a Bulgarian might feel himself part of a larger linguistic community within which speakers could readily understand one another. This view is brought out by the compiler of the Russian Primary Chronicle who, after recounting how Cyril and Methodius translated the Scriptures into Slavonic, adds, 'The Slavonic tongue is one; and the Slavonic tongue and the Russian are one.' The Bulgarians also used the same word *ęzyk* in the sense of 'language', 'people' and 'race', Greek *glōssa* and *ethnos*. This is not based upon normal Greek usage, as are many of the oddities of Old Slavonic semantics. It may reflect an identification of language and nationality in Bulgarian thought.

In the Byzantine empire Greek was the language of administration, public life and culture. It was also that of the majority of the population. But a very substantial minority spoke other languages, and often wrote in them as well. And those who did speak Greek spoke a very different Greek from the language of literature and public utterance. Greek diglossy has a long history, going back to the later Hellenistic age. By the ninth and tenth centuries many of the major structural changes in the language which turned Ancient Greek into Modern Greek had taken place. The official and literary language, however, continued to be that of late antiquity, that is Atticising literary *koinē*. The difference must not be confused with that between demotic and katharevousa Greek today, which involves questions of public education, political affiliation etc. A nearer, though not a very close, parallel would be the situation in German Switzerland, where private life is conducted in Swiss German, public life in literary German. The Greek speaker, however, unlike the modern Swiss or the medieval Bulgarian, did not feel himself to be part of a larger linguistic unity. There was no language closely resembling Greek. It was unique, *sui generis*, and it was the language of the New Testament and the Church, the language of Hellenic civilisation, and the language of diplomatic relations with foreign powers. Use of it had nothing to do with ethnic origins, but was in its speakers' eyes a mark of high civilisation.

Next there is the relation of the individual to the various groups of which he is a member. The Byzantine, if he did not belong to an ethnic or linguistic or religious minority, was curiously isolated. On the one hand there was his family, usually a nuclear family, on the other the state and the Church. Intermediate groups were weak or non-existent. Cities existed indeed, but no longer as communities with internal self-government. The kind of patriotism or commitment which they had evoked was a thing of the past. Except for marginal areas, tribal, clan or cantonal social units were totally absent. A man might be a member of a village commune, which enjoyed a limited autonomy in its internal affairs, formed a fiscal unit for taxation purposes, and could even act as a legal personality (for instance the inhabitants of the village of Radochosta, near Hierissos, who were involved in litigation with the monastery of Rudaba over a plot of land in 1008).[1] In the course of the tenth century these were being penetrated and in various ways taken over by large landowners, in spite of the series of legal enactments designed to keep them in being. This process had certainly begun in the previous century. The Byzantine family, as envisaged by the law, was a nuclear family of parents and children. Whatever sentimental links there might be with more distant kinsmen they did not form part of the same legal or economic unit. To be sure there were extended families, holding and cultivating their land as a single unit. But they were the exception. And the curious situation revealed by certain financial documents, by which a single *stasis* — roughly 'farm' — could be divided between a number of owners not related to one another, suggests that the extended family holding had been commoner earlier and was in process of disappearing.[2]

For a Bulgarian at this time tribal and clan membership probably still meant something. We hear little or nothing of such matters in the sources. But only a short time before the period under discussion

Slavonic tribes were political realities in Danubian Bulgaria, and even more in Thrace and Macedonia. The centralising policy of the Khans from Krum to Boris cannot have altogether effaced all memory of this organisation of society. It was probably reflected in local differences in clothing and decoration, dialect, song, dance, poetry etc., differences which are very marked between different regions of Bulgaria today, and which many scholars consider to be of great antiquity.[3] So far as the sources enable one to judge, the village commune of free peasants was a more widespread institution in Bulgaria than in the Byzantine empire in the ninth and tenth centuries, though there too it was in process of dissolution. Finally, the extended family as an economic and legal unit appears to have been widespread in Bulgaria, as no doubt in other southern Slav lands, in which it survived here and there until the nineteenth century. It is still a reality in Albania.[4] The evidence consists almost entirely of documents regarding property in Bulgarian lands after the Byzantine conquest. If the extended family was widespread then, *a fortiori* it was widespread in the Bulgarian Kingdom, from which no such documents survive. It is interesting in this connection to note that Theophylact, Greek Archbishop of Ohrid at the end of the eleventh century, comments on the size of Bulgarian loaves—enough to feed ten or more grown men.[5] Is this evidence for the average size of Bulgarian households?

Bulgarian dress was distinct from Byzantine. A tenth century text included in the Miracles of St George speaks of a Bulgarian wearing native costume— στολὴ Βουλγαρική.[6] When Symeon proclaimed himhimself emperor he adopted Byzantine imperial costume and no doubt imposed Byzantine dress on his court. But a contemporary Byzantine source records that at the time of his death his two younger sons Ivan and Benjamin 'still wore Bulgarian dress'. In what did the difference consist? A tenth-century Byzantine source—which must be quoting a much earlier text—declares that Bulgarian dress was taken over from the Avars[7] From the late sixth-century *Strategicon* of Maurice and from archaeological evidence we learn that the Avars wore long kaftans of leather or fur descending to the knees, linen tunics, trousers and moccasin-like boots. Both Avar and Bulgarian dress were certainly influenced by Iranian models. Liutprand of Cremona in the tenth century speaks of Bulgarian envoys in Constantinople having their hair cut *ungarico more* and wearing bronze chain belts.

Byzantine sources sometimes speak of Bulgarians as wearing skins. This is in part a mere insult, which is belied by what we know of

Bulgarian textile production. But furs, and above all sheepskin cloaks, were no doubt worn by all Bulgarians in winter. It was such a sheepskin cloak or rug that a twelfth-century metropolitan of Philippopolis sent to his friend in Constantinople, calling it by its Slavonic name of λοσνίχιον (ložnik). The portrait of Basil II on the frontispiece of his Psalter, now in the Marcian Library in Venice, depicts conquered Bulgarians grovelling at his feet. They are wearing long, sleeved robes of red, two shades of blue, purple and white, with belts, and bracelets or armbands on their upper arms. But the motif of the conquered enemy is a traditional one, and the artist may merely have copied his model, without any direct knowledge of what Bulgarians might wear. A miniature painting in the *Menology* prepared for Basil II, now in Paris, shows Bulgarian officers wearing kaftan-like garments down to the knees, belts and tight trousers. Bulgarian dress in more recent times shows many common features with Serbian and Ukrainian dress, which are probably to be interpreted as part of a common Slavonic inheritance. And some ethnographers have detected similarities between the local dress of north-eastern Bulgaria where the Proto-Bulgars first settled — and that of the Chuvash people on the upper Kama, who are the descendants of the Volga Bulgars. In these they have seen Bulgar, as distinct from Slavonic, traits. The *Responsa* of Nicholas I indicate that Bulgarian men wore trousers — or possibly gaiters — and some kind of head-cloth or turban. It is difficult in the absence of descriptions or reliable representations to go much further than this. Byzantine male costume of the period comprised breeches and a *chiton* or shirt coming half-way down the thighs, worn with a belt over which the upper classes wore a long rectangular *himation* pinned with a fibula on the right shoulder, leaving the arm free. Cloaks, capes, hoods and the like were worn in bad weather. Women wore a long dress reaching to the ground and belted. High boots were worn by both sexes. The clothes of the upper classes were richly embroidered and in winter sometimes trimmed with fur. Bulgarian and Byzantine could be distinguished at first sight. When King Boris II fled from Constantinople to Bulgaria, he was killed by a Bulgarian frontier-guard, who mistook him for a Greek because of his dress (Cedrenus II 335).

Both Bulgarians and Byzantines were likely to be outwardly ortho-dox Christians, though a Bulgarian was not unlikely to be in fact a dualist Bogomil. But Bulgarians shared a body of folk-tale and legend, of belief in various kinds of goblins and fairies, of semi-pagan ritual connected with agriculture, which was different from and in some ways richer than that of the medieval Greek world. Where we find common beliefs and practices shared by the Bulgarians in later times with the Serbs and the Ukrainians, there is considerable probability that it is a relic of a common Slavonic culture. Where this agreement in legend and rite extends to the western Slavs or to the Russians, as is the case with the belief in *vile* and the rites connected with them, the probability becomes overwhelming. So a lively and varied folklore of his own marked off the Bulgarian from the Byzantine. The Byzantine, on the other hand, is much more likely to have had a local saint or martyr whose cult provided a focus for his religious life. Connected with this difference is a whole series of observances associated with birth, marriage and death in which the two peoples varied. Byzantine practices comprised much that was pre-Christian or non-Christian in origin.[8] Bulgarian practice in later times shows the familiar link with that of other Slav peoples, particularly Serbs and Ukrainians, which is suggestive of common Slavonic origin.

Bulgarian diet was distinct from that of the Byzantine world. Little or no olive oil, more cheese and milk products, less fish but more meat, millet in place of wheat, and so on. Pulses played a large part in the diet of both communities, though the varieties may not always have been the same. Much that is common to all the Balkan peoples today, such as the tomato, the different varieties of pepper, maize, the potato, the aubergine, and rice, is of later introduction. Before the levelling produced by these new food plants, the differences in diet between the northern and southern Balkans were much greater than in modern times. The extensive fruit-growing characteristic of modern Bulgaria is also a relatively recent development. In the ninth and tenth centuries the number and variety of cultivated fruits was probably less in Bulgaria than in most provinces of the Byzantine empire.

In many ways then, which we cannot always discern clearly today, everyday life was different in Bulgaria and in Byzantium. These differences must have produced an immediate sense of strangeness and disorientation in the man or woman who moved from the one region to the other, long before the deeper differences had time to make their impression.

11   Conclusions

No single factor has emerged as determining the different course of events in Byzantium and Bulgaria in the ninth and tenth centuries. As usual in such cases, we are left with a series of factors, reflecting, no doubt, the complexity of human affairs. But it is in a way an unsatisfactory situation for the historian to find himself in, as it buries the problem of historical causation under a mountain of contingent causes operating in different directions. What one can do, however, is try to single out those factors whose effect appears to have been deepest and most lasting, and try to establish some kind of priority among them. E. H. Carr, whose life work has been concerned with a period where the historian has to cope with too much rather than too little information, speaks of the

> professional compulsion . . . to establish some hierarchy of causes which would fix their relation to one another, perhaps to decide which cause, or which category of causes, should be regarded 'in the last resort' or 'in the final analysis' (favourite phrases of historians) as the ultimate cause, the cause of all causes . . . the historian is known by the causes which he invokes.[1]

Bulgaria, although almost within sight of the Mediterranean, had evidently a lower level of agricultural and industrial production and of trade than the provinces of the Byzantine empire. Though we need not take at their face-value the occasional Byzantine references to the Bulgarians as skin-clad savages, the record is eloquent enough. The failure to develop a monetary economy points both to a low level of exchange and a small internal market, and to the inability of the state to accumulate precious metals. The limited internal market need not imply that the primary producer made no surplus over and above what was needed to keep himself and his family alive. The surplus could be creamed off by taxation or by various feudal dues. We know too little of Bulgarian taxation to make any guess as to its economic effects. There was probably a fixed assessment on each unit of agricultural land, on the Byzantine pattern, but payable in kind. Such a taxation structure should have encouraged increased production, other things being equal. The failure to accumulate treasure is a feature shared by all European states other than the

Byzantine empire in the early Middle Ages. The gold of Europe and the Near East flowed inexorably to Constantinople and Baghdad.

It might be thought that the primary reason for the economic backwardness of Bulgaria was the physical destruction resulting from the long years of invasion and devastation. This no doubt played its part. But the infrastructure of ancient agriculture and industry was neither complex nor dependent on heavy capital investment. Particular items such as olive or mulberry trees involved a wait of a generation from planting to first crop. But these were not the object of monoculture. They were grown along with a variety of other crops, often inter-sown with cereals and the like. There were few elaborate irrigation or drainage works to restore. And the cities, though damaged, were not razed to the ground like Carthage. They could have been used and up to a point were used by the newcomers. But, as has been seen, the Slavs generally preferred at first to settle near, not in, the physical shells of late Roman cities.

Production requires not only land and raw materials, but skilled labour, and sometimes high expertise. The Slavs and Bulgars when they first appeared in the Balkans lacked skilled craftsmen and technicians. But this shortage could soon have been made up from the numerous prisoners, defectors and immigrants from the Byzantine world, whose skills would be in even more demand on account of their rarity. Where it was important, Bulgarian technology fell little short of that of Byzantium. Krum's 30,000 men in full armour, or the stone-carvers and ceramic artists of Preslav, remind us that there was nothing inevitable about Bulgarian backwardness. It was a historical, not an ethnological phenomenon.

What did prevent Bulgaria from taking over Byzantine civilisation, as the Japanese took over industrial capitalist civilisation, was above all the structure and organisation of Bulgarian society itself. The Slavs, whatever may have been their organisation in their homeland, were broken up into an infinity of tiny political units during the long years of expansion. The Slav principalities were not only small, they were egalitarian. Even their enslaved prisoners of war were absorbed into the community after a certain number of years. They were not without private property, but it may be doubted how far they recognised individual, as opposed to communal, property in land. Their principalities formed confederations and alliances, but these were short-lived in the period of migration: each group moved and settled on its own. Once they established themselves in the Balkans larger and more lasting political units appear. And social and economic differentiation within each community becomes greater. Had they been living in a political vacuum the Balkan Slavs would in due course have created one or several large states, with permanent boundaries and more or less fixed political and administrative structure. This was done by the western Slavs in Moravia in the early ninth century (the Moravian state established by Samo in the seventh century seems to have been quite ephemeral), in Bohemia later in the same century, and in Poland in the tenth century. But such a development would have been difficult in the immediate neighbourhood of the Byzantine empire and on territory which the empire regarded as its own. In the outcome the Slav settlers in peninsular Greece were Hellenised and absorbed, those in the north-east Balkans became subject to the Bulgars, and only in the north-west Balkans were they able to develop their own political organisations in some degree of independence.

Such a society in its early days was incapable of accumulating and concentrating the reserves of wealth necessary for the Byzantine way of life. Its basic units—the villages—were largely autarkic, and there was no established class divorced from primary production and able to enjoy leisure and large material resources. After the formation of the Bulgarian state and the extension of its control over most of the northern Balkans the possibility of such a development existed, and was indeed to some extent realised. Boris and Symeon wanted their kingdom to be on a par with the empire. They strove according to their abilities to make Preslav a second Constantinople, with a monarch appointed by God, a patriarch, churches and palaces, the outward trappings of power and the ornaments of advanced civilisation. But in the first place they could only maintain political independence by concentrating a great part of the surplus production of their country in unproductive military activities. And secondly the proximity of the empire distorted their own developing economy by attracting Bulgarian agricultural and other products to Byzantine markets, and turning the country into a producer of raw materials. As the boyars and the Slav chieftains became great territorial magnates they found it more profitable to send their surplus products to Constantinople and Thessalonika in exchange for the prestigious luxury products of Byzantine industry than to encourage the development of industry and commerce in their own cities, which remained small and relatively undeveloped. In this way the grandiose dreams of Boris and Symeon ended in the dreary reality of Peter's long reign, when Bulgaria became a harmless Byzantine protectorate, whose citizens shed their blood to keep the Magyars from reaching the imperial city on the Bosphorus. And after Peter's death the logic of history and the traditions of the Roman empire led the Byzantines to take over their protectorate and reassert their sovereignty over territory which had been lost to them for nearly four centuries.

Even then the take-over proved harder than anyone in Constantinople imagined. Cowed and impoverished, the Bulgarians resisted, and it took a further generation of bitter fighting, under the command of a great military emperor, before the last sparks of Bulgarian independence appeared to be extinguished. They were not in fact extinguished, and Byzantine rule in Bulgaria was marked by a series of revolts which have no parallel in other provinces of the empire and which led, towards the end of the twelfth century, to the re-establishment of an independent Bulgarian Kingdom. And, later, after five centuries of absorption in the Ottoman empire, the Bulgarian state re-emerged in 1878 as a viable political unit.

Some of the more superficial differences between life in Bulgaria and in the Byzantine empire have been outlined in Chapter Ten. But the argument of this book is that there were other, more profound differences between the two societies which were reflected in the situation of the average Bulgarian and the average Byzantine. Some of these may be recapitulated here.

First, Byzantine society was 'totalitarian'; there were few groups of any significance intermediate between the empire on the one hand, and a man and his immediate family on the other. It was not so in Bulgaria, where the creation of a single political community was relatively recent, and where the old political organisation of the Slavs in village communities, tribes and principalities cannot have vanished overnight. A man's membership of such a lower group could for most of his life be far more important than the fact that he was a subject of the king in Pliska or Preslav. We know woefully little of the day-to-day administration of Bulgaria. But what we do know suggests that while the king's government carried out—or tried to carry out—the 'law and order' functions of the state, many of its other functions were performed by older groups still playing a quasi-political role. We never hear, for instance, of local officers of the king's judiciary in Bulgaria. Disputes were presumably settled by village assemblies and tribal authorities, with only occasional interference by the central government. The same must have been true of most of those functions of the state concerned with the distribution of resources on a local scale, minor public works and so on.

Again, a Byzantine, as such, was alone in the world, both as a member of that Christian empire which liked to call itself 'the new Israel', and as the heir to Greek tradition. True, there were Christian communities which were outside the political control of the empire. But in the ninth and tenth centuries the average Byzantine had no contact with them and little knowledge of them. In any case their separation from the Byzantine Christian community was regarded as accidental and temporary. Similarly there were Greek-speaking groups outside the empire, notably in Sicily and in Crete. But these were areas of recent Arab conquest which would no doubt be regained by the empire in due course—Crete was in fact regained in the middle of the tenth century. A Bulgarian, on the other hand, was aware, however vaguely, of belonging to a larger, Slavonic community, with which he shared his language and many elements in his culture. Even the Slavonic liturgy which he heard in his church was composed by men from Thessalonika and first used in remote Moravia. We must not exaggerate this sense of Slavonic unity and give it nineteenth-century overtones. Yet it was there. Svjatoslav's pagan Russian soldiers may have swept through Bulgaria with fire and sword, but at least men could understand what they were saying.

A further point is concerned with the relationship of man to the land. In the Byzantine empire land was a saleable commodity. It could also be rented on various terms, mortgaged etc., and there was a great body of law, much of it of venerable antiquity, which governed such transactions. No doubt most land remained in the hands of the same family or the same community for generations. But the possibility of its alienation was nevertheless there. In a community without money, or in which money found only a very limited use, land is virtually inalienable, not because the law forbids transference of ownership, but because there is in general nothing to exchange it for. Such must have been the case in Bulgaria in the ninth and tenth centuries. Hence the bond between a family, or a village community, and the land which it cultivated must have been closer than in Byzantium, and must have appeared to those most concerned to be part of the eternal order of things. Nevertheless the political and economic forces which drove the powerful to extend their control over their weaker neighbours, and the weak to seek the protection of the strong, continued to operate and to create in Bulgaria what we may loosely term a feudal society.

Yet they could not easily operate by the direct transference of owner-ship of land, and where they did that transference would have an aspect of illegality and of naked force. In fact various attributes of ownership must often have passed to powerful magnates while the legal title re-mained with the original owners. We hear a good deal of the social and economic tensions created in Byzantium by the growth of great estates at the expense of peasant land holdings. In Bulgaria, though we hear little of them, these tensions must have been all the greater for the fact that land was not thought of as a commodity.

Finally, the relative inalienability of land is only an aspect of another important respect in which the situation of the individual in Bulgaria differed from that of his counterpart in Byzantium. In a moneyless society a man cannot easily rise in status through economic activity. In the Byzantine empire it was very easy to raise one's status in this way. True, the position of the merchant was formally a humble one, how-ever rich he might become. But in fact through the contacts he esta-blished in the machinery of government he could come to occupy an important situation. The persons to whom the control of Bulgarian trade with the empire was given in 924 are said to have been merchants, and to have been familiars of Stylianos Zaoutzes, the father-in-law and favourite of Leo VI. Other forms of entrepreneurial activity brought more immediate and tangible rewards. The story of St Philaretos, a prosperous peasant or minor landowner in Asia Minor who in the early ninth century rose to great wealth and influence by skilful use of his economic power in an agrarian community is illuminating. He was what in more recent times might have been called a kulak. He can have had few counterparts in Bulgaria. In fact social mobility in general must have been much less in Bulgaria than in Byzantium, and that at a time when the most drastic and radical changes were taking place in Bulgarian society and the Bulgarian state. This relative rigidity explains in part the failure of Bulgaria to become a second Byzantium.

The consolidation in the reigns of Boris and Symeon—exactly 75 years—of a style of life which owed much, including its Christianity, to Byzantine models, but was in many respects quite un-Byzantine, had given the Bulgarians a consciousness of their own distinctive-ness which they retained throughout the two centuries of Byzantine rule. I have described this as the development of Bulgarian nationality. Its most striking symptom—and one which set up a barrier against the penetration of Byzantine culture—was the use of Slavonic rather than Greek as the language of administration, worship and literature. The second Bulgarian Kingdom of the thirteenth and fourteenth centuries was in a way more Byzantinised than the first. Its princes and notables inter-married with Greek families. Its men of letters were sometimes as much at home in Greek as in Slavonic. Yet it never became Hellenised. Nor did it become provincial. Its monarchs and statesmen seldom acted as Byzantine puppets or felt themselves to be the instruments of Byzantine policy. The growth of Bulgarian nationality, with its own peculiar profile, helped to end the Byzantine myth of oecumenicity, the concept that the empire was a unique instrument of providence whose boundaries, in the fullness of time, must be those of the inhabited world.

Though the conversion of Prince Vladimir of Kiev was a stroke of Byzantine diplomacy whose immediate purpose may have been strategic, the christianising of Russia and the drawing of that great country into the orbit of Mediterranean and European civilisation was largely the work, either directly or through their writings, of men from Bulgaria. And the whole pattern of Russian public life was strongly influenced by Bulgarian models. The Princes of Kiev, and later the Princes of Muscovy, belonged to the Byzantine Commonwealth, to use Obolensky's phrase. But politically, in their literary cultures, and in the details of their everyday life, the Russians maintained a distance and independence which had been foreshadowed by the Bulgaria of Boris and Symeon, whose literature and ideas they took over and made their own.

Lastly, in the Bogomil heresy the Bulgarians, building their own edifice out of Byzantine materials, developed a view of the universe which answered the hopes — and the despair — of the underdogs of the feudal world better than the subtle dogma and the hierarchical structure of official Christianity. How far the spread of dualist doctrines in medieval Europe is due to direct Bulgarian influence is a hard question to which the present writer would not presume to offer an answer. Certainly Bulgarian missionaries played a role in the spread of Bogomilism in Serbia and Bosnia, where its hold became peculiarly tenacious. Their contribution to the growth of the Cathar movement in Italy and France is much less certain. Yet the French *bougre* and its English derivative preserve even today the memory of an intellectual and social movement of protest originating in the first Bulgarian Kingdom and stimulated by its confrontation with the empire of east Rome.

Chronological Table
Bibliography
Notes
Index

Chronological Table

741	Accession of Constantine V. Further Byzantine victories over Arabs.
756-75	Constantine V tries to expel Bulgars from Balkans. Nine campaigns in which invasion of Bulgarian Thrace is combined with naval expedition to Danube.
763	Crushing defeat of Khan Telets by Constantine V at Anchialus.
777	Khan Telerig flees to Constantinople, accepts baptism, and is married to a cousin of Leo IV.
784	Empress ·Irene visits Berrhoea (Stara Zagora) and christens it Irenopolis.
792	Khan Kardam defeats Constantine VI at Marcellae.
791-6	Charlemagne invades Avar territory in Pannonia.
c 800	Avar empire collapses under attack by Franks, Slavs and Bulgars. Krum, leader of Bulgar revolt in Pannonia, becomes Khan of an empire extending from Black Sea to Theiss, and marching with Frankish empire.
807	Nicephorus I opens hostilities against Bulgaria, but is defeated by Krum near Strymon.
809	Krum captures Serdica. Nicephorus sacks and burns Pliska.
811	26 July: Krum defeats Byzantine army and kills Nicephorus.
812	Krum captures Develtos and Mesembria.
813	Bulgarian siege of Constantinople. Krum captures Adrianople and transfers population north of Danube.
814	13 April: death of Krum.
815-6	Khan Omurtag concludes Thirty Years Peace with Byzantium.
827	Bulgarians invade Frankish Croatia.
828	Louis the German leads expedition against Bulgarians.
829	Bulgarians invade Frankish Pannonia.
c 831	Bulgarians occupy Serdica and Philippopolis and annex central Macedonia.
832	Peace treaty between Franks and Bulgarians.
852	Accession of Khan Boris. Bulgarians invade Frankish territory.
860	Surprise Russian attack on Constantinople.
c 862	Bulgarian alliance with Frankish emperor Louis the German.
864	Byzantine military threats force Boris to renounce

Frankish alliance and to accept Christianity from Constantinople. Revolt of boyars ruthlessly suppressed.

868   Boris asks Louis the German to send a bishop and priests and requests Pope Nicholas I to appoint an independent Patriarch of Bulgaria. *Responsa* of Nicholas I and arrival of Roman clergy in Bulgaria.

870   Anti-Photian Council of Constantinople returns Bulgaria to jurisdiction of Patriarch of Constantinople. Roman clergy expelled from Bulgaria. Archbishop of Bulgaria consecrated by Patriarch Ignatius.

882   Methodius visits Constantinople at invitation of Basil I.

885   Death of Methodius in Moravia. His disciples welcomed to Bulgaria by Boris.

886   Clement sent to Ohrid.

889   Abdication of Boris in favour of his eldest son Vladimir-Rasate. Anti-Christian movement among boyars.

893   Deposition of Vladimir-Rasate and accession of Symeon. Slavonic proclaimed official language of church and state in Bulgaria.

894   Transfer of Bulgarian trade from Constantinople to Thessalonika. Symeon invades Thrace.

895   Leo VI invites Magyars to invade Bulgaria. Symeon calls in Pechenegs, who drive Magyars from Moldavia to Pannonia.

896   Symeon defeats Byzantines at Bulgarophygon. Peace concluded, with annual tribute for Bulgaria.

904   Capture of Thessalonika by Arabs under Leo of Tripoli.

907   2 May: death of Boris.

912   Death of Leo VI. His successor Alexander cuts off tribute to Bulgaria and insults Bulgarian envoys. Symeon invades Thrace and appears before walls of Constantinople.

913   4 June: death of Alexander. Regency council appointed for boy emperor Constantine VII. Symeon once again appears before Constantinople. Negotiations between Symeon and Patriarch Nicolaus Mysticus. August: coronation of Symeon as King of the Bulgarians in Constantinople, and probable betrothal of his daughter to Constantine VII.

914   Palace revolution in Constantinople. Nicolaus Mysticus

	removed from regency council. Agreement with Symeon repudiated. Symeon invades Thrace and takes Adrianople.
915-6	Bulgarian operations near Dyrrhachium and Thessalonika.
917	Byzantine invasion of Bulgaria. 20 August: Symeon routs Byzantines at Achelous and sweeps into Thrace.
918	Byzantine diplomacy entangles Bulgaria in war with Serbia. Bulgarian occupation of Thessaly.
920	Romanus Lecapenus crowned co-emperor with Constantine VII, who marries his daughter.
921-2	Bulgarian army before Constantinople.
923	Bulgarians recapture Adrianople.
924	Bulgarian army before Constantinople. Autumn: meeting of Symeon and Romanus Lecapenus at Cosmidium.
c 926	Archbishopric of Bulgaria raised to independent patriarchate. Bulgarian army defeated in Croatia by King Tomislav.
927	27 May: death of Symeon and accession of his son Peter. Autumn: Peter marries Maria Lecapena. Byzantines recognise Bulgarian patriarchate and undertake to pay annual subsidy to Bulgaria.
934	Magyars invade Bulgaria.
940s	Growth of Bogomil heresy in Bulgaria.
943	Magyars invade Bulgaria.
958-60	Magyars invade Bulgaria.
965	Death of Maria Lecapena. Nicephorus Phocas refuses to pay Bulgarian subsidy, makes raids into Bulgaria and negotiates alliance with Svjatoslav of Kiev.
967	Svjatoslav overruns Dobrudja.
968	Pechenegs, at Bulgarian request, attack Kiev. Svjatoslav withdraws from Bulgaria.
969	Svjatoslav returns, captures Preslav and Philippopolis, occupies eastern Bulgaria and threatens Constantinople, with Magyars, Bulgars and Pechenegs as allies.
970	John Tzimisces defeats Svjatoslav at Arcadiopolis.
971	Byzantines annex eastern Bulgaria, capture Preslav, and defeat Svjatoslav at Silistria. Boris II abdicates and Bulgaria is proclaimed a Byzantine province.

970s	Establishment of independent state in western Bulgaria under Samuel, David, Moses and Aaron.
980	Samuel entitles himself King of the Bulgarians and begins regular invasions of northern Greece.
986	Samuel captures Larissa, defeats Basil II, and recaptures Preslav and Pliska.
989	Samuel captures Berrhoea in Macedonia. Conversion of Vladimir, son of Svjatoslav.
990-4	Basil II recaptures Berrhoea and many other Macedonian cities.
995	Basil II goes to eastern front. Samuel defeats Byzantine army near Thessalonika.
996	Byzantines recapture Larissa and Bulgarians abandon northern Greece.
1001-3	Basil II returns to Bulgarian front and recaptures many points in Thrace and Macedonia.
1004	Basil II besieges Vidin. Samuel sacks Adrianople. Basil II captures and garrisons Vidin. Bulgarians defeated near Skopje.
1005	Byzantines recapture Dyrrhachium.
1006-14	Byzantine campaigns in western Bulgaria.
1014	29 July: disastrous Bulgarian defeat at Cimbalongus. Death of Samuel.
1014-8	Collapse and disintegration of Bulgaria.
1015	Basil II takes Ohrid.
1016	Basil II besieges Pernik.
1017	Further Byzantine victories.
1018	Bulgarian King John Vladislav attacks Dyrrhachium and is killed. Pernik surrenders to Byzantines. Basil receives surrender of Queen Maria and Bulgarian royal family at Ohrid, makes triumphant progress through conquered territory, and goes on to Athens.
1019	Last Bulgarian resistance overcome.

Bibliography

1   There is no book which systematically examines the institutions and way of life of the Byzantine empire and Bulgaria during the crucial ninth and tenth centuries from a comparative standpoint, though there are many discussions of their political relations and of Byzantine policy on the northern frontier. Chapters 3, 4 and 5 (pp. 69-163) of D. Obolensky, *The Byzantine Commonwealth: Eastern Europe 500-1453*, London, 1971 provide a penetrating and thought-provoking treatment of some of the topics of the present book. P. Mutafchiev, 'Der Byzantinismus im mittelalterlichen Bulgarien', *Byzantinische Zeitschrift* 30 (1929-30), 387-94, D. Angelov, 'Die gegenseitigen Beziehungen und Einflüsse zwischen Byzanz und dem mittelalterlichen Bulgarien', *Byzantino-Slavica* 20 (1959), 40-49; id., 'Vizantijski vlijanija vŭrkhu srednovekovna Bŭlgarija', *Istoricheski Pregled* 4 (1947-8), 401-16, and 5 (1948-9), 587-601 pose questions rather than suggest answers. The geographical background is still best set out by J. Cvijic, *La péninsule balkanique: géographie humaine*, Paris, 1918, particularly pp. 45-79.

2   There are many general histories of the Byzantine empire. The best is G. Ostrogorsky, *History of the Byzantine State*, trans. by Joan Hussey, second edn, Oxford, 1968; Ostrogorsky confines himself to political history. More wide-ranging, though less sure in judgement, are A.A. Vasiliev, *History of the Byzantine Empire*, 2 vols. Madison, Wisconsin, 1958; L. Bréhier, *Le monde byzantin*, 3 vols., Paris, 1947-50 (paperback reprint now available); S. D. Skazkin (ed.), *Istorija Vizantii*, 3 vols., Moscow, 1967 (a German translation of this important Marxist work is in preparation); K. A. Amantos, *Historia tou Byzantinou Kratous*, 2 vols., second/third edn, Athens, 1957-63; J. M. Hussey (ed.), *The Cambridge Medieval History*, vol. IV, 2 parts, Cambridge, 1966, 1967 (a work of collaboration, of very uneven merit, and occasionally out of date); D. A. Zakythinos, *Hē Byzantinē Autokratoria 324-1071*, Athens, 1969; D. Angelov, *Istorija na Vizantija*, 3 vols., Sofia, 1959-67 (interesting as giving a Bulgarian Marxist point of view). R. J. H. Jenkins, *Byzantium: The Imperial Centuries*, London, 1966 deals with the period from 610 to 1071. P. Whitting (ed.), *Byzantium: An Introduction*, Oxford, 1971 is based on a series of lectures broadcast by the B.B.C. in 1968.

3   Among studies of Byzantine civilisation, which presume at least an outline knowledge of Byzantine history, there are several excellent short works by English scholars. N. H. Baynes, *The Byzantine Empire*, London, 1925 and S. Runciman, *Byzantine Civilisation*, London, 1933. Both date

slightly, but are nevertheless essential reading. N. H. Baynes and H. St.
L. B. Moss (eds.), *Byzantium*, Oxford, 1948 has the unevenness characteristic of books written by many hands. J. M. Hussey, *The Byzantine
World*, London, 1957 is perhaps the best introduction. Ch. Diehl, *Les
grands problèmes de l'histoire byzantine*, Paris, 1943 is a disappointing
work written by a great scholar in his old age and during the occupation
of his country. H. Hunger, *Das Reich der neuen Mitte*, Graz-Vienna-
Cologne, 1965 is long and suggestive, but rather narrowly concerned
with religion. H. Haussig, *A History of Byzantine Civilisation*, trans. by
J. M. Hussey, London, 1971 is unhistorical and confused, but for those
who read with critical alertness contains many striking observations.
A. P. Kazhdan, *Vizantijskaja kul'tura*, Moscow, 1968, is an unpretent-
ious but first-class examination of the distinguishing traits of Byzantine
civilisation. Ph. Koukoulès, *Byzantinōn bios kai politismos*, 6 vols.,
Athens, 1948-57 is an impressive compilation of material from Byzantine
literature on a great variety of topics; the author tends to put together
side by side evidence from the fourth and the fourteenth centuries without
distinction; but for those who can make their own distinctions this un-
wieldy work is an inexhaustible mine of information.

4   The economic history of the Byzantine empire is given rather stepmotherly treatment in general economic histories of the Middle Ages,
such as R. H. Bautier, *The Economic Development of Medieval Europe*,
London, 1971; G. A. J. Hodgett, *Social and Economic History of Medieval
Europe*, London, 1972. There are useful chapters in the *Cambridge
Economic History of Europe* vols. I-III, 1954-61. Many important
studies are collected in G. Ostrogorsky, *Privreda i društvo u vizantiskom
carstvu*, Belgrade, 1969. Of basic importance for land tenure and agrarian
economy is P. Lemerle, 'Esquisse pour une histoire agraire de Byzance.
Les sources et les problèmes', *Revue Historique* 219 (1958), 32-74, 254-
84, and 220 (1958), 43-94. Leo VI's *Book of the Prefect* has given rise
to several important studies, of which the most valuable are A. Stöckle,
Spätrömische und byzantinische Zünfte, Leipzig, 1911; G. Mickwitz,
*Die Kartellfunktionen der Zünfte und ihre Bedeutung bei der Entstehung
des Zunftwesens*, Helsinki, 1936; and M. Ja. Szuzjumov, *Vizantijskaja
Kniga Eparkha*, Moscow, 1967. A. P. Kazhdan, *Derevnja i gorod v
Vizantii ix-x vv*, Moscow, 1960 is illuminating on many matters
concerning the economic life of the middle Byzantine period. On taxation
see F. Dölger, *Beiträge zur Geschichte der byzantinischen Finanzver-
waltung*, Leipzig, 1927; G. Ostrogorsky, *Die ländliche Steuergemeinde
des byzantinischen Reiches im IOten Jahrhundert*, second edn, Amster-
dam, 1969; E. Schilbach, *Byzantinische Metrologie*, Munich, 1970,
248-63. On coinage see P. Grierson,'Coinage and Money in the Byzantine Empire 498-c. 1090', *Settimane di Studio del Centro Italiano di
Studi sull'Alto Medioevo VIII*, Spoleto, 1961, 411-53.

5   The administrative structure of the Byzantine empire in the period under review is the subject of two admirable studies: J. B. Bury, *The Imperial Administrative System in the Ninth Century*, London, 1911 and Hélène Glykatzi-Ahrweiler, 'Recherches sur l'administration de l'empire byzantin aux ixe-xie siècles', *Bulletin de Correspondance Hellénique* 84 (1960), 1-109. There is much useful information on the administration of the European provinces in A. Bon, *Le Péloponnèse byzantin jusqu'en 1204*, Paris, 1951. On imperial ideology see O. Treitinger, *Die oströmische Kaiser und Reichsidee*, Jena, 1938, reprinted Darmstadt, 1956. An unpublished Oxford thesis by Dr J. D. Howard-Johnston, 'Studies in the Organisation of the Byzantine Army in the Tenth and Eleventh Centuries' provides the best treatment of problems concerning the Byzantine army. On the navy cf. Hélène Ahrweiler, *Byzance et la mer*, Paris, 1966.

6   On science, literature and thought in the middle Byzantine empire see J. M. Hussey, *Church and Learning in the Byzantine Empire 867-1185*, London, 1937; P. Tatakis, *La philosophie byzantine*, Paris, 1949; P. Lemerle, *Le premier humanisme byzantin*, Paris, 1971; K. Krumbacher, *Geschichte der byzantinischen Literatur*, second edn, Munich, 1897 (indispensable as a reference book, though now out of date in many respects); H. G. Beck, *Kirche und theologische Literatur im byzantinischen Reich*, Munich, 1959; Gy. Moravcsik, *Byzantinoturcica*, vol. I, second edn, Berlin, 1958 (on the Byzantine historians). On the visual arts there are many books available, such as D. Talbot Rice, *Art of the Byzantine Era*, London, 1963; id., *The Appreciation of Byzantine Art*, London, 1972; C. Delvoye, *L'art byzantin*, Paris, 1967; V. Lazarev, *Storia della pittura bizantina*, Turin, 1967; J. Beckwith, *Early Christian and Byzantine Art*, London, 1970; W. F. Volbach and J. Lafontaine-Dosogne, *Byzanz und der christliche Osten*, (Propyläen-Kunstgeschichte Bd. 3), Berlin, 1968. There is much important material on the classical tradition in Byzantine art in K. Weitzmann, *Studies in Classical and Byzantine Manuscript Illumination*, Chicago, 1971.

7   Works dealing particularly with Byzantium during the period under study include S. Runciman, *The Emperor Romanus Lecapenus and his Reign*, Cambridge, 1929; E. E. Lipshits, *Ocherki istorii vizantijskogo obshchestva i kul'tury: VIII—pervaja polovina IX veka*, Moscow, 1961; A. Vasiliev, *The Russian Attack on Constantinople*, Cambridge, Mass., 1946; F. Dvornik, *The Photian Schism: History and Legend*, Cambridge, 1948; G. Kolias, *Léon Choerosphactès*, Athens, 1939; A. Toynbee, *Constantine Porphyrogenitus and his Age*, London, 1973.

8   On the invasions and settlements of barbarian peoples in the Balkans in the sixth and seventh centuries the best outline is given by P. Lemerle,

'Invasions et migrations dans les Balkans depuis la fin de l'époque romaine jusqu'au VIIIe siècle', *Revue Historique* 211 (1954), 265-308. V. I. Velkov, *Gradŭt v Trakija i Dakija prez kŭsnata antichnost*, Sofia, 1959 surveys the literary and archaeological evidence concerning the cities of the northern Balkans from the fourth to the sixth century; an English translation is announced for publication. On the Huns cf. E. A. Thompson, *A History of Attila and the Huns*, Oxford, 1948; L. Hambis, *Attila et les Huns*, Paris, 1972. The problems regarding the Avars are fully discussed by A. Kollautz and H. Miyakawa, *Geschichte und Kultur eines völkerwanderungszeitlichen Nomadenvolkes. Die Jou-Jan der Mongolei und die Awaren in Mitteleuropa*, 2 vols., Klagenfurt, 1970. The literature on the Slavonic settlements in the Balkans is vast. F. Dvornik, *The Slavs: Their early History and Civilisation*, Boston, 1959 provides a good introduction. M. Vasmer, *Die Slaven in Griechenland*, Berlin, 1941 surveys the evidence on Slav settlement in Greece. V. Tŭpkova-Zajmova, 'Sur les rapports entre la population indigène des régions balkaniques et les barbares au VIe-VIIe siècles', *Byzantinobulgarica* 1 (1962), 67-78 and V. I. Velkov, 'Les campagnes et la population rurale en Thrace au IVe-VIe siècle', *ibid.*, 31-66 deal particularly with the territory of future Bulgaria. An international symposium on 'The Slavs and the Mediterranean World' was held in Sofia in 1970; the proceedings have not yet been published.

J. Herrmann, 'Byzanz und die Slawen am äussersten Ende des westlichen Ozeans', *Klio* 54 (1972), 309-19 draws attention to Byzantine influences among the western Slavs in the sixth and seventh centuries. The history and civilisation of these western Slavs, particularly in present-day Germany, is exhaustively studied in J. Herrmann (ed.), *Die Slawen in Deutschland*, second edn, Berlin, 1972; new datings obtained by pollen-analysis, dendrochronology and the C14 method make most earlier studies unreliable.

9   The starting point for all serious study of medieval Bulgaria is V. N. Zlatarski's monumental *Istorija na bŭlgarskata dŭrzhava prez srednite vekove*, 4 vols., Sofia, 1918-40. It covers the period from the beginning of the Bulgarian Kingdom to 1280. The first two volumes are concerned with the period under study. Zlatarski provides a detailed historical narrative supported by an exhaustive and critical examination of the sources. He is interested in what the French call '*histoire événementielle*' rather than in institutions, still less in social or economic history. Archaeological evidence thus hardly falls within his field of view. But within the limits set by his time and the school to which he belonged—he lived from 1866 to 1935 and studied at St Petersburg under Lamansky and Vasilevsky— he did first-class work on which all subsequent studies inevitably depend.

The best account available in English of early Bulgarian history is S. Runciman, *A History of the First Bulgarian Empire*, London, 1930.

It gives a lively and lucid picture, based principally on Zlatarski. More recent works include P. Mutafchiev, *Istorija na bŭlgarskija narod* vol. I, Sofia, 1943 (often polemical in tone, and like Zlatarski uninterested in structures); N. S. Derzhavin, *Istorija Bolgarii* vols. 1 and 2, Moscow, 1945, 1946 (an uneven but often illuminating treatment by a distinguished Russian Slavist who sometimes neglects events in favour of structures); P. N. Tret'jakov (ed.), *Istorija Bolgarii*, vol. 1, Moscow, 1954 (brief but clear); D. Kosev (ed.), *Istorija na Bŭlgarija*, vol. 1, Sofia, 1914 (rather disappointing collective work by Bulgarian Marxist scholars, whose interests lie mainly in a later period. D. Angelov and M. Andreev, *Istorija na bŭlgarskata feodalna dŭrzhava i pravo*, Sofia, 1968 discusses the political structure and legal system of medieval Bulgaria. A new work by V. Beševliev, *Die protobulgarische Periode der bulgarischen Geschichte*, is reported in course of printing.

10   The economic and social history of medieval Bulgaria is treated by Derzhavin, Tret'jakov and Kosev. I. Sakăzov, *Bulgarische Wirtschaftsgeschichte*, Berlin-Leipzig, 1929 provides a useful summary of the little that we know, though he does not make adequate use of archaeological evidence. D. Angelov, *Obrazuvane na bŭlgarskata narodnost*, Sofia, 1971 provides a full and many-sided discussion of the development of Bulgarian nationality in the middle ages, with references to the extensive Bulgarian literature on the subject; students who know Bulgarian should not fail to read this book, which will introduce them to all the current problems. See also the collective work *Etnogenezis i kulturno nasledstvo na bŭlgarskija narod*, Sofia, 1971. S. Lishev's works—*Za stokovoto proizvodstvo vŭv feodalna Bŭlgarija*, Sofia, 1957; *Za genezisa na feodalizma v Bŭlgarija*, Sofia, 1963; *Bulgarskijat srednovekoven grad*, 1970—are remarkable for their sophisticated use of archaeological material. They deal mainly with a later period than that under review, but the early chapters of each book are relevant. X. Tŭpkova-Zajmova, *Nashestvija i etnicheski promeni na Balkanite prez vi-vii v*, Sofia, 1966, makes a careful examination of the literary and archaeological sources on the movements of peoples in the Balkans before and up to the foundation of the Bulgarian Kingdom. The same subject is treated more briefly but authoritatively by P. Lemerle, 'Invasions et migrations dans les Balkans depuis la *fin* de l'époque romaine jusqu'au VIIIe siècle', *Revue Historique* 211 (1954), 265-308.

11   On the religious history of Bulgaria in the Middle Ages the best guides are the relevant chapters of Dvornik, *Les Slaves, Byzance et Rome au ixe siècle*, Paris, 1926; A. P. Vlasto, *The Entry of the Slavs into Christendom*, Cambridge, 1970; F. Dvornik, *Byzantine Missions among the Slavs: SS. Constantine-Cyril and Methodius*, New Brunswick, N. J., 1970. On Clement of Ohrid and his influence see I. Snegarov, *Sveti*

Kliment Okhridski, Sofia, 1927; Y. S. Kiselkov, *Sveti Kliment Okhridski*, Sofia, 1941; D. Angelov (ed), *Kliment Okhridski*, Sofia, 1968 (an uneven but valuable collective work). On the Bogomil movement the best introductions are D. Obolensky, *The Bogomils: a Study in Balkan Neo-Manichaeism*, Cambridge, 1948 and D. Angelov, *Bogomilstvoto v Bŭlgarija*, third edn, Sofia, 1969.

12   The archaeological material is scattered through a variety of publications. On the material remains of the early Slavs in Europe see L. Niederle, *Manuel de l'antiquité slave*, 2 vols., Paris, 1923-6; Marija Gimbutas, *The Slavs*, London, 1971. V. Beševliev and J. Irmscher (eds.), *Antike und Mittelalter in Bulgarien*, Berlin, 1960 provides a good introduction to medieval archaeology in Bulgaria with full references to the literature. Important publications since 1960 include Zh. Vŭzharova, *Slavjanski i slavjanobŭlgarski selishta v bŭlgarskite zemi ot kraja na vi-xi v*, Sofia, 1965; S. Michailov, *Pliska, die Hauptstadt des ersten bulgarischen Reiches*, Berlin, 1960; S. Stanchev, *Veliki Preslav*, 2 vols., Sofia, 1966; *Sbornik Preslav*, 2 vols., Sofia, 1968. Reports of current archaeological work in Bulgaria are published in the periodical *Arkheologija*. On medieval Bulgarian costume see J. Ivanov, 'Le costume des anciens Bulgares', *L'art byzantin chez les Slaves: Recueil Th. Uspensky*, I, Paris, 1930, 325-51.

13   On medieval Bulgarian literature and art see E. Georgiev, *Raztsvetŭt na bŭlgarskata literatura v ix-x v*, Sofia, 1962; P. Dinekov (ed.), *Istorija na bŭlgarskata literatura. I: Starobŭlgarskata literatura*, Sofia, 1962; B. D. Filow, *Geschichte der altbulgarischen Kunst bis zur Eroberung des bulgarischen Reichs durch die Türken*, Berlin-Leipzig, 1932; N. Mavrodinov, *Starobŭlgarskata zhivopis*, Sofia, 1946; N. Mavrodinov, *Starobŭlgarskoto izkustvo*, Sofia, 1959; K. Mijatev, *Arkhitekturata v srednovekovna Bŭlgarija*, Sofia, 1965; W. F. Volbach and J. Lafontaine-Dosogne, *Byzanz und der christliche Osten* (Propyläen-Kunstgeschichte Bd. 3), Berlin, 1968, 241-57, Abb. 192-215; M. Bitchev, *L'architecture en Bulgarie*, Sofia, 1961; *Medieval Bulgarian Culture*, Sofia, 1964; Ts. Kristanov and I. Dujchev, *Estestvoznanieto v srednovekovna Bŭlgarija*, Sofia, 1954.

14   A corpus of the written sources for the history of Bulgaria in the Middle Ages is in course of publication: *Izvori za bŭlgarskata istorija*, Sofia, 1954-   . The texts in Greek, Latin, Slavonic or oriental languages are accompanied by a Bulgarian translation. Another collection of source material relevant to the theme of this book is F. Barišić and others (eds.), *Vizantiski izvori za istoriju naroda Jugoslavije*, tom 1, Belgrade, 1955. The inscriptions of the first Bulgarian Kingdom are published with full introduction and commentary by V. N. Beševliev, *Die protobulgarischen*

Inschriften, Berlin, 1963; the editor's rich annotation is a mine of information on early Bulgarian history. Much miscellaneous source material is published by J. Ivanov, *Bŭlgarski starini iz Makedonija*, second edn, Sofia, 1931. The earliest Bulgarian legal code is edited by V. Ganev, *Zakon sudnyj ljudĭm*, Sofia, 1959. I. Dujchev, *Iz starata bŭlgarska knizhnina*, 2 vols., Sofia, 1943 is a handy collection of Old Slavonic texts with valuable introductions and modern Bulgarian translations.

15   Among monographs dealing with short periods or topics in early Bulgarian history V. Gjuzelev, *Knjaz Boris pŭrvi*, Sofia, 1969 is a popular but well-founded account of the life and times of Boris, beautifully illustrated. G. Sergheraert (Christian Gérard), *Syméon le Grand (895-927)*, Paris, 1960 is a much inferior study of Symeon, to be used with caution. Alkmene Stavridou-Zaphraka, *Hē synantēsē Symeōn kai Nikolaou Mystikou (Augoustos 913) sta plaisia tou Byzantinoboulgarikou antagōnismou*, Thessalonika, 1972 examines in detail the problems connected with the 'coronation' of Symeon by the Patriarch in Constantinople in 913. The numerous studies of I. Dujchev on medieval Bulgarian history and literature touch on every aspect of the subjects and are models of careful scholarship. They are collected in *Prouchvanija vŭrkhu bŭlgarskoto srednovekovie*, Sofia, 1945; *Medioevo bizantino-slavo*, 3 vols., Rome, 1965-9; *Slavia Orthodoxa*, London, 1970. G. G. Litavrin, *Bolgarija i Vizantija v xi-xii vv*, Moscow, 1960 deals primarily with the period of Byzantine occupation of Bulgaria, but contains much of interest concerning the period of Bulgarian independence. F. Dölger, *Byzanz und die europäische Staatenwelt*, Ettal, 1953 includes several important studies of Byzantine-Bulgarian political relations in the late ninth and early tenth centuries.

NOTES

2   The Balkans in Late Antiquity and the Origin of Bulgaria

1 Cf. E. Gren, *Kleinasien und der Ostbalkan in der wirtschaftlichen Entwicklung der romischen Kaiserzeit*, 1941.
2 Cf. H. Thompson, 'Athenian Twilight: A.D. 267-600', *Journal of Roman Studies* 49 (1959), 61-72.
3 Cf. V. Georgiev, 'The Genesis of the Balkan Peoples', *Slavonic and East European Review* 44 (1965-6), 285-97.
4 Olympiodorus frg. 27.
5 Jerome *ep.* 60.4.
6 Cyril of Scythopolis, ed. E. Schwartz, 193.24ff.; John Moschus, Migne *PG* 87.3 3025B; Theodore of Petra, *Life of Theodosius*, Migne *PG* 114.495B; *Antonini Placentini Itinerarium* 183.
7 *Expositio totius mundi et gentium* 50; Justinian *Novel* 26 pr.
8 Cf. C. Weigand, *Die Aromunen*, 2 vols., Leipzig 1894-5; M. Gyóni, 'La transhumance des Valaques balcaniques au Moyen Age', *Byzantinoslavica* 12 (1950), 29ff.; C. Daicovici, E. Petrovici, G. Stefan, *Die Entstehung des rumänischen Volkes und der rumänischen Sprache*, Bucarest, 1964; H. Mihăescu, 'Die lateinische Sprache in Sudosteuropa', *Zeitschr. f. Balkanologie* 6 (1968), 128-36.
9 Cf. C. Höeg, *Les Saracatsans*, 2 vols., Paris-Copenhagen, 1925-6; V. Marinov, *Prinos kŭm izuchavaneto na proizkhoda, bita i kulturata na Karakachanite v Bulgarija*, Sofia, 1964; id., 'Podvizhno pastirstvo v Bŭlgarija i na balkanskija poluostrov', *Izvestija na Etnografskija Institut i Muzej* 8 (1965), 79ff.; J.K. Campbell, *Honour, family and patronage: a study of institutions and moral values in a Greek mountain community*, Oxford, 1964.
10 On the fate of the cities of the Balkans, and in particular of Bulgaria, during the Avar and Slav invasions cf. V. I. Velkov, *Gradŭt v Trakija i Dakija Prez Kŭsnata antichnost*, Sofia, 1959 — an admirable work which unfortunately does not go beyond 600; V. Beševliev, 'Les cités antiques en Mésie et en,Thrace et leur sort à l'époque du haut moyen âge', *Études Balkaniques* 5 (1966), 207-20 — where full references to the literature will be found; and the opening chapters of S. I. Lishev, *Bŭlgarskijat srednovekoven grad*, Sofia, 1970.
11 Cf. V. Beševliev, 'Aus der Geschichte der Protobulgaren', *Études Balkaniques* 6 (1970), 39-56.
12 Cf. V. N. Zlatarski, 'Izvestieto na Mikhail Sirijski za preselenieto na Bŭlgarite', *Izvestija na Bŭlgarskoto Istorichesko Druzhestvo* 4 (1915), 38-52.

13 On the relations of the Proto-Bulgars with the various Slav tribes of Moesia and on the frontiers on the earliest Bulgarian state cf. the discussion by I. Dujčev, 'Obedinenieto na slavjanskite plemena v Mizija prez VII u.', *Izsledvanija vchest na Marin Drinov*, Sofia, 1960, 417-28.
14 Cf. Zh. N. Vŭzharova, 'Slavjani i Prabŭlgari (Tjurko-bŭlgari) v svetlinata na arkheologicheskite danni', *Arkheologija* 13 (1971), 1-21; id., 'Pamjatniki Bolgarii kontsa VI-IX u, i ikh etnicheskaja prinadlezhnost', *Sovetskaja Arkheologija*, 1968, 3, 148-59; id., *Slavjanski i Slavjanobŭlgarski selishta v bŭlgarskite zemi ot Kraja na VI-XI u.*, Sofia, 1965.
15 V. Beševliev, *Die protobulgarischen Inschriften*, Berlin, 1963, No. 4.

3 Bulgaro-Byzantine Relations in the Ninth and Tenth Centuries

1 Cf. the most recent examination of the evidence by Alkmene Stavridou-Zaphraka, *Hē synantēsē Symeon kai Nikolaou Mystikou (Augoustos 913) sta plaisia tou Byzantinoboulgarikou antagōnismou*, Thessaloniki, 1972.
2 Migne *PG* 111.449 ff.
3 On Bulgar primogeniture cf. most recently G. Tsankova-Petkova, 'Vlijanija na vizantijskite politicheski institutsii u Bŭlgarite prez XI vek', *Studia Balcanica* 2 (1970), 98-9.
4 Cf. E. Georgiev, 'Prabŭlgarskoto letopisanie', *Izsledvanija v chest na Marin Drinov*, Sofia, 1960, 369-80.
5 Cf. I. Zaimov, *Bitolski nadpis na Ivan Vladislav, samodurzhets Bŭlgarski*, Sofia, 1970, 79 ff.
6 Cf. L. Petit, Typicon de Grégoire Pacourianos pour le monastère de Petritzos: Supplement to *Vizantijskij Vremennik* 11 (1904), xi ff.
7 Cf. I. Dujčev, 'Tsentry vizantijsko-slavjanskogo obshchenija i sotrudnichestva', *Trudy Otdela Drevnerusskoj Literatury* 19 (1963), 107-29.

4 The Land

1 *Les fondements géographiques de l'histoire de l'Islam* Paris, 1968, 204.
2 Strabo 12.577.
3 Cf. L. Robert, *Journal des Savants*, 1961, 147.
4 On the *Geoponica*, of which we do not yet possess a satisfactory critical edition cf. J. L. Teall, 'The Byzantine Agricultural Tradition', *Dumbarton Oaks Papers* 25 (1971), 33-59, esp. 40-44. Translations into Pehlevi, Arabic, Syriac, Armenian and Latin of the work or of its principal source bear witness to the wide influence of Byzantine agricultural theory.
5 *Vita Clementis* 23.68.
6 On the importance of millet among the Slavs of the north-east Balkans

cf. Zh. N. Vŭzharova, *O proiskhozhdenij bolgarskikh pakhotnykh orudij*, Moscow, 1956, 42.
7 *Book of the prefect 9.6.*
8 Cf. Zh. N. Vŭzharova, *Slavjano-bŭlgarskoto selishte kraj selo Popino, Silistrensko*, Sofia, 1956, 92-4.
9 Cf. J. L. Teall, 'The Byzantine Agricultural Tradition', *Dumbarton Oaks Papers* 25 (1971), 51; G. Duby, *L'économie rurale et la vie des campagnes dans l'occident médiéval*, 1962, 71-9.
10 I. Dujčev, *Iz starata bŭlgarska knizhnina* I, 73.
11 Ibid., 80.
12 Cf. Zh. N. Vŭzharova, *O proiskhozhdenii bolgarskikh pakhotnykh orudij*, Moscow, 1956, passim.
13 The literature on Byzantine land-tenure is immense. Cf. *exempli gratia* : G. Ostrogorsky, *Pour l'histoire de la féodalité byzantine, Brussels*, 1954; P. Lemerle, 'Esquisse pour une histoire agraire de Byzance', *Revue Historique,* 219 (1958), 32-74, 254-84 and 220 (1958), 43-94 (these two studies are fundamental to all modern discussions of the problems); A. P. Kazhdan, *Derevnja i gorod v Vizantii IX-X vv*, Moscow, 1960; Germaine Rouillard, *La vie rurale dans l'empire byzantin*, Paris, 1953; S. Vryonis, 'Byzantium: the social basis of the decline in the eleventh century', *Greek, Roman and Byzantine Studies* 2 (1959) 159-175; K. I. Watanabe, 'Problèmes de féodalité byzantine. Une mise au point sur les diverses discussions', *Hitotsubashi Journal of Arts and Sciences* 5/1 (Jan. 1965), 31-40 and 6/1 (Sept. 1965), 7-24.
14 N. G. Svoronos, 'Recherches sur le cadastre byzantin: le cadastre de Thèbes', *Bulletin de Correspondance Hellénique* 83 (1959), 1-145.
15 Ed. M. H. Fourmy and M. Leroy, *Byzantion* 9 (1934), 113 ff.
16 P. Noailles and A. Dain, *Les Nouvelles de Léon VI le Sage*, Paris, 1944, 376.
17 A convenient summary of the laws in question can be found in D. A. Zakythinos, *Hé Byzantinē autokratoria 324-1071*, Athens, 1969, 252-64.
18 J. Ivanov, *Bŭlgarski starini iz Makedonija*, Sofia, 1931, 547-62.
19 *Anonymi (P. Magutri) Gesta Hungarorum*, ed, Aem. Jakulovich, (Scriptores Rerum Hungaricarum 10), Budapest, 1937, 49-50; *Legenda S. Gerbardi episcopi*, ed. E. M. Madzsar (Scriptores Rerum Hungaricarum 11) Budapest, 1938, 489-90.

5 Cities

1 *Novel* 46, Noailles-Dain, *op. cit.*, 185.
2 A summary of the evidence for and against continuity of occupation of various city-sites will be found S. N. Lishev, *Bŭlgarskijat srednovekoven grad*, Sofia, 1970, 5-26.
3 Cf. E. Kirsten, *Die byzantinische Stadt, Berichte zum XI Internationalen*

Byzantinisten-Kongress, München, 1959, V. 3, Anm. II, 69-72, where a survey of the evidence is given.
4 *Nova Tactica,* ed. H. Gelzer in *Georgii Cyprii descriptio orbis Romani,* Leipzig, 1890, 61-83.
5 For a survey of the economic and demographic situation of Asia Minor in the eleventh century cf. S. Vryonis, *The Decline of Medieval Hellenism in Asia Minor,* Berkeley-Los Angeles-London, 1971, 1-68. There is no comparable survey for an earlier period.
6 References to sources in P. Tivčev, 'Sur les cités byzantines aux XIe-XIIe siècles', *Byzantinobulgarica* 1 (1962), 145-82 and in P. Charanis, 'Observations on the Demography of the Byzantine Empire', *Proceedings of the XIIIth International Congress of Byzantine Studies,* Oxford, 1967, 460.
7 Cf. D. Krůndžalov, 'Is the fortress at Aboba identical with Pliska, the oldest capital of Bulgaria?', *Slavia Antiqua* 13 (1966), 429-49, for a careful statement of the case against the identification.
8 Theophanes 490.26; George the Monk, II, 774.19.
9 Cf. V. Beševliev, *Die protobulgarischen Inschriften,* Berlin, 1963, 276.
10 German translation in V. Beševliev and J. Irmscher, *Antike und Mittelalter in Bulgarien,* Berlin, 1960, 235.
11 V. Beševliev, *Die protobulgarischen Inschriften,* Berlin, 1963, 190-206.
12 V. Beševliev, *Die protobulgarischen Inschriften,* Berlin, 1963, Nos. 3, 81, 85.

6 Industry and Trade

1 Cf. A. Rudakov, *Ocherki vizantijskoj kul'tury po dannym grecheskoj agiografii,* Moscow, 1971, 154-74.
2 Cf. R. H. Bautier, *The Economic Development of Medieval Europe,* 1971, 64.
3 Theophilus Presbyter, *De diversis artibus* 2.16, p, 47, Dodwell.
4 Theophilus Presbyter, *De diversis artibus* 2.13; 2.15, pp. 45, 46, Dodwell.
5 P. Lemerle, A. Guillou, N. Svoronos, *Actes de Lavra, I. Des origines à 1204* Paris, 1970, 324.
6 V. Beševliev, *Die protobulgarischen Inschriften,* Berlin, 1963, 202.
7 Cf. I. Changova, 'Kům prouchvaneto na preslavskata risuvana keramika', *Arkheologija* 1972, 33-9.
8 Cf. M. Stancheva and L. Doncheva-Petkova, 'Srednovekovna bitova keramika ot Eskus pri s. Gigen', *Arkheologija* 1972, 22-32.
9 *Book of the Prefect* 9.6.
10 Their nature is discussed by V. N. Zlatarski, *Istorija na bŭlgarskata dŭrzhava prez srednite vekove* I, 1918, 415-20.
11 Cf. H. Antoniadis-Bibicou, *Recherches sur les dovanes a Byzance,* Paris, 1963.

7   Political Structure

1   Cf. R. Browning and B. Laourdas, *Epeteris tēs Hetaireias Byzantinōn Spoudōn* 27 (1957), 151-212; for a discussion cf. P. Lemerle, *Le premier humanisme byzantin*, Paris, 1971, 246-51.

2   S. E. Malov, *Pamjatniki drevne-tjurkskoj pis'mennosti; Teksty i issledovanija*, Moscow, 1951; id., *Enisejskaja pis'mennost' Tjurkov: Teksty i perevody*, Moscow, 1952.

3   On the interpretation of this and other Proto-Bulgar royal titles cf. V. Beševliev, *Die protobulgarischen Inschriften*, Berlin, 1963, 249-51.

4   Cf. I. Dujčev, 'Les boljars dits intérieurs et extérieurs de la Bulgarie médiévale', *Medioevo bizantino-Slavo*, 1, Rome, 1965, 231-44.

5   For a brief discussion of the problem cf. V. Beševliev, *Die protobulgarischen Inschriften*, Berlin, 1963, 282-3.

6   Einhard, *Annales*, s. ann. 818.

7   V. Beševliev, 'Zur Datierung und Deutung der protobulgarischen Inschrift vor dem Reiterrelief von Madara, Bulgarien', *Byzantinische Zeitschrift* 47 (1954), 117.

8   Einhard, *Annales*, 210.

9   These problems are discussed by V. N. Zlatarski, *Istorija na bŭlgarskata dŭrzhava prez srednite vekove*, II, 226-31.

10   For a list cf. V. Beševliev, *Die protobulgarischen Inschriften*, Berlin, 1963, 46-7.

11   See the discussion in Hélène Glykatzi-Ahrweiler, 'Recherches sur l'administration de l'empire byzantin aux IXe-XI[e]siècles', *Bulletin de Correspondance Hellénique* 84 (1960), 3-4.

12   Cf. the inventories in V. Beševliev, *Die protobulgarischen Inschriften*, Berlin, 1963, 229-44.

13   Cf. Hélène Ahrweiler, *Byzance et la mer*, Paris, 1966, 87-9.

14   On these questions see the interesting discussion in S. N. Lishev, *Za stokovoto proizvodstvo vŭv feodalna Bŭlgarija*, Sofia, 1957, 9-48.

8   Religion

1   Cf. Gy. Moravcsik, *Byzantinoturcica*, Second edn, II, 1958, 296; V. Beševliev, *Die protobulgarischen Inschriften*, Berlin, 1963, 150, where references to the literature are to be found.

2   *Scriptor incertus de Leone Armenio*, p. 342.

3   Cf. G. Lenczyk, *Materialy Archeologiczne* 5 (1964), 5-61.

4   Tacitus, *Germ.* 8.3; *Hist.* 4.61.3; Statius *Silv.* 1.4.90, Cass. Dio 67.5.

5   On early Slavonic religious beliefs and practices cf. I. Dujčev, 'Slavjano-bolgarskie drevnosti', *Byzantinoslavica* 11 (1950), 7-31.

6   Cf. R. Jakobson, 'Slavic Epic Verse', *Oxford Slavonic Papers* 3 (1952), reprinted in *Selected Writings* 4 (1966), 414-63.

7   *Ep.* 6, pp. 200-248 Valettas.

8 V. Beševliev, *Die protobulgarischen Inschriften*, No. 15.
9 Ibid., No. 87.
10 Ibid., No. 78.
11 T. Totev, 'Nov starobŭlgarski pismen pametnik ot Preslav', *Izvestija na Arkheologicheskija Institut* 29 (1966), 64.
12 Cf. M. Arnaudov, *Die bulgarischen Festbräuche*, Leipzig, 1917; I. Georgieva, 'Njakoi antichni sledi v bŭlgarskite narodni vjarvanija i obichai', *Izvestija na Bŭlgarskoto Istorichesko Druzhestvo* 27 (1970), 21ff.
13 Cf. on this point the arguments of D. Obolensky, *The Bogomils: A Study in Balkan Neo-Manichaeism*, Cambridge, 1948, 154-67.
14 Cf. Y. Ivanov, *Bogomilksi knigi i legendi*, Sofia, 1925; D. Angelov, 'Apokrifnata knizhnina kato otrazhenie na feodalnata dejstvitelnost i svetogleda na eksploatiranata klasa v srednovekovna Bŭlgarija', *Istoricheski Pregled* 7 (1949-50), 493-508.
15 On Bogomilism the literature is extensive and much of it is of little value. Two recent important works are D. Obolensky, *The Bogomils: A Study in Balkan Neo-Manichaeism*, Cambridge, 1948 and D. Angelov, *Bogomilstvoto v Bŭlgarija*, third edn, Sofia, 1969. Both have full bibliographies.
16 G. Ostrogorsky, *History of the Byzantine State*, second edn, Oxford, 1968, 217.

9   Culture

1 *Life of St Theodore of Sykeon* 5.18, 10.1, 26.12 Festugière; *Life of St Christodoulos of Patmos*, 113 Sakkelion.
2 Commentary on Canon 62 of Council in Trullo.
3 For a discussion of the sources and the problems cf. F. Fuchs, *Die höheren Schulen von Konstantinopel*, Leipzig, 1926, 18ff.; S. Impellizeri, 'L'umanesimo bizantino del ix secolo e la genesi della Biblioteca di Fozio', *Revista di studi bizantini e neo-ellenici* N. S. 6-7 (1969-70), 9-69; P. Lemerle, *Le premier humanisme byzantin,* Paris, 1971, 148-76, 242-66.
4 On Arethas cf. S. Kougeas, *Ho Kaisareias Arethas*, Athens, 1913; P. Lemerle, *op. cit.* 205-41. His *Scripta Minora* have recently been edited by L. G. Westerink, 2 vols., Leipzig, 1968, 1971.
5 On tenth-century encyclopedism cf. P. Lemerle, *op. cit*, 267-300; A. J. Toynbee, *Constantine Porphyrogenitus and his Age*, London, 1973, 575-605.
6 Cf. R. J. H. Jenkins, 'The Classical Background of the Scriptores post Theophanem', *Dumbarton Oaks Papers* 8 (1954), 13-30; id., 'The Hellenistic Origins of Byzantine Literature', *Dumbarton Oaks Papers* 17 (1963), 39-52.
7 The most illuminating treatment is still that by V. N. Lazarev, *Istorija*

vizantijskoj zhivopisi, Moscow, 1947, I, 74-103; cf. also K. Weitzmann, *Studies in Classical and Byzantine Manuscript Illumination*, Chicago, 1971, 176-223.

8 Cf. V. Beševliev, *Die protobulgarischen Inschriften*, Berlin, 1963, 263-5.

9 Cf. V. Beševliev, 'Vizantijski triumfalni obichai, aklamatsii i titli u Bŭlgarite prez ix. v', *Izvestija na Etnografskija Institut i Muzej* 3 (1958), 2-38.

10 V. Beševliev, *Die protobulgarischen Inschriften*, Berlin, 1963, No. 47.

11 *Synaxarium ecclesiae Constantinopolitanae*, ed. H. Delehaye, Brussels, 1902, 416.

12 Theophylact, Martyrium SS xv illustrium martyrum, Migne, *P. G.* 126.191ff.

13 For the text cf. P. A. Lavrov, *Materialy po istorii vozniknovenija drevnej slavjanskoj pis'mennosti*, The Hague, 1966, 162ff.

14 On the problems of liturgical poetry cf. R. Jakobson, 'The Slavic response to Byzantine poetry', *Actes du XIIe Congrès International d'Études Byzantines*, Ohrid, 1961, 1.249-65.

15 On all these texts the basic work is still M. Weingart, *Byzantské Kroniky v literatuře církevně-slovanské*, 2 vols., Bratislava, 1922-3.

16 On the whole question of Bulgarian translations from Byzantine Greek there is an admirable survey by I. Dujčev, 'Les rapports littéraires byzantino-slaves', *Actes du XIIe Congrés International d'Études Byzantines*, Ohrid, 1961, 1.411-29, reprinted with additions in *Medioevo Bizantino-slavo*, 2, Rome, 1968, 3-27, 589-94.

17 Cf. R. Aitzetmüller, *Das Hexaemeron des Exarchos Johannes*, Graz, 1958- (in progress).

18 Cf. K. Kuev, *Chernorizets Khrabur,* Sofia, 1967, where a full bibliography will be found.

19 Cf. A. Vaillant and P..Puech, *Le Traité contre les Bogomiles de Cosmas le Prêtre*, Paris, 1945.

20 Cf. E. Georgiev, *Raztsvetŭt na bŭlgarskata literatura v ix-x v*, Sofia, 1962, 275; N. S. Derzhavin, *Istorija Bolgarii* 2, Moscow, 1946, 80-82.

21 Cf. L. Masing, 'Studien zur Kenntnis des Izbornik Svjatoslava vom Jahre 1073 nebst Bemerkungen zu den jüngeren Handschriften', *Archiv für slavische Philologie* 8 (1885) and 9 (1886).

22 A. P. Vlasto, *The Entry of the Slavs into Christendom*, Cambridge, 1970, 178.

23 Cf. A. D. Momigliano in *Paganism and Christianity in the Fourth Century*, London, 1962.

24 Cf. I. Dujčev, 'Poesia epica bulgara con reminiscenze dell'epoca medioevale', *La Poesia epica e la sua formazione*, Rome, 1970, 447-66.

25 Cf. A. Grabar, *La peinture religieuse en Bulgarie*, Paris, 1928, 183ff.; N. Mavrodinov, 'Vŭnshnata ukrasa na starobŭlgarskite tsŭrkvi', *Izvestija*

na Bŭlgarskoto Arkheologichesko Druzhestvo 8 (1934); id., *Starobŭlgars-kata zhivopis*, Sofia, 1945, 23ff.
26 Cf. V. Gjuzelev, *Knjaz Boris I*, Sofia, 1969, 22, 44, 53.
27 Ibid. 111.
28 Ibid. 147.
29 Ibid. 426.
30 Ibid. 463.
31 V. Beševliev and J. Irmscher, *Antike und Mittelalter in Bulgarien*, Tafel, 41.
32 F. Dvornik, *Byzantine Missions among the Slavs*, New Brunswick, N.J., 1970, fig. 16-18.
33 J. Poulik, *Dve velkomoravské rotundy*, Prague, 1963, pl. 26.
34 J. Poulik, op.cit.; V. Hrubý, *Staré Mésto-Velkomoravsky Velehrad*, Prague, 1965, 184-190.

10 Everyday Life

1 P. Lemerle, A. Guillou, N. Svoronos, *Actes de Lavra I*, Paris, 1970, No. 14.
2 On this matter cf. A. P. Kazhdan, *Agrarnye otnoshenija v Vizantii xiii-xiv vv*, Moscow, 1952, 74-6; G. G. Litavrin, *Bolgarija i Vizantija v xi-xii vv*, Moscow, 1960, 63-6.
3 Cf. S. Stojkov, *Bŭlgarskata dialektologija*, Sofia, 1968; I. Koev, *Bŭlgarskata vezbena ornamentika*, Sofia, 1951; V. Naslednikova, *Istorija na bŭlgarskija kostjum*, Sofia, 1970.
4 Cf. Margaret Hasluck, *The Unwritten Law in Albania*, Cambridge, 1974, 25ff.
5 Migne, *P. G.* 126.217D.
6 J. B. Aufhauser, *Miracula S. Georgii*, Leipzig, 1913, 18-40.
7 *Suda* I. p. 483 Adler.
8 A fascinating but rather uncritical catalogue is to be found in Ph. Koukoulès, *Byzantinōn bios kai politismos*, 4, Athens, 1951, 1-248.

11 Conclusions

1 *What is History. The G. M. Trevelyan Lectures delivered in the University of Cambridge 1961*, Harmondsworth, 1964, 89-90.

Index

Aachen, Charlemagne's basilica, 109
Aboba, ruins of, 95-6; see also Pliska
Abydos, 61, 74
Achelous river, battle of (917), 63, 64, 70
Adrianople, 24, 39, 49-51, 60, 66, 91, 92, 94; battle of (378), 26
Aegean islands and sea, 52, 94, 136, 138
Agriculture, 79-87; Anatolian, 79; Bulgarian, 80-81; cereal crops, 79, 80, 82; fodder crops, 79; fruit trees, 79-81; implements, 82; leguminous crops, 80; olives, 79; stock breeding, 81; vegetables, 81; vines, 79, 80
Alans, the, 24, 26, 27, 123, 140
Albania and the Albanians, 22-4, 43, 54, 61; language, 23
Alexios I Comnenus, 78, 116
Anchialos, 37, 43, 48, 50, 51, 54, 63, 94, 98; naval base, 137
Angelarius, Moravian missionary, 154, 155
Antae, the, 30, 31
Apostolic Canons, 177-8
Arabs, the, 27, 39, 41, 45, 52, 54, 61, 62, 77, 81, 82, 91, 123, 136, 138, 181, 182
Arcadiopolis (Lüle Burgaz), 50; battle of (970), 72
Archontes, 93, 123, 127, 136
Arethas, Metropolitan of Caesarea, 18, 171, 179
Arkona (Rügen), Temple of the Wends, 141
Armaments, production of, 106, 114
Armenia and Armenians, 61, 77, 78, 103, 163, 182
Arnulf, King of Bavaria, 157
Arpad, Magyar leader, 59
Ashot of Taron, 74
Asia Minor, 101, 123, 136, 142,

185; bishoprics, 94; long-distance trade, 94
Asparukh, Bulgar leader, 46-8, 100, 126-7, 143, 158
Athanasius, St, 105, 180
Athens, 22, 39, 52, 90-4, 103; and the Goths, 26; excavation of Agora, 17
Attica, 40, 41
Attila, 28, 45, 96
Auxentius, bishop of Silistria, 99
Avars, the, 35-9, 42-9, 52, 54, 68, 82, 90-1, 99, 124, 159, 189; and the Romans, 37-8; and the Slavs, 36-8; Khagans, 36

Bachkovo, monastery, 78
Baian, Khagan of the Avars, 36, 38, 43
Balčik, 98, 143
Balkan chain, 22, 23, 26, 33, 38, 47, 48, 72, 126
Balsamon, Theodore, 170
Balshi (Albania), Greek inscription, 158
Bardanes, 175
Bardas Phocas, 72
Bardas Sclerus, 72, 73
Basil I, emperor, 18, 56, 117, 119, 149, 151, 152, 154, 156, 179, 185
Basil II, emperor, 70, 72, 73; war against western Bulgaria, 74-5, 99; Psalter, 190
Basilica (codification of law), 119
Belgrade, 129, 154; bishopric, 129, 154; see also Singidunum
Benjamin, son of Symeon, 69
Berrhoea see Stara Zagora
Beševliev V, 18, 23, 45, 61, 128, 129, 143, 174
Bibliotheca (Photius), 170, 178
Bishoprics, 129
Blachernae, Symeon's coronation ceremony at, 62

230

Paul, bishop of Populonia, 149, 150
Paulicians, 54, 55, 145, 151, 152, 163, 165, 166, 168, 185
Pechenegs, the, 59-60, 63, 66, 69, 71; mercenaries, 72
Peloponnese, the, 40, 41, 49, 51-3, 75, 78
Perbund, Slav prince, 41
Persia and Persians, 36-9, 44, 62, 82, 91, 123
Perun (Slav god), 141
Peryn: pre-Christian building, 141
Peter, King of Bulgaria, 68-72, 74, 99, 160, 164, 165, 179, 184, 194-5
Peter Deljan, 111
Peter of Sicily, 162
Peter the Cardinal, 152
Peter the Kavkhan, 148-51
Petronas, Byzantine general, 55
Philaretos, St, 197
Philippi, 21, 51, 92, 94
Philippopolis (Plovdiv), 24, 39, 50, 51, 72, 91, 94, 99-100, 143; bishopric, 129
Phocas, emperor, 37, 38
Photius, patriarch, 18, 56, 145-9, 151-3, 167, 168, 170, 171, 178, 179
Pippin, son of Charlemagne, 48
Pliska, Bulgar capital, 18, 47-51, 57, 63, 74, 77, 81, 82, 95-7, 100, 101, 112, 146, 149-54, 156, 158, 160, 195; basilica and palace church, 161, 184; bronzework, 185
Ploughs, 82
Political structure, 116-39; Byzantine, 116-23, 130-32; civil servants, 121-2; codification of laws, 119-20; court ceremonies, 119; emperor's functions and duties, 117-9; emperor's powers, 116; hierarchy of officials, 120; *Kleisourai*, 123; provincial governors, 120; senate, 121; state departments, 120; *tagmata*, 132; *theme* system, 116, 122-3, 130-2; usurpations, 118-19
Bulgaria, 123-9; army, 125-6;

133-5; episcopal sees, 129; Khans, 123-8; laws, 124-5; officers of state, 125, 128; provinces and governors, 127, 129-30
Pottery, 31, 32, 47, 104, 112, 113
Preslav: Bulgar royal residence, 51; capital of Bulgaria, 57, 59, 61, 63, 67, 69-74, 95-8, 100, 101, 112, 128, 140, 154, 155, 158, 160, 161, 176, 177, 179, 183, 194, 195; bishopric, 129; churches, 184, 185; excavations, 185; monasteries, 157, 159, 161; schools, 177; sculptures and carvings, 185
Prochiron (summary of the law), 119, 179
Procopius Crenites, 59
Proto-Bulgars, 112, 123, 132, 133, 140, 183, 190; inscriptions, 174; language, 128; settlements, 18
Prouchontes, 93

Radislav, governor of Belgrade, 154
Rasate *see* Vladimir
Rastislav, King of Moravia, 145
Responsa (Nicholas I), 134-5, 140, 148-9, 190
Rhodope mountains, 22, 70
Rila mountains, 138; monastery, 159
Roman Church, 56
Roman empire, 15, 21-6, 32-3, 37-8, 45, 78; garrisons on Danube, 25-6, 28, 33, 34; posts and forts, 25, 34, 35; roads, 24-5
Romano-Celtic communities, 77
Romanus II, emperor, 70, 119
Romanus, governor of Skopie, 74
Romanus Lecapenus, 64-7, 69, 70, 118-19, 168
Rügen, temples, 141
Rugievit, Wendish god, 141
Rumania and Rumanians, 42-3
Russia and Russians, 16, 69, 71-4, 94, 100, 136, 139, 142, 145, 158, 191, 196, 198; missions